GONE FISHING

GONE FISHING

An Anthology of Fishing Stories

Michael Hordern
and Abigail Morgan

CASTLE BOOKS

Published in 1995 by
CASTLE BOOKS
A division of Book Sales, Inc.
114 Northfield Avenue
Edison, NJ 08837

Published by arrangement with Michael O'Mara Books Ltd,
9 Lion Yard, Tremadoc Road, London SW4 7NQ

ISBN 0-7858-0508-7

Designed and typeset by Florencetype Ltd, Stoodleigh, Devon

MANUFACTURED IN THE UNITED STATES OF AMERICA

ACKNOWLEDGMENTS

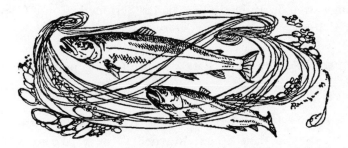

The publisher has made every effort to contact the copyright holders of material reproduced in this book, and wishes to apologize to those he has been unable to trace. Grateful acknowledgment is made for permission to reprint the following:

Nobody Said Anything by Raymond Carver. Copyright © 1974 by Raymond Carver; copyright renewed 1993 by Tess Gallagher. Reprinted by permission of International Creative Management, Inc.

'Pike' by Ted Hughes. Reprinted by permission of the author. Also extract from *Poetry in the Making* by permission of the author.

Angling Adventures of An Artist by John Shirley-Fox. Reprinted by permission of John Murray Publishers Ltd.

Rod and Line by Arthur Ransome. Reprinted by permission of Random House UK Limited.

Salar the Salmon by Henry Williamson. Printed by permission of the estate of the late Henry Williamson.

Highland River by Neil Gunn. Reprinted by permission of the Estate of Neil Gunn and Random House UK Limited. First published by

The Porpoise Press, Edinburgh 1937 and in London by Faber and Faber Ltd.

Big Two-Hearted River by Ernest Hemingway. Reprinted by permission of The Hemingway Foreign Rights Trust and Scribner, an imprint of Simon & Schuster, from IN OUR TIME by Ernest Hemingway. Copyright 1925 Charles Scribner's Sons. Copyright renewed 1953 by Ernest Hemingway.

The Little Fishes by H.E. Bates. Reprinted by permission of the Estate of H. E. Bates.

Coming Up for Air by George Orwell. Reprinted by permission of the Estate of the late Sonia Brownell Orwell, Martin Secker & Warburg, and Harcourt Brace & Company.

A River Runs Through It by Norman Maclean. Copyright © The University of Chicago 1976.

CONTENTS

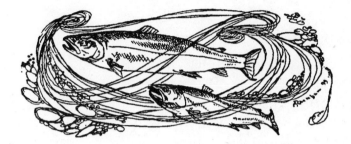

INTRODUCTION

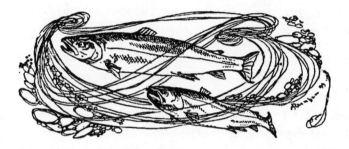

I CAUGHT my first fish when I was five and I have often thought that had I been allowed to take it home to show my mother I might never have been infected with a passion for fishing. It was a tiddler caught with nothing more than a worm on a hook. My elder brother, Shrimp, all of eleven years old and very superior, decreed that it must be released back into the water. 'Put it back, Michael. It's too small.' I obeyed him but I fixed in my mind to go back the next day to catch another and I've been going back ever since. Hooked!

Something binds me to this sport but, after more than eighty years, I still don't know exactly what it is; there is the lure of the riverbank, with its extraordinary variety of wildlife, the taste of the trout fried on the riverbank with a nub of butter and the twist of salt that I always carry, or is it simply the pull of the fish one never quite caught? I don't know, but it has been a devouring passion which over the years I have very roughly documented in my fishing diaries. These are thick, old exercise books the first of which was bought, so it reminds me, at Gillett's Stationers and Printers, Market Street, Brighton, in 1929.

Fishing language is a kind of private language impenetrable to the non-fisherman, laced with the exotic names of flies and technical discussions of the characteristics of different streams and pools. My diaries are monuments to long, wet luckless days, the making of a decent fly, the weight of a salmon or trout and, from time to time, the odd remark about a fishing companion. Very long and often boring and I am sure, only of interest to another fisherman but they do, I believe, sometimes catch something of the joy of fishing – I would almost say an exaltation comparable with the rare moment on stage when it all seems to come together.

This is an entry from my diary for 1935 which should have been written in red ink!

> *I've caught a salmon! And on the Dart too. The Brownriggs lent us Wild Goose for the week and Shrimp and Dacia and a girlfriend of D's and a man friend of S's and I occupied the cottage for a misty, heavenly week. Major Cooke-Hurle kindly gave me a day on his water and on that great day, Wednesday June 12th I got into a salmon in the flats above Eagles Rock. It was the thrill I had been waiting for all these years. My knees knocked and my heart thumped and I felt so ill that for some time I honestly wished I had never hooked it. I could see myself weeping beside a broken cast in ten minutes' time. I knew how I should feel but I gave the fish hell and in about 7 minutes I had my gaff out but he saw it and fled: With the gaff between my teeth, looking and swearing like a pirate, I played him for another 2 or 3 minutes. I wish I could have seen and heard myself.*
>
> *Then he was on the bank. 'Michael Hordern', I said in a loud voice, 'has killed a salmon.' I wanted very badly to cry as I used to when I got good fish. I was too thrilled to go on fishing but picked up the fish and hurried back to Dartmeet. I was across the Dart at one place at great risk to life, limb, rod and salmon just for the pleasure of impressing two trip-pers on the opposite bank. I succeeded. 'Coo,' they said as I went by, 'what is it?' 'Oh,' I said nonchalantly 'a salmon, you know.' Mrs Cross (who kept the filling station at Dartmeet) embraced me voluminously and was as pleased as I was. Not the least pleasant part of it was the 'schloop' noise it made as it fell on the granite floor of Wild Goose, a noise I had so often hoped to hear. . .*

The photographs Mrs Cross took of me dishevelled, triumphant and holding my ten-pound catch unfortunately never came out but the ones that Dacia took of me the next day did.

Fishing has always been for me something private and being soli-tary is a part of the pleasure. I tend to go on my own and talk to the trout. As an actor it is the most perfect pastime, particularly when a show is up and running and a wonderful antidote to the essential social element of acting, which is all about teamwork. You have your days free and some of our best theatres are on very good stretches of water. I often find the odd ally during a rehearsal period. Tom Stoppard has become an occasional piscatorial companion since working with him on his first play, *Enter A Free Man* in 1968, and Richard Burton always used to show a certain interest in the water, though I think he mainly enjoyed poaching.

I couldn't say which has been my greater passion; acting or fishing. I have sympathy with Trigorin in Chekhov's play *The Seagull*. Trigorin is a famous writer and, indeed, he is obsessive about writing. He cannot, however, see why the young, naive Nina thinks it must be so wonderful to be a writer. To him it is somewhere between an albatross, always hanging about his neck, and a gift of which he is the slightly reluctant recipient and host. He would much rather talk about fishing, his real love, but of course, Nina cannot understand that.

TRIGORIN   *I love fishing. There's no greater pleasure I know than sitting on the bank at the end of the day and watching the float.*

NINA   *But I think for anyone who has experienced the pleasure of creating something, all other pleasures must pale into insignificance.*

ARKADINA   *[laughing] You must not talk like that. When anyone talks high-flown language to him, he hasn't the least idea what to say.*

I think I'm on Trigorin's side and I chuckle at Arkadina's remark. It is just such tiny insights which reveal Chekhov to be the great writer he is.

Perhaps one of the most memorable and determined anglers I've known was a woman, Peggy Howard whom I started fishing with in my late teens. She was mad keen and lived on Dartmoor. Salmon and sea trout were her catch. We met for the first time late one night fishing on the Dart. I was on the curve of the river and she was on the opposite bank. We had fished like this all the week but had never spoken. As usual I was talking to myself as I fished when I struck up a little song. It may have been 'Rubus the River' or a piece of opera,

I don't remember, but when I stopped she took up the song where
I had left off. A friendship was made and we fished like this for years
but always, in a way, alone. To give you some idea of what kind of
woman she was and how the fishing bug can grab one, I recorded
this in my diary;

Dart August 1938

*Peggy just told me the most terrible fishing story ever. She hooked a
salmon at dusk, as I did, with her Peal rod. It got the wrong side of the
big rock in the middle of the pool and in order to free it she swam rod
and all in the dark to the rock. She freed the fish which then went down
to the tail of the pool. To keep on terms with it, she again swam down
to the tail and twisted her ankle badly in the rocks but continued to play
it sitting on a stone. When the fish was dead beat she saw that the cast
was twisted round and round its head and before landing it she decided,
I can't quite think why, that this must be unwound. This she did only
to discover too late that the salmon wasn't hooked at all and all that held
it was the cast round its gill, once free of the line, the fish floated away
out of her reach.*

*She returned the next morning to retrieve some line she'd left on the
bank and was amazed to see in the shallow water her salmon drifting
away 'dead'. So she grasped it around the tail, lifted it from the water
but it gave an almighty flip and was gone for good!*

As the playwright, Oliver Goldsmith told Samuel Johnson: 'If you
were to make little fish talk, they would talk like whales'.

I know what inspires me to write my diary: I don't want all those
experiences, all that pain and pleasure, to go unrecorded. Even if
I am the only one who ever reads my diary, I just want to get it
down, to capture the immediacy of the experience. I want to be able
to relive the excitement of the act of fishing; to prevent the experience being lost or transformed by any uncertain memory. It is that
sense of what it is to fish that I look for in books about fishing.
Abstract discussion of the theory of fishing is not, to my mind, 'real'
writing on fishing.

This is what I find in the limpid poetry of Ted Hughes, the lively
wit of Arthur Ransome, and the sense of personal struggle that per-
vades Hemingway's description of his battles with fish. In the best
writing about fishing, there is this enthusiasm for the fish, the need
to 'catch' it on paper. To be able to write on nature, on the curve

of the trout as Harry Plunkett Greene does in his book, *Where The Bright Waters Meet* is beyond me. But my favourite 'fish' writer is Arthur Ransome. I spent a very happy year filming Ransome's *Rod and Line*, for Granada Television in 1981. We fished mainly in the Lake District - the Hodder, the Dove, the Swale and through the changing seasons. He was a lively man who had a lively life. You can't cheat with Ransome and there was to be no cheating in the filming. Having a camera focused on one, even for the most vain among us can be crippling. It destroys that sense of communing with the fish alone to which I have referred before. Fortunately, Ransome understood the 'fishless' afternoon but though we had barren days, what we didn't bank on experiencing was the unusual problem of too many fish. Occasionally I had to slow down. Ransome accounted for this as well,

> *The benign moment is difficult to define or explain, though every fisherman knows it. It is like one of those sudden silences in a general conversation when, in England, we say, 'An angel passes' and in Russia, in the old days, they used to say, 'A policeman is being born'. The day is not that day but another. Everything feels and looks different. The fisherman casts not in the mere hope of rising a fish but, knowing that he will rise one, concerned only to hook it when it comes. He knows that even the hooking of it is even more likely than at other times.*

The moment of catching a fish unites all lovers of fishing in the same, but perhaps ultimately, indescribable joy. I certainly cannot do it and I admire writers who can and who can evoke the lesser but profound pleasures associated with fishing such as watching the river wildlife.

There are some things I feel one ought to be able to do while fishing but simply can't. I have tried to learn my lines or resolve the meaning of life but I find I cannot do it.

Ted Hughes, an avid fisherman, composed a poem for me about a day when he and I and a few friends went fishing in unpropitious circumstances. There was snow still on the bank and the season was just opening and though I did not expect that we would catch anything, I thought it would be quite enjoyable to cast. Most of the day had passed when suddenly, Ted felt a fish and, handing me the rod, insisted I land it. So I cast out my fly and started to play the fish. There wasn't much playing to be done. It soared about in the water a bit and I played to my audience of five when I realised it was absolutely as dead as a doornail. No one came to my rescue so I waded out with my net, brought it ashore, to find it was not only dead, but frozen rock-solid! They had got it out of the freezer and somehow hooked it on to my line when I wasn't looking!

Ted's poem is a very long spoof epic, depicting a Herculean battle of wills. The fishing party is transformed into the cast of *King Lear*, Ted modestly playing The Fool with a demented laugh. Two of the verses go:

> *And so these shadows of the stage*
> *That God could hardly see*
> *Shattered the ice and waded deeper*
> *Into tragedy,*
> *Like Herons in an afterlife*
> *Where not a fish could be.*

> *Till suddenly, 'I've got a fish!'*
> *The Fool let out a screech.*
> *Lear, like the old man of the sea*
> *Came staggering up the beach.*
> *'It's absolutely fresh!' he gasped*
> *'O my God, what a peach!'*

and it ends:

> *Now let us praise the flies of the creator*
> *And such a fly that brought up such a fish*
> *Straight to the Fisher's wish*
> *Out of the depths of a refrigerator.*

I am very proud of it and have it – the poem, not the fish – framed on my wall.

More seriously, my favourite Hughes' poem is, 'The Pike', in which he succeeds in making me 'see' the fish and it is my favourite fishing poem. However, my favourite fish being the trout, I particularly love Wordsworth's description of the 'bold brook' in 'The Excursion':

> *On whose capricious surface is outspread*
> *Large store of gleaming crimson-spotted trouts;*
> *Ranged side by side, in regular ascent.*

With the start of each new season, I watch the weather closely. I still manage to go out on the Lambourn, occasionally with my brother Shrimp. Sixty years on, he's still a better fisherman than me. We both still have that 'want' to bring the fish home, stumbling and shouting at each other across the bank. I think of the fish as my noble enemy and I want him for my supper. Particularly if it is trout. It is both a fight and a dance and there is always that one that got away.

I am very fortunate: my cottage overlooks the Lambourn in a beautiful part of Berkshire and I have fished for near eighty years. It is a passion that has never loosened its grip on me and one I hope to pass on to my grandson, Nicholas. I read my diaries from time to time, but I must confess that I haven't added to it in recent years. Somehow, the detail is still interesting to me from long ago fishing victories: the pleasure that it was a ten pound salmon and not the nine pound I thought I remembered it to be. The diaries have decided many a dispute and, though no literary masterpiece, they plot an idyllic fishing career. In *Coming up for Air*, Orwell writes: 'There isn't a cowpond or backwater that I can't see a picture of if I shut my eyes and think.' This is also true of me.

If you share my passion for fishing, I hope you will enjoy *Gone Fishing*.

from

THE PLEASURES OF PRINCES
Gervase Markham

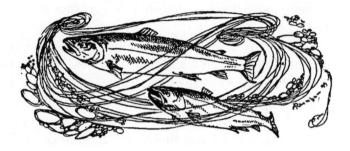

I was introduced to Gervase Markham's The Pleasures of Princes *by Tom Stoppard. He gave it to me after I had appeared in his play* Jumpers *and I found it fascinating. It is thought Markham was born in 1568 in Nottinghamshire. He became a soldier, going with the Earl of Essex's expedition to Ireland. He was a horsebreeder on which subject, in 1593, he wrote a 'Discourse'.*

He wrote several other books including, in 1613, The English Husbandman *which did not include anything on angling. However, the next year he published,* The Second Book of English Husbandman *which did include a section called 'Discourse on the General Art of Fishing with the Angle' from which this extract is taken. I like it because it is so practical. Here is a man who knew that angling was a serious business, not to be taken lightly. Even what you wear has a bearing on how successful your day's fishing is going to be.*

My daughter Joanna could make a very good fly in her youth and I once caught a monster fish on 'The Spaniard's Curse' which she tied at eleven years of age. Christened 'Joanna's Fancy' her most successful attempt was sent to Harvey's to register and so pleased must they have been to have it, they never sent it back. For the fisherman, the making of a fly is always fascinating.

'The Art of Angling' from *The Pleasures of Princes*

Of Angling, the virtue, use and antiquity

SINCE pleasure is a rapture and since all are now the sons of pleasure, and every good is measured by the delight it produces – what work can be more thankful to a man than the discourse of that pleasure which is most comely, most honest, and gives the most liberty to divine meditation, and that without all question is the art of angling which has been the sport or recreation of God's saints, of most holy fathers, and of many worthy and reverend divines, both dead and alive.

For its use carried in it neither covetousness, deceit, nor anger, the three main spirits which rule in all other pastimes. For in diceplay, cards, bowls or any sports where money is the goal, their handmaids are theft, blasphemy, bloodshed. What else can account for man's avarice than a familiar robber, each seeking to win by deceit and spoil others of that bliss of means which God had bestowed to support them and their families?

But in this art of angling there is no such evil, no such sinful violence, for the greatest thing it covets is, for much labour, a little fish, hardly so much to suffice nature in a reasonable stomach. For the angler must entice, not command, his reward, and that which is worth millions to his contentment, another may buy for a groat in the market. His deceit works not upon man but upon those creatures whom it is lawful to beguile for honest recreation or needful uses, and rage and fury are strangers to this civil pastime. It was first invented, taught and shall be ever maintained for patience only; and yet not only by patience but by her other three sisters who have a commanding power in this exercise – justice, temperance and fortitude.

Justice directs and points out those places where men may with liberty use their sport without doing injury to their neighbours nor incurring the censure of incivility. Temperance lays down the measure of action and moderates desire in such good proportion that no excess is found in the overflow of their affections. Lastly, fortitude enables the mind to endure the travel and exchange of weathers with a healthful ease and to despair little at the expense of time but persevere with a constant imagination to obtain in the end both pleasure and satisfaction.

Now for the antiquity thereof, for all pleasures, like gentry, are held to be most excellent which are most ancient. It is said by some writers to be found out by Ducalion and Pialia, his wife after the flood. Others wrote that it was the invention of Saturn after the peace concluded between him and his brother Tytan; others, that it came from Bellus, the son of Nimrod, who first invented all holy and virtuous recreations. And all these, though they savour of fiction, yet they differ not from truth for, most certainly, Ducalion, Saturn and Bellus are taken for figures of Noah and his family, and the invention of the art of angling is truly said to come from the sons of Seth of which Noah was most principal.

Thus you see it is good, having no coherence with evil; worthy of use in as much as it is mixed with a delightful profit, and most ancient as being the creation of the first patriarchs.

Now I will proceed to the art itself and the means to attain it.

Of the angle-rod, lines, corks, hooks and other tools for angling

In as much as the first groundwork or substance of this art of angling consists in the implements belonging to it, and unless a man is possessed of them which are most exact, nimble or necessary for the same, his labour is vain. For as much as the angle-rod is the greatest, principal and sole director of all other tools belonging thereunto, I think it not amiss to begin with the choice and order thereof according to the opinions of the best noted anglers which have been in times past or present. For the choice then of your angle-rod, some anglers are of the opinion that the best should be composed of two pieces, a main body and a small pliant top. The main body would be of a fine grown ground witchen or a ground elm of at least nine or ten feet in length, straight, smooth, without knots and not differing much at either end in substance or thickness. It would be gathered at the fall of the leaf and laid up in some dry place where it may lie straight and self-season: for to bake them in the fire, when they are green is not so good, but after they are well dried and have self-seasoned *then* bake them in the fire and set them so straight that even an arrow cannot surpass them, is excellent: then you may take the upper rind and what with the smoke and their age, their colour will be so dark that they will not reflect into the water, which is a principal observation.

Your rod having been made straight and seasoned, you shall, at the upper end thereof, with an augur or hot iron, a hot iron is better, burn a hole, about three inches deep and a finger wide. Then on the outside of the rod, from the top of the hole to the bottom, you shall wrap it about with either strong double twisted thread, well waxed or pitched, or with shoemakers' thread doubled many times and well waxed with shoemakers' wax, and the last end fastened under the last fold, so closely that it does not loosen: this will keep the rod from cleaving or breaking where the hollow was made.

Having made the stock, fix the top into the hole, which would be a very small ground-hazel, growing upwards from the earth, very smooth and straight, which would be cut at the latter end of the year and lie in season all winter, the upper rind by no means being taken off, neither the rod put into the fire but only seasoned in a dry place, where it may lie straight and have both wind and some air from the fire to reach it. This top must be pliant and bending, yet of such sufficient strength that it will not break with any reasonable jerk, but if it is bent in any way will return to its former straightness. This top-wand would be a yard and a half, or an ell at least in length, and the smallest end would be fastened with a wrap of hair, a strong loop of hair, about an inch long, to which you may at pleasure fasten your fishing line: and the bigger end of the top must be thrust into the socket of the stock and made so fast that it does not loosen nor shake out with any shaking or other reasonable violence. The witchen or ground-elm are the best to frame these main stocks, yet I have seen very good stocks made of sallow, beech or poplar: for the lighter your rod is (so be it strong) the better it is and easier to use.

There are other approved good anglers which allow only that rod which is composed of one entire piece, and think them stronger, nimbler and less casual. These rods they would have chosen are straight and well-grown ground-hazel, being from the bottom to the top finely rush-grown, the upper end being small, pliant and bending. This rod would be gathered at the fall of the leaf, when some of the leaves are fallen and some sticking: as soon as you have cut them up, cut away the leaves and small sprigs, but not so near that you hurt the bark (for that must not be stirred, as well for the strength of the rod as for the colour which being dark will not readily catch the eye of the fish and offend). Then bringing your rods home, lay them upon a level floor, and pressing them down with weights, to keep them from warping, let them lie and season all winter: then, in the springtime, take them up for your purpose, which is only to make the knots smooth and to fix your loop of hair to the upper end. Now the longest of all these rods is the best, so be it straight and well grown, for most commonly they are so short that they well serve only for fishing in little narrow brooks or else in a boat in great waters.

There are other anglers, and many of the best and approved judgments, which allow the angle-rod of many pieces: as those which are made of cane, each piece exceeding another one degree, in such even proportion that being fixed, and thrust on within another they will show as one even, and most straight rush-grown body without any crookedness or other outward evil favouredness: these pieces would not be above four foot in length and three such pieces are sufficient for the stock of the rod, besides the top, now for those ends which are the sockets into which you fix the other canes, you shall hoop them about with fine plates of brass, an inch and a half broad, well soldered and smoothly filed which will keep the cane from cleaving: and for the top of this rod, the round whalebone is thought the best and surely in my concept it is, both for this and any rod whatsoever, for it is tough, strong and most pliant. These rods most commonly are made to have the small canes thrust down into the wide canes, so that a man may walk with them as with a staff and when he pleases draw them forth and use them as occasion rises: the only exception which is taken at these kind of rods is the bright colour of the cane, which reflecting into the water, often scares the fish and makes them afraid to bite. But if you fish in deep and thick waters, there is no such matter, for the shadow of the rod is not discerned through the sun, only in shallow and clear brooks it is a little hindrance and therefore he who is a master in this art will umber and darken the rod by rubbing it over a gentle fire with a little capons-grease and brown of Spaine mixed together.

Now for your lines, you shall understand that they are to be made of the strongest, longest and best grown horsehair that can be got, not that which grows on his mane, nor upon the upper part of or setting of his tail, but that which grows from the middle and inmost part of his dock, and so extends itself down to the ground, being the biggest and strongest hairs on the horse; neither are these hairs to be gathered from poor, lean and diseased jades of little price or value, but from the fattest, soundest and proudest horse you can find, for the best horse has the best hair, neither would your hair be gathered from nags, mares or geldings, but from stone horses only, of which the black hair is the worst, the white or grey best, and other colours indifferent: those lines which you make for small fish, as gudgeon, whiting or minnow, would be composed of three hairs: those which you make for perch, or trout, would be of five hairs: and those for the chub or barbel, would be of seven. To those of three hairs you shall add one thread of silk: and to those of seven three threads of silk. You shall twist your hairs neither too hard nor too slack, but even so as they may twine and couch close one within another, and no more, without either snarling or gaping one from another. The ends you shall fasten together with a Filbers knot, which is your ordinary fast knot, folded about four times, both under and above, for this will not loosen in the water, but being drawn together will continue when all other knots fail, for a smooth stiff hair will yield and go back if not drawn together artificially. Your ordinary line would be between three and four fathoms in length, yet for as much as there is diversity in the length of rods, in the depths of waters and in the places of standing to angle in, it shall be good to have lines of different lengths and to take those fitted for your purpose.

These lines, though natural hairs being white or grey are not offensive, yet it shall not be amiss to colour them according to the seasons of the year, for so they will least scare the fish, and entice them sooner to the bite. And of all the colours, water-green is the best which is made in the following way: take a bottle of alome-water and put into it a handful of marigolds and let them boil until a yellow scum rises upon the water and then take half a pound of green copperas and as much verdigris, beaten to a fine powder, and put it with the hair into the water, and let it boil again and then let it cool for half a day: then take out your hair and lay it to dry and you shall see it turn a delicate green colour, which is indeed the best water-green that may be. This colour is excellent to angle with in all clear waters where the line lies plain, and most discovered, and will continue from the beginning of the spring to the beginning of winter. Now if you will have your lines of a yellow colour, you shall boil your hair in alome-water, mixed only with marigolds and a handful of turmeric; but if you cannot get turmeric, then you shall stamp so much of green walnut leaves, and mix it with the water, and steep your hair in it for twenty four hours at least. Lines of this colour are good to angle with in waters that are clear yet full of

weeds, sedge and such like, for it is not unlike the stalks of these
weeds, and it will well continue to angle with all the first part of the
winter, as from before Michaelmas till after Christmas.

If you will have your lines of a russet colour, you shall take a
quarter of alamo-water, and as much strong lye, then put thereto
a handful of soot, and as much brown of Spaine; and after it has
boiled for an hour or two, set it by to cool, and when it is cold steep
your hair in it for a day and a night, and then hang it up to dry;
these coloured lines are good to angle with in all deep waters,
whether they be rivers or standing pools, as ponds and such like and
are most in use from Christmas till after Easter. Now if your lines are
of a brown or duskish colour, you shall take a pound of umber, and
half as much of soot, and seeth it in a bottle of ale, then when it is
cold steep your hairs in it for a day and a night and then hang them
up to dry, and the colour will be perfect, yet if you want it darker
put more umber into it. These lines are excellent to angle with in
waters that are black, deep and muddy, be they either running or
standing waters, and will continue all seasons of the year, only in
bright waters are they too black, and cast too large a shadow. Lastly,
if you would have your lines of a tawny colour, you take lime and
water and mix it together, and steep your hair in it for half a day and
then take it and steep it for twice as long in tanner's ouze, and then
hang it up to dry, and the colour shall be perfect. These lines are best
to angle with in moorish and heathy waters which are of a reddish
colour and will serve for that purpose all seasons of the year. If with
this colour, or the green, you mixed a silver thread it would not be
amiss, and with the other colours a gold thread is good also: and
note, that at each end of your line you make a loop, one to fasten
to the top of your rod being the larger, and the other to fasten your
hook line unto, which would be somewhat lesser.

After your lines are made, you shall make your corks in this manner: take the best and thickest cork you can get, and with a fine razor
pare it smooth and cut it in the fashion of a long Katherine Pear, big
and round at one end and long and slender at the other, and according to the strength of your line, make your work bigger or lesser,
as for a line of three hairs, a cork of an inch and a half in length, and
as much in compass in the thickest part is big enough: and for a
line of more hairs, a cork of more length and compass will become
it. And indeed to speak truly for as much as it serve but only for a

direction to your eye to know when the fish bites, and when you shall strike, the lesser your cork is, the better it is, and breeds less fright in the water, in so much that many anglers will fish without any cork, with a bare quill only, but is not so certain, nor gives so sure direction as the cork does.

After you have shaped your cork, you shall with a hot iron bore a hole lengthwise through the middle and into that hole thrust a quill and draw your line through the quill and fasten both together with a wedge of the hard end of the goose-feather: and note that both your quill and your wedge be white, for that breeds the least offence on the water, then place the smaller end of your cork down towards your hook, and the bigger end towards your rod, that the smaller end, sinking down with the hook, the bigger may float aloft, and bear the quill upward, which when at any time, you see pulled down into the water, then you may safely strike, for it is an assured sign that the fish has bitten. There are other anglers which make their corks in the fashion of a Nun-gigge, small at both ends, and big in the middle, and it is not much to be disliked, only it is apt to sink sooner, and you may thereby strike before the fish have fully bitten. Others shape their corks in the fashion of a whirl, or of a little apple, round, flattish of both sides, and this cork is best of angle for the greatest fishes, because it is not so apt to sink, and will float till the hook is fastened, and the fish begins to shut away with the bait, so that a man then striking can seldom or never loose his labour.

Next to your corks are your hooks, and they are diverse in shape, and fashion, some big, some little, some in between, according to the angle at which you fish, the best substance to use is either old Spanish Needles, or else strong wire drawn as near as possible that height of temper, which being nailed and allayed in the fire, you may bend and bow at your pleasure. Now for the best softening of your wire if you make your hooks of old needles, you shall need but to hold them in a candle flame till they are red hot, and then let them cool and they will be soft and pliant enough, but if you make your hooks of strong Spanish wire, you shall roll it round and then lay it upon burning charcoal, turning it up and down till it is red hot, then let it gently cool and it will be soft enough.

Now for the making of your hooks from the biggest to the least, that is to say, from that which takes the loach, to that which takes the salmon, and let them lie before you for examples; then look what sort

of hooks you intend to make and with a fine file, first make the point
of your hook, which should not be too sharp for then it will catch
hold of things that it should not, nor too blunt, lest it fail to take
hold when needs be therefore make it less sharp than a fine needle,
and more sharp than a small pin. When you have made the point with
a thin knife, you shall cut out and raise up the beard which you shall
make greater or less, according the size of the hook, and the strength
of the wire: for you must by no means cut the beard so deep as to
weaken the hook, but it must be as strong in that place as any other.
When the point and beard are made, you shall with a pair of pliers
turn and compass the hook making it round, circular-wise, somewhat
more than semi-circle, and observe that the rounder the compass the
better proportioned the hook. This done, leave as much as you think
convenient for the shank, and then cut it off from the rest of the wire:
which done, you shall beat the end down flat and somewhat broader
than the rest, and so polish and smooth it all over. Then, heating it red
hot in a little pan of charcoal, put it suddenly into the water, which
will bring your hook to full strength and hardness.

For single hooks, take a length of your twisted hairs, containing
that number which is fit for the hook, and having made a strong
loop at one end, lay the other end where there is no bough, upon
the inside of your hook, then with strong red silk, either single or
double according the size of the hook being well waxed, whip and
warp the hook round about as thick, close and straight as can be, in
the sort of way you see men whip their bow-strings, and in the same
manner make the ends of your silk fast. Then cut the silk with a pair
of scissors and hairs off close by the hook, and you may be sure that
they will not loosen with any reasonable force. After your hook is
fastened to your line, you shall then plumb your line, by fixing certain pieces of lead, according to the size of your line about it, some
being a quarter of an inch in length, some bigger, some smaller,
according to the weight of your hook and size of your cork, for these
plummets are but only to carry down your hook, and lay it in the
bottom, neither being so heavy to make the cork dip into the water:
your first plummet would be twelve or fourteen inches from the
hook, the rest not above five or seven at the most, although some
anglers use nine, and some more, as their fancy takes them. There
are several fashions of plummets used, as one long, another, square,
and the third in a diamond form, but all tending to one end, have

but one use, and the long ones are accounted the best, so that they are neatly set to, and the ends smooth, and closely laid down, so that they do not tangle the line by catching on the weeds, or other trash in the bottom of the water.

Thus you have seen the best choice of rods, lines, corks and hooks and how to fix and couple them together to do their jobs, now we must speak of other necessary implements, which should accompany the painful angler. And they are: he shall have a large musket-bullet, through which is fixed a double twisted thread, and makes a strong loop, which he may at pleasure hang upon his hook and therewith sound the depth of every water, and so know how to plumb his lines and place his corks in their due places. Then he shall have a large ring of lead at least six inches in compass and made fast to a small long line, through which thrusting your angle-rod, and let it fall down into the water by your hair line, it will help to loose your hook if it catches upon weeds or stones in the water. Then he shall have a fine smooth board of some curious wood for show sake, being as big as a trencher and cut battlement-wise at each end; on which he shall fold his lines. His hooks he shall have in a dry closed box: he shall have a little badge of red cloth to carry his worms in and mix them with a little fresh mould and fennel; then he shall have either a close stopped horn in which he shall keep maggots, bobs, palmers and such like, or a hollow cane in which he may put them and scarabs: he shall have a closed box for all sorts of live flies and another for needles, silk, thread, wax and loose hairs, then a roll of pitched thread to mend the angle-rod if it happens to break, a file, a knife, a pouch with many purses in which you can place all your many instruments. Lastly, you shall have a little fine wanded pebbe to hang by your side, in which you shall put the fish which you catch and a small round net fastened to a pole end, with which you can land a pike or other great fish; to have also a little boat or cot if you angle in great waters to carry you up and down to the most convenient places for your pastime, is also necessary and fit for an angler. And thus I have shown you the substance of the Angler's instruments.

Of the Angler's apparel and inward qualities

Touching the Angler's apparel (for it is a respect as necessary as any other whatsoever) it should by no means be garish, light coloured or shining, for whatsoever has a glittering hue reflects upon the water and immediately frightens the fish and makes them fly from his presence, no hunger being able to tempt them to bite, when their eye is offended; and of all creatures there are none more sharp sighted than fish. Let then your apparel be plain and comely, of dark colour, as russet, tawny, or such like, close to your body, without any new fashioned slashes, or hanging sleeves, waving loose, like sails about you, for they are like blinks which will ever chase your game far from you. Let it be for your own health, and ease sake, be warm, and well lined, that neither the cold air nor water offends you. Keep your head and feet dry, for these cause ague and worse infirmities.

Now for the inward qualities of the mind, some writers are able to reduce them into twelve heads, which indeed whosoever enjoys cannot choose but be very complete in much perfection, yet I must draw them into many more branches. The first, and most special is that a skilful angler ought to be a general scholar and seen in all the liberal sciences as a grammarian, to know how either to write or discourse of his art in true terms, without affection or rudeness. He should have sweetness of speech, to persuade and entice other to delight in an exercise so much laudable. He should have strength of argument, to defend and maintain his profession against envy or slander. He should have knowledge of the sun, moon and stars, that by their aspects he may guess the season of the weather, the breeding of storms, and from what coasts the winds are delivered. He should have a knowledge of countries, and well used to high ways that by taking the readiest paths to every lake, brook or river, his journeys may be more certain and less wearisome. He should have knowledge of all sorts of proportions, whether circular, square, or diametrical, that when he shall be questioned of his diurnal progress, he may give a graphical description of the angles and channels of rivers, how they fall from their heads, and what compasses they fetch in their several windings.

He must also have the perfect art of numbering, that in the sounding of lakes or rivers, he may know how many feet or inches each contains and by adding or subtracting or multiplying the same, he may yield the reason of every river's swift or slow current. He would not be unskilful in music, that whensoever either melancholy, heaviness of thought, or the perturbations of his own fancies stir up some sadness in him, he may remove the same with some godly hymn or anthem, of which David gives him ample examples. He must be of a well settled and constant belief to enjoy the benefit of his expectation, for then to despair it were better never to put in practice: and he must ever think where the waters are pleasant and likely that there the Creator of all things has stored up much of his plenty: and though your satisfaction be not as ready as your wishes, yet you must hope still, that with perseverance you shall reap the fulness of your harvest. Then he must be full of love, both to his pleasure and to his neighbour: to his pleasure, which otherwise would be irksome and tedious and to his neighbour that he neither give offence in any particular not be guilty of any general destruction: then he must be exceedingly patient and neither vex nor excruciate himself with losses or mischances, as in losing the prey when it is almost in the hand or by breaking his tools by ignorance or by negligence but with a pleased sufferance amend errors and think mischances instructions to better carefulness.

He must then be full of humble thoughts into disdaining when occasion commands to kneel, lie down or wet his fingers as often as there is any advantage given thereby, to the gaining the end of his labour. Then he must be strong and valiant, neither to be amazed with storms nor frightened by thunder but to hold them according to their natural causes and the pleasure of the highest. Neither must he like the fox which preys upon lambs employ all his labour against the smaller fry, but like the lion that seizes elephants, think the greatest fish which swim a reward little enough for the pains which he endures. Then must he be liberal and not working only for his own belly as if it could never be satisfied. He must with much cheerfulness bestow the fruits of his skill among his honest neighbours, who being partners of his gain, will doubly renown his triumph, and that is ever a pleasing reward to virtue.

Then must he be prudent, that apprehending the reasons why the fish will not bite, and all other casual impediments which hinder his sport and knowing the remedies for the same, he may direct his labours to be without trouble. Then he must have a moderate contention of mind, to be satisfied with indifferent things and not out of an avaricious greed think every thing too little, be it never so abundant. Then he must be of a thankful nature, praising the author of all goodness and showing a large gratefulness for the least satisfaction. Then must he be of a perfect memory, quick and prompt to call into his mind all the needful things which are any way in his exercise to be employed, least by omission of any, he frustrate his hopes and make his labour effectless. Lastly, he must be of a strong constitution of body, able to endure much fasting and not of a gnawing stomach, observing hours, in which if it be unsatisfied, it troubles both the mind and the body and looses that delight which makes the pastime only pleasing.

Thus having shown the inward virtues and qualities which should accompany a perfect angler, it is now time to give you certain cautions, which being carefully observed, you shall with more ease obtain the fullness of your desires. First therefore, when you go to angle, you shall observe that all your tools, lines or implements be (as the seaman says) fit and ready, for to have them ravelled, ill made or unready are great hindrances to your pleasure. Then look that your baits be good, sweet, fine and agreeing with the season: for if they be otherwise improper in any of their natures, they are useless and you have been better off at home than by the river. Then you must not angle in unseasonable times, for the fish not being inclined to bite, it is a strange enticement that can compel them. Then you must be careful neither by your apparel, motions, or too open standing to give fright to the fish, for when they are scared they fly from you, and you seek society in an empty house. Then must you labour in clear and untroubled waters, for when the brooks are white, muddy and thick, either through inundations or other trouble, it is impossible to get any thing with the angle. Then to respect the temper of the weather, for extreme wind or extreme cold takes from fish all manner of appetite: so does likewise too violent heat, or rain that is great, heavy and beating, or any storms, snows, hails or blusterings especially that which comes from the east which is the worst of all. Those which blow from the south are best and those which come from the north or west are indifferent: there are many other observations but they shall follow in due course.

from

THE COMPLEAT ANGLER
Izaak Walton

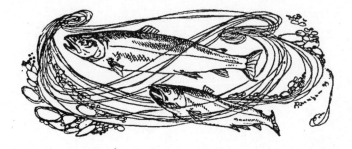

Izaak Walton wrote his masterpiece The Compleat Angler *in 1653 and it is the fisherman's Bible but − and here I commit sacrilege − I have never liked it. I find it hard to read and I think a lot of what he says just is not true. However, I would not dare to omit it and so I leave it to Sir Edward Grey, eminent statesman and fisherman to introduce this piece.*

'Walton, of course, stands first; his book has become a classic, and has been read and remembered now long enough for us to be sure that it will remain so. This, no doubt, is due to his literary skill, and to that distinguished something called style, which Walton had, and without which no book lives long. . . There is a quiet and benign light in his writing, which draws us to it, and makes us choose to linger over it. It must not, however, be forgotten that Walton wrote other books not about angling: these, too, are of literary excellence, and we still have to account for the fact, that it is by The Compleat Angler *that Walton is best remembered. It may be that the others would not have been forgotten; but unless he had written* The Compleat Angler *Walton would never have been as well known as he is. It is his best book, and I like to think that it is so, because the happiness of the subject was specially suited to his kind and quiet spirit.'*

VENATOR. Oh me ! look you, master, a fish ! a fish ! Oh, alas, master, I have lost her.

PISCATOR. Ay, marry, Sir, that was a good fish indeed: if I had had the luck to have taken up that rod, then 'tis twenty to one he should not have broke my line by running to the rod's end, as you suffered him. I would have held him within the bent of my rod, unless he had been fellow to the great Trout that is near an ell long, which was of such a length and depth, that he had his picture drawn, and now is to be seen at mine host Rickabie's, at the George in Ware, and it may be, by giving that very great Trout the rod, that is, by casting it to him into the water, I might have caught him at the long run, for so I use always to do when I meet with an overgrown fish; and you will learn to do so too, hereafter, for I tell you, scholar, fishing is an art, or, at least, it is an art to catch fish.

VENATOR. But, master, I have heard that the great Trout you speak of is a Salmon.

PISCATOR. Trust me, scholar, I know not what to say to it. There are many country people that believe hares change sexes every year: and there be very many learned men think so too, for in their dissecting them they find many reasons to incline them to that belief. And to make the wonder seem yet less, that hares change sexes, note that Dr. Mer. Casaubon affirms, in his book 'Of credible and incredible things,' that Gasper Peucerus, a learned physician, tells us of a people that once a year turn wolves, partly in shape, and partly in conditions. And so, whether this were a Salmon when he came into fresh water, and his not returning into the sea hath altered him to another colour or kind, I am not able to say; but I am certain he hath all the signs of being a Trout, both for his shape, colour, and spots; and yet many think he is not.

VENATOR. But, master, will this Trout which I had hold of die? for it is like he hath the hook in his belly.

PISCATOR. I will tell you, scholar, that unless the hook be fast in his very gorge, 'tis more than probable he will live, and a little time, with the help of the water, will rust the hook, and it will in time wear away, as the gravel doth in the horse-hoof, which only leaves a false quarter.

And now, scholar, let's go to my rod. Look you, scholar, I have a fish too, but it proves a logger-headed Chub: and this is not much amiss, for this will pleasure some poor body, as we go to our lodging to meet our brother Peter and honest Coridon. Come, now bait your hook again, and lay it into the water, for it rains again; and we will even retire to the Sycamore-tree, and there I will give you more directions concerning fishing, for I would fain make you an artist.

VENATOR. Yes, good master, I pray let it be so.

PISCATOR. Well, scholar, now we are sate down and are at ease, I shall tell you a little more of Trout-fishing, before I speak of the Salmon, which I purpose shall be next, and then of the Pike or Luce.

You are to know, there is night as well as day fishing for a Trout; and that, in the night, the best Trouts come out of their holes. And the manner of taking them is on the top of the water with a great lob or garden-worm, or rather two, which you are to fish with in a stream where the waters run somewhat quietly, for in a stream the bait will not be so well discerned. I say, in a quiet or dead place, near to some swift, there draw your bait over the top of the water, to and fro, and if there be a good Trout in the hole, he will take it, especially if the night be dark, for then he is bold, and lies near the top of the water, watching the motion of any frog or water-rat, or mouse, that swims betwixt him and the sky; these he hunts after, if he sees the water but wrinkle or move in one of these dead holes, where these great old Trouts usually lie, near to their holds; for you are to note, that the great old Trout is both subtle and fearful, and lies close all day, and does not usually stir our of his hold, but lies in it as close in the day as the timorous hare does in her form; for the chief feeding of either is seldom in the day, but usually in the night, and then the great Trout feeds very boldly.

And you must fish for him with a strong line, and not a little hook; and let him have time to gorge your hook, for he does not usually forsake it, as he oft will in the day-fishing. And if the night be not dark, then fish so with an artificial fly of a light colour, and at the snap: nay, he will sometimes rise at a dead mouse, or a piece of cloth, or anything that seems to swim across the water, or to be in motion. This is a choice way, but I have not oft used it, because it is void of the pleasures that such days as these, that we two now enjoy, afford an angler.

And you are to know, that in Hampshire, which I think exceeds all England for swift, shallow, clear, pleasant brooks, and store of Trouts, they used to catch Trouts in the night, by the light of a torch or straw, which, when they have discovered, they strike with a Trout-spear, or other ways. This kind of way they catch very many: but I would not believe it till I was an eye-witness of it, nor do I like it now I have seen it.

VENATOR. But, master, do not Trouts see us in the night?

PISCATOR. Yes, and hear, and smell too, both then and in the day-time: for Gesner observes, the Otter smells a fish forty furlongs off him in the water: and that it may be true, seems to be affirmed by Sir Francis Bacon, in the eighth century of his *Natural History*, who there proves that waters may be the medium of sounds, by demonstrating it thus: 'That if you knock two stones together very deep under the water, those that stand on a bank near to that place may hear the noise without any diminution of it by the water.' He also offers the like experiment concerning the letting an anchor fall, by a very long cable or rope, on a rock, or the sand, within the sea. And this being so well observed and demonstrated as it is by that learned man, has made me to believe that Eels unbed themselves and stir at the noise of thunder, and not only, as some think, by the motion or stirring of the earth which is occasioned by that thunder.

And this reason of Sir Francis Bacon has made me crave pardon of one that I laughed at for affirming that he knew Carps come to a certain place, in a pond, to be fed at the ringing of a bell or the beating of a drum. And, however, it shall be a rule for me to make as little noise as I can when I am fishing, until Sir Francis Bacon be confuted, which I shall give any man leave to do.

And lest you may think him singular in this opinion, I will tell you, this seems to be believed by our learned Doctor Hakewill, who in his *Apology of God's power and providence*, quotes Pliny to report that one of the emperors had particular fish-ponds, and, in them, several fish that appeared and came when they were called by their particular names. And St. James tells us, that all things in the sea have been tamed by mankind. And Pliny tells us, that Antonia, the wife of Drusus, had a Lamprey at whose gills she hung jewels or ear-rings; and that others have been so tender-hearted as to shed tears at the death of fishes which they have kept and loved. And these observations, which will to most hearers seem wonderful, seem to have a further confirmation from Martial, who writes thus:

Piscator, fuge; ne nocens, etc.

Angler! would'st thou be guiltless? then forbear;
For these are sacred fishes that swim here,
Who know their sovereign, and will lick his hand,
Than which none's greater in the world's command;
Nay more, they've names, and, when they called are,
Do to their several owner's call repair.

All the further use that I shall make of this shall be, to advise anglers to be patient, and forbear swearing, lest they be heard, and catch no fish.

And so I shall proceed next to tell you, it is certain that certain fields near Leominster, a town in Herefordshire, are observed to make the sheep that graze upon them more fat than the next, and also to bear finer wool; that is to say, that that year in which they feed in such a particular pasture, they shall yield finer wool than they did that year before they came to feed in it; and coarser, again, if they shall return to their former pasture; and, again, return to a finer wool, being fed in the fine wool ground: which I tell you, that you may the better believe that I am certain, if I catch a Trout in one meadow, he shall be white and faint, and very like to be lousy; and, as certainly, if I catch a Trout in the next meadow, he shall be strong, and red, and lusty, and much better meat. Trust me, scholar, I have caught many a Trout in a particular meadow, that the very shape and the enamelled colour of him hath been such as hath joyed me to look on him: and I have then, with much pleasure, concluded with Solomon, 'Everything is beautiful in his season.'

★ ★ ★

The Salmon is accounted the King of freshwater fish; and is ever bred in rivers relating to the sea, yet so high, or far from it, as admits of no tincture of salt, or brackishness. He is said to breed or cast his spawn, in most rivers, in the month of August: some say, that then they dig a hole or grave in a safe place in the gravel, and there place their eggs or spawn, after the melter has done his natural office, and then hide it most cunningly, and cover it over with gravel and stones;

and then leave it to their Creator's protection, who, by a gentle heat which he infuses into that cold element, makes it brood, and beget life in the spawn, and to become Samlets early in the spring next following.

The Salmons having spent their appointed time, and done this natural duty in the fresh waters, they then haste to the sea before winter, both the melter and spawner; but if they be stopt by flood-gates or weirs, or lost in the fresh waters, then those so left behind by degrees grow sick and lean, and unseasonable, and kipper, that is to say, have bony gristles grow out of their lower chaps, not unlike a hawk's beak, which hinders their feeding; and, in time, such fish so left behind pine away and die. 'Tis observed, that he may live thus one year from the sea; but he then grows insipid and tasteless, and loses both his blood and strength, and pines and dies the second year. And 'tis noted, that those little Salmons called Skeggers, which abound in many rivers relating to the sea, are bred by such sick Salmons that might not go to the sea, and that though they abound, yet they never thrive to any considerable bigness.

But if the old Salmon gets to the sea, then that gristle which shews him to be kipper, wears away, or is cast off, as the eagle is said to cast his bill, and he recovers his strength, and comes next summer to the same river, if it be possible, to enjoy the former pleasures that there possest him; for, as one has wittily observed, he has, like some persons of honour and riches which have both their winter and summer houses, the fresh rivers for summer, and the salt water for winter, to spend his life in; which is not, as Sir Francis Bacon hath observed in his *History of Life and Death*, above ten years. And it is to be observed, that though the Salmon does grow big in the sea, yet he grows not fat but in fresh rivers; and it is observed, that the farther they get from the sea, they be both the fatter and better.

Next, I shall tell you that though they make very hard shift to get out of the fresh rivers into the sea, yet they will make harder shift to get out of the salt into the fresh rivers, to spawn, or possess the pleasures that they have formerly found in them: to which end, they will force themselves through floodgates, or over weirs, or hedges, or stops in the water, even to a height beyond common belief. Gesner speaks of such places as are known to be above eight feet high above water. And our Camden mentions, in his *Britannia*, the like wonder to be in Pembrokeshire, where the river Tivy falls into the

sea; and that the fall is so downright, and so high, that the people
stand and wonder at the strength and sleight by which they see the
Salmon use to get out of the sea into the said river; and the manner
and height of the place is so notable, that it is known, far, by the
name of the Salmon-leap. Concerning which, take this also out of
Michael Drayton, my honest old friend; as he tells it you, in his
Polyolbion:

> And when the Salmon seeks a fresher stream to find;
> (Which hither from the sea comes, yearly, by his kind,)
> As he towards season grows; and stems the watry tract
> Where *Tivy*, falling down, makes an high cataract,
> Forc'd by the rising rocks that there her course oppose,
> As tho' within her bounds they meant her to inclose;
> Here when the labouring fish does at the foot arrive,
> And finds that by his strength he does but vainly strive;
> His tail takes in his mouth, and, bending like a bow
> That's to full compass drawn, aloft himself doth throw,
> Then springing at his height, as doth a little wand
> That bended end to end, and started from man's hand,
> Far off itself doth cast; so does the Salmon vault:
> And if, at first, he fail, his second summersault
> He instantly essays, and, from his nimble ring
> Still yerking, never leaves until himself he fling
> Above the opposing stream.

This Michael Drayton tells you, of this leap or summersault of
the Salmon.

And, next, I shall tell you, that it is observed by Gesner and others,
that there is no better Salmon than in England; and that though
some of our northern counties have as fat, and as large, as the river
Thames, yet none are of so excellent a taste.

And as I have told you that Sir Francis Bacon observes, the age
of a Salmon exceeds not ten years; so let me next tell you, that his
growth is very sudden: it is said, that after he is got into the sea,
he becomes, from a Samlet not so big as a Gudgeon, to be a Salmon,
in as short a time as a gosling becomes to be a goose. Much of this has
been observed, by tying a riband, or some known tape or thread, in
the tail of some young Salmons which have been taken in weirs as they
have swimmed towards the salt water; and then by taking a part of

them again, with the known mark, at the same place, at their return from the sea, which is usually about six months after; and the like experiment hath been tried upon young swallows, who have, after six months' absence, been observed to return to the same chimney, there to make their nests and habitations for the summer following; which has inclined many to think, that every Salmon usually returns to the same river in which it was bred, as young pigeons taken out of the same dovecote have also been observed to do.

And you are yet to observe further, that the He-salmon is usually bigger than the Spawner; and that he is more kipper, and less able to endure a winter in the fresh water than the She is: yet she is, at that time of looking less kipper and better, as watry, and as bad meat.

And yet you are to observe, that as there is no general rule without an exception, so there are some few rivers in this nation that have Trouts and Salmon in season in winter, as 'tis certain there be in the river Wye in Monmouthshire, where they be in season, as Camden observes, from September till April. But, my scholar, the observation of this and many other things I must in manners omit, because they will prove too large for our narrow compass of time, and, therefore, I shall next fall upon my directions how to fish for this Salmon.

And, for that: First you shall observe, that usually he stays not long in a place, as Trouts will, but, as I said, covets still to go nearer the spring-head: and that he does not, as the Trout and many other fish, lie near the water-side or bank, or roots of trees, but swims in the deep and broad parts of the water, and usually in the middle, and near the ground, and that there you are to fish for him, and that he is to be caught, as the Trout is, with a worm, a minnow, which some call a penk, or with a fly.

And you are to observe, that he is very seldom observed to bite at a minnow, yet sometimes he will, and not usually at a fly, but more usually at a worm, and then most usually at a lob or garden-worm, which should be well scoured, that is to say, kept seven or eight days in moss before you fish with them: and if you double your time of eight into sixteen, twenty, or more days, it is still the better; for the worms will still be clearer, tougher, and more lively, and continue so longer upon your hook. And they may be kept longer by keeping them cool, and in fresh moss; and some advise to put camphire into it.

Note also, that many used to fish for a Salmon with a ring of wire on the top of their rod, through which the line may run to as great a length as is needful, when he is hooked. And to that end, some use a wheel about the middle of their rod, or near their hand, which is to be observed better by seeing one of them than by a large demonstration of words.

And now I shall tell you that which may be called a secret. I have been a-fishing with old Oliver Henly, now with God, a noted fisher both for Trout and Salmon; and have observed, that he would usually take three or four worms out of his bag, and put them into a little box in his pocket, where he would usually let them continue half an hour or more, before he would bait his hook with them. I have asked him his reason, and he has replied, 'He did but pick the best out to be in readiness against he baited his hook the next time': but he has been observed, both by others and myself, to catch more fish than I, or any other body that has ever gone a-fishing with him, could do, and especially Salmons. And I have been told lately, by one of his most intimate and secret friends, that the box in which he put those worms was anointed with a drop, or two or three, of the oil of ivy-berries, made by expression or infusion; and told, that by the worms remaining in that box an hour, or a like time, they had incorporated a kind of smell that was irresistibly attractive, enough to force any fish within the smell of them to bite. This I heard not long since from a friend, but have not tried it; yet I grant it prob-able, and refer my reader to Sir Francis Bacon's *Natural History*, where he proves fishes may hear, and, doubtless, can more probably smell: and I am certain Gesner says, the Otter can smell in the water; and I know not but that fish may do so too. 'Tis left for a lover of angling, or any that desires to improve that art, to try this conclusion.

I shall also impart two other experiments, but not tried by myself, which I will deliver in the same words that they were given me by an excellent angler and a very friend, in writing: he told me the latter was too good to be told, but in a learned language, lest it should be made common.

'Take the stinking oil drawn out of polypody of the oak by a retort, mixed with turpentine and hive-honey, and anoint your bait therewith, and it will doubtless draw the fish to it.' The other is this: 'Vulnera hederæ grandissimæ inflicta sudant balsamum oleo gelato,

albicantique persimile, odoris verò longè suavissimi.' ' 'Tis supremely
sweet to any fish, and yet assa fœtida may do the like.'

But in these I have no great faith; yet grant it probable; and have
had from some chymical men, namely, from Sir George Hastings and
others, an affirmation of them to be very advantageous. But no more
of these; especially not in this place.

I might here, before I take my leave of the Salmon, tell you, that
there is more than one sort of them, as namely, a Tecon, and another
called in some places a Samlet, or by some a Skegger; but these, and
others which I forbear to name, may be fish of another kind, and differ as we know a Herring and a Pilchard do, which, I think, are as
different as the rivers in which they breed, and must, by me, be left to
the disquisitions of men of more leisure, and of greater abilities than
I profess myself to have.

And lastly, I am to borrow so much of your promised patience,
as to tell you, that the trout, or Salmon, being in season, have, at
their first taking out of the water, which continues during life, their
bodies adorned, the one with such red spots, and the other with such
black or blackish spots, as give them such an addition of natural
beauty as, I think, was never given to any woman by the artificial
paint or patches in which they so much pride themselves in this age.
And so I shall leave them both.

from

THE EXCURSION
William Wordsworth

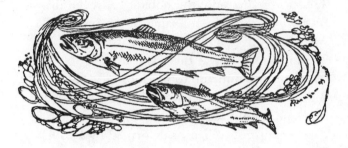

Published in 1814 The Excursion *is in fact the middle section of what was to have been a three-part poem 'on man, on nature and on human life'. Simply, it is a beautiful poem and concerns my favourite fish – the trout.*

'A blessed lot is yours!'
He said, and with that exclamation breathed
A tender sigh; – but, suddenly the door
Opening, with eager haste two lusty Boys
Appeared – confusion checking their delight.
– Not Brothers they in feature or attire;
But fond Companions, so I guessed, in field.
And by the river-side – from which they come,
A pair of Anglers, laden with their spoil.
One bears a willow-pannier on his back,
The Boy of plainer garb, and more abashed
In countenance, – more distant and retired.
Twin might the Other be to that fair Girl
Who bounded tow'rds us from the garden mount.
Triumphant entry this to him! – for see,
Between his hands he holds a smooth blue stone,
On whose capacious surface is outspread

Large store of gleaming crimson-spotted trouts;
Ranged side by side, in regular ascent,
One after one, still lessening by degree
Up to the dwarf that tops the pinnacle.
Upon the Board he lays the sky-blue stone
With its rich spoil: their number he proclaims;
Tells from what pool the noblest had been dragged;
And where the very monarch of the brook,
After long struggle, had escaped at last –
Stealing alternately at them and us
(As doth his Comrade too) a look of pride.
And, verily, the silent Creatures made
A splendid sight together thus exposed;
Dead – but not sullied or deformed by Death,
That seemed to pity what he could not spare.

    But oh! the animation in the mien
Of those two Boys! Yea in the very words
With which the young Narrator was inspired,
When, as our questions led, he told at large
Of that day's prowess! Him might I compare,
His look, tones, gestures, eager eloquence,
To a bold Brook which splits for better speed,
And, at the self-same moment, works its way
Through many channels, ever and anon
Parted and reunited: his Compeer
To the still Lake, whose stillness is to the eye
As beautiful, as grateful to the mind.

from

CHALK-STREAM STUDIES
Charles Kingsley

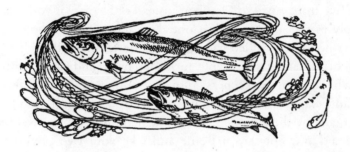

Charles Kingsley spent most of his life at Eversley in Hampshire. He wrote a number of novels of which his most famous is The Water Babies *(1863) written for his son Grenville. Apart from demonstrating his indignation at how poor children were treated by society, it also revealed his love of rivers. Five years earlier he had contributed to Fraser's magazine what is now recognized as a classic in the fly fishing world,* Chalk-Stream Studies, *a description of the Hampshire streams he loved so well.*

Susan Chitty in her splendid biography of Kingsley, The Beast and the Monk, *makes me see him striding about the country, not dressed in the clothes of a parish priest which he only wore on Sunday, but 'in grey breeches and gaiters, thick shooting boots and parti-coloured tie,' like a gamekeeper. Still preserved is his fly-wallet — rather like a needle book, it has a stitched leather cover and pages of cream-coloured flannel stuck with flies.*

COME, then, you who want pleasant fishing days. Come to pleasant country inns, where you can always get a good dinner; or, better still, to pleasant country houses, where you can always get good society; to rivers which will always fish, brimfull in the longest droughts of summer, instead of being, as those mountain ones are, very like a turnpike-road for three weeks, and then like bottled porter for three

GONE FISHING

days; to streams on which you have strong south-west breezes for a
week together on a clear fishing water, instead of having, as on those
mountain ones, foul rain 'spate' as long as the wind is south-west, and
clearing water when the wind chops up to the north, and the chill
blast of 'Clarus Aquilo' sends all the fish shivering to the bottom;
streams, in a word, where you may kill fish (and large ones) four days
out of five from April to October, instead of having, as you will most
probably in the mountain, just one day's sport in the whole of your
month's holiday. Deluded friend, who suffered in Scotland last year a
month of Tantalus his torments, furnished by art and nature with rods,
flies, whisky, scenery, keepers, salmon innumerable, and all that man
can want, except water to fish in; and who returned, having hooked
accidentally by the tail one salmon – which broke all and went to sea
– why did you not stay at home and take your two-pounders and
three-pounders out of the quiet chalk brook which never sank an inch
through all that drought, so deep in the caverns of the hills are hidden
its mysterious wells? Truly, wise men bide at home, with George
Riddler, while 'a fool's eyes are in the ends of the earth.'

Repent, then; and come with me, at least in fancy, at six o'clock
upon some breezy morning in the end of June, not by roaring railway nor by smoking steamer, but in the cosy four-wheel, along
brown heather moors, down into green clay woodlands, over white
chalk downs, past Roman camps and scattered blocks of Sarsden
stone, till we descend into the long green vale where, among groves
of poplar and abele, winds silver Whit. Come and breakfast at the
neat white inn, of yore a posting-house of fame. The stables are now
turned into cottages; and instead of a dozen spruce ostlers and
helpers, the last of the postboys totters sadly about the yard and looks
up eagerly at the rare sight of a horse to feed. But the house keeps
up enough of its ancient virtue to give us a breakfast worthy of
Pantagruel's self; and after it, while we are looking out our flies, you
can go and chat with the old post-boy, and hear his tales, told with
a sort of chivalrous pride, of the noble lords and fair ladies before
whom he has ridden in the good old times gone by – even, so he
darkly hints, before 'His Royal Highness the Prince' himself. Poor
old fellow, he recollects not, and he need not recollect, that these
great posting houses were centres of corruption, from whence the
newest vices of the metropolis were poured into the too-willing ears
of village lads and lasses, and that not even the New Poor-Law itself

has done more for the morality of the South of England than the substitution of the rail for coaches.

Now we will walk down through the meadows some half mile,

> While all the land in flowery squares,
> Beneath a broad and equal-blowing wind
> Smells of the coming summer,

to a scene which, as we may find its antitype anywhere for miles round, we may boldly invent for ourselves.

A red brick mill (not new red brick, of course) shall hum for ever below giant poplar-spires, which bend and shiver in the steady breeze. On its lawn laburnums shall feather down like 'dropping wells of fire,' and from under them the stream shall hurry leaping and laughing into the light, and spread at our feet into a broad bright shallow, in which the kine are standing knee-deep already, a hint, alas! that the day means heat. And there, to the initiated eye, is another and a darker hint of glaring skies, perspiring limbs, and empty creels. Small fish are dimpling in the central eddies; but here, in six inches of water, on the very edge of the ford road, great tails and back-fins are showing above the surface, and swirling suddenly among the tufts of grass, sure sign that the large fish are picking up a minnow-breakfast at the same time that they warm their backs, and do not mean to look at a fly for many an hour to come.

Yet courage; for on the rail of yonder wooden bridge sits, chatting with a sun-browned nymph, her bonnet pushed over her face, her hayrake in her hand, a river-god in coat of velveteen, elbow on knee and pipe in mouth, and rising when he sees us, lifts his wideawake, and holloas back a roar of comfort to our mystic adjuration, –

'Keeper! Is the fly up?'

'Mortial strong last night, gentlemen.'

Wherewith he shall lounge up to us, landing-net in hand, and we will wander up-stream and away.

We will wander – for though the sun be bright, here are good fish to be picked out of sharps and stop-holes – into the water tables, ridged up centuries since into furrows forty feet broad and five feet high, over which the crystal water sparkles among the roots of the rich grass, and hurries down innumerable drains to find its parent stream between tufts of great blue geranium, and spires of purple loosestrife, and the delicate white and pink comfrey-bells, and the avens – fairest and most modest of all the water-side nymphs, who hangs her head all day long in pretty shame, with a soft blush upon her tawny cheek. But at the mouth of each of those drains, if we can get our flies in, and keep ourselves unseen, we will have one cast at least. For at each of them, on some sharp-rippling spot, lies a great trout or two, waiting for beetle, caterpillar, and whatsoever else may be washed from among the long grass above. There, and from brimming feeders, which slip along, weed-choked, under white hawthorn hedges, and beneath the great roots of oak and elm, shall we pick out full many a goodly trout. There, in yon stop-hole underneath that tree, not ten feet broad or twenty long, where just enough water trickles through the hatches to make a ripple, are a brace of noble fish, no doubt; and one of them you may be sure of, if you will go the proper way to work, and fish scientifically with the brace of flies which I have put on for you – a governor and a black alder. In the first place, you must throw up into the little pool, not down. If you throw down, they will see you in an instant, and besides, you will never get your fly close under the shade of the brickwork, where alone you have a chance. What use throwing into the still shallow tail, shining like oil in the full glare of the sun?

'But I cannot get below the pool without –'

Without crawling through that stiff shrubbed hedge, well set with trees, and leaping that ten-foot feeder afterwards. Very well. It is this sort of thing which makes the stay-at-home cultivated chalk-fishing as much harder work than mountain angling, as a gallop over a stiffly-enclosed country is harder than one over an open moor. You can do it or not, as you like; but if you wish to catch large trout on a bright day, I should advise you to employ the only method yet discovered.

There, you are through; and the keeper shall hand you your rod. You have torn your trousers, and got a couple of thorns in your shins. The one can be mended, the other pulled out. Now, jump the feeders. There is no run to it, so – you have jumped in. Never mind: but keep the point of your rod up. You are at least saved the lingering torture of getting wet inch by inch and as for cold water hurting anyone –

Now make a circuit through the meadow twenty yards away. Stoop down when you are on the ridge of each table. A trout may be basking at the lower end of the pool, who will see you, rush up and tell all his neighbours. Now, kneel down; take off that absurd black chimney-pot which you are wearing, I suppose, for the same reason as Homer's heroes wore their koruthous and phalerous, to make yourself look taller and more terrible to your foes.

Shorten your line all you can – you cannot fish with too short a line up-stream; and throw, not into the oil-basin near you, but right up into the darkest corner. Make your fly strike the brickwork and drop in. – So? No rise? Then, don't work or draw it, or your deceit is discovered instantly. Lift it out, and repeat the throw.

What? You have hooked your fly in the hatches? Very good. Pull at it till the casting-line breaks, put on a fresh one, and to work again. There! you have him. Don't rise! fight him kneeling; hold him hard, and give him no line, but shorten up anyhow. Tear and haul him down to you before he can make to his home, while the keeper runs round with the net. . . . There, he is on shore. Two pounds, good weight. Creep back more cautiously than ever, and try again. . . . There. A second fish, over a pound weight. Now we will go and recover the flies off the hatches; and you will agree that there is more cunning, more science, and therefore more pleasant excitement, in 'foxing' a great fish out of a stop-hole, than in whipping far and wide over an open stream, where a half-pounder is a wonder and a triumph. And as for physical exertion, you will be able to compute for yourself how much your back, and knees, and fore-arm will ache by nine o'clock to-night, after some ten hours of this scrambling, splashing, leaping, and kneeling upon a hot June day. This item in the day's work will of course be put to the side of loss or of gain, according to your temperament; but it will cure you of an inclination to laugh at us Wessex chalk-fishers as cockneys.

So we will wander up the streams, taking a fish here and a fish there, till – Really it is very hot. We have the whole day before us; and the fly will not be up till five o'clock at least; and then the real fishing will begin. Why tire ourselves beforehand? The squire will send us luncheon in the afternoon, and after that expect us to fish as long as we can, see, and come up to the hall to sleep, regardless of the ceremony of dressing. For is not the green drake on? And while he reigns, all hours, meals, decencies, and respectabilities must yield to his caprice. See, here he sits, or rather tens of thousands of him, one on each stalk of grass. Green drake, yellow drake, brown drake, white drake, each with his gauzy wings folded over his back, waiting for some unknown change of temperature, or something else, in the afternoon, to wake him from his sleep, and send him fluttering over the stream; while overhead the black drake, who has changed his skin and reproduced his species, dances in the sunshine, empty, hard and happy, and we will chat over chalk-fishing.

The first thing, probably, on which you will be inclined to ask questions, is the size of the fish in these streams. We have killed this morning four fish averaging a pound weight each. All below that weight we throw in, as is our rule here; but you may have remarked that none of them exceeded half a pound; that they were almost all about herring size. The smaller ones I believe to be year-old fish, hatched last spring twelvemonth; the pound fish, two-year olds. At what rate these last would have increased depends very much, I suspect, on their chance of food. The limit of life and growth in cold-blooded animals seems to depend very much on their amount of food. The boa, alligator, shark, pike, and I suppose the trout also, will live to a great age and attain an enormous size, give them but range enough; and the only cause why there are trout of ten pounds and more in the Thames lashers, while one of four pounds is rare here, is simply that the Thames fish has more to eat. Here, were the fish not sufficiently thinned out every year by anglers, they would soon become large-headed, brown, and flabby, and cease to grow. Many a good stream has been spoilt in this way, when a squire has unwisely preferred quantity to quality of fish.

And if it be not the quantity of feed, I know no clear reason why chalk and limestone trout should be so much larger and better flavoured than any others. The cause is not the greater swiftness of the streams; for (paradoxical as it may seem to many), a trout likes swift water no more than a pike does, except when spawning or cleaning afterwards. At those times his blood seems to require a very rapid oxygenation, and he goes to the 'sharps' to obtain it: but when he is feeding and fattening, the water cannot be too still for him. Streams which are rapid throughout never produce large fish; and a hand-long trout, transferred from his native torrent to a still pond, will increase in size at a ten times faster rate. In chalk streams the largest fish are found oftener in the mill-heads than in the mill-tails. It is a mistake, though a common one, to fancy that the giant trout of the Thames lashers lie in swift water. On the contrary, they lie in the very stillest spot of the whole pool, which is just under the hatches. There the rush of the water shoots over their heads, and they look up through it for every eatable which may be swept down. At night they run down to the fan of the pool, to hunt minnow round the shallows; but their home by day is the still deep; and their preference of the lasher pool to the quiet water above is due merely to the greater abundance of food. Chalk trout, then, are large not merely because the water is swift.

Whether trout have not a specific fondness for lime; whether water of some dozen degrees of hardness is not necessary for their development? are questions which may be fairly asked. Yet is not the true reason this – that the soil on the banks of a chalk or limestone stream is almost always rich - red loam carrying an abundant vegetation, and therefore an abundant crop of animal life, both in and out of the water? The countless insects which haunt a rich hay meadow, all know who have eyes to see; and if they will look into the stream they will find that the water-world is even richer than the air-world.

Every still spot in a chalk stream becomes so choked with weed as to require mowing at least thrice a year, to supply the mills with water. Grass, milfoil, water crowfoot, hornwort, starwort, horsetail, and a dozen other delicate plants, form one tangled forest, denser than those of the Amazon, and more densely peopled likewise. . . .

The four great trout-fly families are, *Phryganeæ*, *Ephemeræ*, *Sialidæ*, *Perlidæ*; so you have no excuse for telling – as not only cockneys, but really good sportsmen who write on fishing, have done – such fibs as, that the green drake comes out of a caddis-bait, or give such vague generalities as, 'this fly comes from a water-larva.'

These are, surely, in their imperfect and perfect states, food enough to fatten many a good trout: but they are not all. See these transparent brown snails, *Limneæ* and *Succinæ*, climbing about the posts; and these other pretty ones, coil laid within coil as flat as a shilling (*Planorbis*). Many a million of these do the trout pick off the weed day by day and no food, not even the leech, which swarms here, is more fattening. The finest trout of the high Snowdon lakes feed almost entirely on leech and snail – baits they have none – and fatten till they cut as red as a salmon.

Look here too, once more. You see a grey moving cloud about

that pebble bed, and underneath that bank. It is a countless swarm of 'sug,' or water-shrimp; a bad food, but devoured greedily by the great trout in certain overstocked preserves.

Add to these plenty of minnow, stone-loach, and miller's thumbs, a second course of young crayfish, and for one gormandizing week of bliss, thousands of the great greendrake fly; and you have food enough for a stock of trout which surprise, by their size and number, an angler fresh from the mountain districts of the north and west. To such a fisherman the tale of Mr. ★★★ of Ramsbury, who is said to have killed in one day in his own streams on Kennet, seventy-six trout, all above a pound, sounds like a traveller's imagination; yet the fact is, I believe, accurately true.

This, however, is an extraordinary case upon an extraordinary stream. In general, if a man shall bring home (beside small fish) a couple of brace of from one to three pounds a piece, he may consider himself as a happy man, and that the heavens have not shone, but frowned, upon him very propitiously.

And now comes another and an important question. For which of all these dainty eatables, if for any, do the trout take our flies? And from that arises another. Why are the flies with which we have been fishing this morning so large, of the size which is usually employed on a Scotch lake? You are a North-country fisher, and are wont, upon your clear streams to fish with nothing but the smallest gnats. And yet our streams are as clear as yours – what can be clearer?

Whether fish really mistake our artificial flies for different species of natural ones, as Englishmen hold; or merely for something good to eat, the colour whereof strikes their fancy, as Scotchmen think; a theory which has been stated in detail, and with great semblance of truth, in Mr. Stewart's admirable *Practical Angler*, is a matter about which such good sense has been written on both sides.

Whosoever will, may find the great controversy fully discussed in the pages of *Ephemera*. Perhaps (as in most cases) the truth lies between the two extremes; at least, in a chalk-stream.

Ephemera's list of flies may be very excellent, but it is about ten times as long as would be required for any of our southern streams. Six or seven sort of flies ought to suffice for any fisherman; if they will not kill, the thing which will kill is yet to seek.

To name them:–

    1 The caperer.
    2 The March-brown
    3 The governor
    4 The black alder

And two or three large palmers, red, grizzled, and coch-a-bonddhu, each with a tuft of red floss silk at the tail. These are enough to show sport from March to October; and also like enough to certain natural flies to satisfy the somewhat dull memory of a trout.

But beyond this list there is little use in roaming, as far as my experience goes. A yellow dun kills sometimes marvellously on chalk-streams, and always upon rocky ones. A Turkey-brown ephemera, the wing made of the bright brown tail of the cock partridge, will, even just after the May-fly is off, show good sport in the forenoon, when he is on the water; and so will in the evening the claret spinner, to which he turns. Excellent patterns of these flies may be found in Ronalds: but after all, they are uncertain flies; and, as Harry Verney used to say, 'they casualty flies be all havers,' which sentence the reader, if he understands good Wessex, can doubtless translate for himself.

And there are evenings on which the fish take greedily small transparent ephemera. But, did you ever see big fish rise at these ephemera? and even if you did, can you imitate the natural fly? And if you did, would it not be waste of time? For the experience of many good fishers is, that trout rise at these delicate duns, black gnats, and other microscopic trash, simply *faute de mieux*. They are hungry, as trout are six days in the week, just at sunset. A supper they must have, and they take what comes; but if you can give them anything better than the minute fairy, compact of equal parts of glass and wind, which naturalists call an Ephemera, or Bætis, it will be most thankfully received, if there be ripple enough on the water (which there seldom is on a fine evening) to hide the line; but even though the water be still, take boldly your caperer or your white moth (either of them ten times as large as what the trout are rising at), hurl it boldly into a likely place and let it lie quiet and sink, not attempting to draw or work it; and if you do not catch anything by that means, comfort yourself with the thought that there are others who can.

And now to go through our list, beginning with –

1 The caperer   This perhaps is the best of all flies; it is certainly the one which will kill earliest and latest in the year; and though I would hardly go as far as a friend of mine, who boasts of never fishing with anything else, I believe it will, from March to October, take more trout, and possibly more grayling, than any other fly. Its basis is the woodcock wing; red hackle legs, which should be long and pale; and a thin mohair body, of different shades of red-brown, from a dark claret to a pale sandy. It may thus, tied of different sizes, do duty for half-a-dozen of the commonest flies; for the early claret (red-brown of Ronalds; a nemoura, according to him), which is the first spring-fly; for the red spinner, or perfect form of the march-brown ephemera; for the soldier, the soft-winged reddish beetle which haunts the umbelliferous flowers, and being as soft in spirit as in flesh, perpetually falls into the water, and comes to grief therein; and last but not least, for the true caperers, or whole tribe of phryganidæ. As a copy of them, the body should be of a pale red-brown, all but sandy (but never snuff-coloured, as shop-girls often tie it), and its best hour is always the evening. It kills well when fish are gorged with their morning meal of green drakes; and after the green drake is off, it is almost the only fly at which large trout care to look; a fact not to be wondered at when one considers that nearly two hundred species of English phryganidæ have been already described, and that at least half of them are of the fawn-tint of the caperer. Under the title of flame-brown, cinnamon, or red-hackle and rail's wing, a similar fly kills well in Ireland, and in Scotland also; and is sometimes the best sea-trout fly which can be laid on the water. Let this suffice for the caperer.

2 Of the **March-brown** ephemera there is little to be said, save to notice Ronalds' and *Ephemer*'s excellent description, and *Ephemera*'s good hint of fishing with more than one March-brown at once, viz., with a sandy-bodied male, and a greenish-bodied female. The fly is a worthy fly, and being easily imitated, gives great sport, in number rather than in size; for when the March-brown is out, the two and three pound fish are seldom on the move, preferring leeches, tom-toddies, and caddis-bait in the nether deeps, to lanky ephemeræ at the top; and if you should (as you may) get hold of a big fish on the fly, 'you'd best hit him in again,' as we say in Wessex; for he will be like the Ancient Mariner –

> Long, and lank, and brown
> As is the ribbed sea-sand.

3 **The 'governor.'** In most sandy banks, and dry poor lawns, will be found numberless burrows of ground bees who have a great trick of tumbling into the water. Perhaps, like the honey bee, they are thirsty souls, and must needs go down to the river and drink; perhaps, like the honey bee, they rise into the air with some difficulty, and so in crossing a stream are apt to strike the further bank, and fall in. Be that as it may, an imitation of these little ground bees is a deadly fly the whole year round; and if worked within six inches of the shore, will sometimes fill a basket when there is not a fly on the water or a fish rising. There are those who never put up a cast of flies without one; and those, too, who have killed large salmon on him in the north of Scotland, when the streams are low.

His tie is simple enough. A pale partridge or woodcock wing, short red hackle legs, a peacock-herl body, and a tail – on which too much artistic skill can hardly be expended – of yellow floss silk, and gold twist or tinsel. The orange-tailed governors 'of ye shops,' as the old drug-books would say, are all 'havers;' for the proper colour is a honey yellow. The mystery of this all-conquering tail seems to be, that it represents the yellow pollen, or 'bee bread' in the thighs or abdomen of the bee; whereof the bright colour, and perhaps the

strong musky flavour makes him an attractive and savoury morsel. Be
that as it may, there is no better rule for a chalk stream than this –
when you don't know what to fish with, try the governor.

4 The black alder (*Sialis nigra*, or *Lutaria*).

What shall be said, or not be said of this queen of flies? And what
of *Ephemera*, who never mentions her? His alder fly is – I know not
what; certainly not that black alder, shorm fly, Lord Stowell's fly, or
hunchback, which kills the monsters of the deep, surpassed only by
the greendrake for one fortnight; but surpassing him in this, that she
will kill on till September, from that happy day on which

> You find her out on every stalk
> Whene'er you take a river walk,
> When swifts at eve begin to hawk –

O thou beloved member of the brute creation! Songs have been
written in praise of thee; statues would ere now have been erected to
thee, had that hunch back and flabby wings of thine been 'susceptible
of artistic treatment.' But ugly thou art in the eyes of the uninitiated
vulgar; a little stumpy old maid, toddling about the world in a black
bonnet and a brown cloak, laughed at by naughty boys, but doing
good wherever thou comest, and leaving sweet memories behind
thee; so sweet that the trout will rise at the ghost or sham of thee, for
pure love of thy past kindnesses to them, months after thou hast
departed from this sublunary sphere. What hours of bliss do I not owe
to thee! How have I seen, in the rich meads of Wey after picking out
wretched quarter-pounders all the morning on March-brown and
red-hackle, the great trout rush from every hover to welcome thy first
appearance among the sedges and buttercups! How often, late on in
August, on Thames, on Test, on Loddon-heads, have I seen the three
and four-pound fish prefer thy dead image to any live reality. Have I
not seen poor old Si. Wilder, king of Thames fishermen (now gone
home to his rest), shaking his huge sides with delight over thy mighty
deeds, as his fourteen-inch whiskers fluttered in the breeze like the
horse-tail standard of some great Bashaw, while crystal Thames
murmured over the white flints on Monkey Island shallow, and the
soft breeze sighed in the colossal poplar spires, and the great trout rose
and rose, and would not cease, at thee, my alder-fly? Have I not seen,
after a day in which the earth below was iron, and the heavens above
as brass, as the three-pounders would have thee, and thee alone, in the

purple August dusk, old Moody's red face grow redder with excitement, half-proud at having advised me to 'put on' thee, half fearful lest we should catch all my Lady's pet trout in one evening? Beloved alder fly! would that I could give thee a soul (if indeed thou hast not one already, thou, and all things which live), and make thee happy in all æons to come: but as it is, such immortality as I can I bestow on thee here, in small return for all the pleasant days thou hast bestowed on me.

Bah! I am becoming poetical; let us think how to tie an alder-fly.

The common tie is good enough. A brown mallard, or dark lien-pheasant tail for wing, a black hackle for legs, and the necessary peacock-herl body. A better still is that of Jones Jones Beddgelert, the famous fishing clerk of Snowdonia, who makes the wing of dappled peacock-hen and puts the black hackle on before the wings, in order to give the peculiar hunch-backed shape of the natural fly. Many a good fish has this tie killed. But the best pattern of all is tied from the mottled wing-feather of an Indian bustard; generally used, when it can be obtained, only for salmon flies. The brown and black check pattern of this feather seems to be peculiarly tempting to trout, especially to the large trout of Thames; though in every river where I have tried the alder, I have found the bustard wing *facile princeps* among all patterns of the fly, especially if the legs be made of a dark grouse hackle.

Of palmers (the hairy caterpillars) are many sorts. *Ephemera* gives by far the best list yet published. Ronalds has also three good ones, but whether they are really taken by trout instead of the particular natural insects which he mentions is not very certain. The little coch-a-bonddhu palmer, so killing upon moor streams, may probably be taken for young larvæ of the fox and oak-egger moths, abundant on all moors, upon trefoils, and other common plants; but the lowland caterpillars are so abundant and so various in colour that trout must be good entomologists to distinguish them. Some distinction they certainly make; for one palmer will kill where another does not: but this depends a good deal on the colour of the water: the red palmer being easily seen, will kill almost anywhere and any when, simply because it is easily seen; and both the grizzle and brown palmer may be made to kill by adding to the tail a tuft of red floss silk; for red, it would seem, has the same exciting effect on fish which it has upon many quadrupeds, possibly because it is the colour of flesh. The mackerel will often run greedily at a strip of scarlet cloth; and the most killing pikefly I ever used had a body made of remnants of the huntsman's new 'pink.' Still, there are local palmers. On Thames, for instance, I have seldom failed with the grizzled palmer, while the brown has seldom succeeded, and the usually infallible red never. There is one more palmer worth trying, which Scotsmen, I believe, call the Royal Charlie; a coch-a-bonddhu or furnace hackle, over a body of gold-coloured floss silk, ribbed with broad gold tinsel. Both in Devonshire and in Hampshire this will kill great quantities of fish, wherever furzy or otherwise wild banks or oak-woods afford food for the oak-egger and fox moths, which children call 'Devil's Gold Rings,' and Scotsmen 'Hairy Oubits.'

Two hints more about palmers. They must not be worked on the top of the water, but used as stretchers and allowed to sink, as living caterpillars do; and next, they can hardly be too large or rough, provided that you have skill enough to get them into the water without a splash. I have killed well on Thames with one full three inches long, armed of course with two small hooks. With palmers – and perhaps with all baits – the rule is, the bigger the bait the bigger the fish. A large fish does not care to come to the top of the water except for a good mouthful. The best pike-fisher I know prefers a half-pound chub when he goes after one of his fifteen-pound jack; and the largest pike I ever ran – and lost, alas! – who seemed of any weight above twenty pounds, was hooked on a live white fish of full three-quarters of a pound. Still, no good angler will despise the minute North country flies. In Yorkshire they are said to kill the large chalk trout of Driffield as well as the small limestone and grit fish of Craven; if so, the gentlemen of the Driffield Club, who are said to think nothing of killing three-pound fish on midge flies and cobweb tackle, must be (as canny Yorkshiremen are likely enough to be) the best anglers in England.

In one spot only in Yorkshire, as far as I know, do our large chalk flies kill; namely, in the lofty limestone tarn of Malham. There palmers, caperers, and rough black flies, of the largest Thames and Kennet sizes, seem the only attractive baits; and for this reason, that they are the flies of the place. The cinnamon phryganea comes up abundantly from among the stones and the large peat moss to the west of the tarn abounds, as usual, in house-flies and bluebottles, and is the caterpillars of the fox and oak-egger moths: another proof that the most attractive flies are imitations of the real insects. On the other hand, there are times when midges, and nothing else, will rise fish on our chalk streams. The delicate black hackle which Mr. Stewart praises so highly (and which should always be tied on a square sneck-bind hook), will kill in June and July; and on the Itchen, at Winchester, hardly any flies but small ones are used after the greendrake is off. But there is one sad objection against these 'said midges – what becomes of your fish when hooked on one in a stream full of weeds (as all chalk streams are after June,) save

> One struggle more, and I am free
> From pangs which rend my heart in twain?

Winchester fishers have confessed to me that they lose three good fish out of every four in such cases; and as it seems pretty clear that chalk fish approve of no medium between very large flies and very small ones, I advise the young angler, whose temper is not yet schooled into perfect resignation, to spare his own feelings by fishing with a single large fly – say the governor in the forenoon, the caperer in the evening, regardless of the clearness of the water. I have seen flies large enough for April, raise fish excellently in test and other clear streams in July and August; and what is more drag them up out of the weeds and into the landing-net, where midges would have lost them in the first scuffle.

So much for our leading chalk flies; all copies of live insects. Of the entomology of mountain streams little as yet is known, but a few scattered hints may suffice to show that in them, as well as in the chalk rivers, a little natural science might help the angler.

The well-known fact that smaller flies are required on the moors than in the lowlands, is easily explained by the fact that poorer soils and swifter streams produce smaller insects. The large Phryganeæ, or true caperers, whose caddis-baits love still pools and stagnant ditches, are there rare, and the office of water-scavenger is fulfilled by the Rhyacophiles (torrent-lovers) and Hydropsyches, whose tiny pebble-houses are fixed to the stones to resist the violence of the summer floods. In and out of them the tiny larva runs to find food, making in addition, in some species, galleries of earth along the surface of the stones, in which he takes his walks abroad in full security. In any of the brown rivulets of Windsor forest, toward the middle of summer, the pebble-houses of these little creatures may be seen in millions, studding every stone. To the Hydropsyches (species Montana? or Variegata? of Pictet) belongs that curious little Welsh fly, known in Snowdon by the name of the Gwynnant, whose tesselated wing is best imitated by brown mallard feather, and who so swarms in the lower lakes of Snowdon, that it is often necessary to use three of them on the line at once, all other flies being useless. It is perhaps the abundance of these tesselated Hydropsyches which makes the mallard wing the most useful in mountain districts, as the abundance of the fawn and grey Phryganideæ in the south of England makes the woodcock wing justly the favourite. The Rhyacophiles, on the other hand, are mostly of a shining soot-grey, or almost black. These may be seen buzzing in hundreds over the pools on a wet evening, and with them the sooty Mystacides, called silver-horns in Scotland, from their antennæ, which are of preposterous length, and ringed prettily enough with black and white. These delicate fairies make moveable cases, or rather pipes, of the finest sand, generally curved, and resembling in shape the Dentalium shell. Guarded by these they hang in myriads on the smooth ledges of rock, where the water runs gently a few inches deep. These are abundant everywhere: but I never saw so many of them as in the exquisite Cother brook, near Middleham, in Yorkshire. In that delicious glen, while wading up beneath the ash-fringed crags of limestone, out of which the great ring ouzel (too wild, it seemed, to be afraid of man) hopped down fearlessly to feed upon the strand, or past flower-banks where the golden globe-flower, and the great blue geranium, and the giant campanula, bloomed beneath the white tassels of the bird-cherry, I could not tread upon the limestone slabs without crushing at every step hundreds of the delicate Mystacide tubes, which literally paved the shallow edge of the stream, and which would have been metamorphosed in due time into small sooty moth-like fairies, best represented, I should say, by the soft black-hackle which Mr. Stewart recommends as the most deadly of North-country flies. Not to these, however, but to the Phryganeæ (who, when sticks and pebbles fail, often make their tubes of sand, e.g. P. flava), should I refer the red-cow fly, which is almost the only autumn killer in the Dartmoor streams. A red cow-hair body and a woodcock wing is his type, and let those who want West-country trout remember him.

Another fly, common on some rocky streams, but more scarce in the chalk, is the 'Yellow Sally,' which entomologists, with truer appreciation of its colour, call *Chrysoperla viridis*. It may be bought at the shops; at least a yellow something of that name, but bearing no more resemblance to the delicate yellow-green natural fly, with its warm, grey wings, than a Pre-Raphaelite portrait to the human being for whom it is meant. Copied, like most trout flies, from some traditional copy by the hands of cockney maidens, who never saw a fly in their lives, the mistake of a mistake of a mistake, a sham raised to its tenth power, it stands a signal proof that anglers will never get good flies till they learn a little entomology themselves, and then teach it to the tackle makers. But if it cannot be bought, it can at least be made; and I should advise every one who fishes rocky streams in May and June, to dye for himself some hackles of a brilliant greenish-yellow, and in the most burning sunshine, when fish seem inclined to rise at no fly whatsoever, examine the boulders for the chrysoperla, who runs over them, her wings laid flat on her back, her yellow legs moving as rapidly as a forest-fly's; try to imitate her, and use her on the stream, or on the nearest lake. Certain it is that in Snowdon this fly and the Gwynnant *Hydropsyche* will fill a creel in the most burning north-easter, when all other flies are useless; a sufficient disproof of the Scotch theory – that fish do not prefer the fly which is on the water.

Another disproof may be found in the 'fern web,' 'bracken clock' of Scotland; the tiny cockchafer, with brown wing-cases and dark-green thorax, which abounds in some years in the hay-meadows, on the fern, or on the heads of umbelliferous flowers. The famous Loch-Awe fly, described as an alder-fly with a rail's wing, seems to be nothing but this fat little worthy; but the best plan is to make the wings, either buzz or hackle, of the bright neck-feather of the cock pheasant, thus gaining the metallic lustre of the beetle tribe. Tied thus, either in Devonshire or Snowdon, few flies surpass him – when he is out. His fatness proves an attraction which the largest fish cannot resist.

The Ephemeræ, too, are far more important in rapid and rocky streams than in the deeper, stiller water of the south. It is worth while for a good fish to rise at them there; the more luxurious chalk trout will seldom waste himself upon them, unless he be lying in shallow water, and has but to move a few inches upward.

But these Ephemeræ, like all other naiads, want working out. The species which Mr. Ronalds gives, are most of them by his own

confession, very uncertain. Of the Phryganideæ he seems to know
little or nothing, mentioning but two species out of the two hundred which are said to inhabit Britain; and his land flies and beetles
are in several cases quite wrongly named. However, the professed
entomologists know but little of the mountain flies; and the angler
who would help to work them out would confer a benefit on science, as well as on the 'gentle craft.' As yet the only approach to such
a good work which I know of, is a little book on the trout flies of
Ripon, with excellent engravings of the natural fly. The author's
name is not given; but the book may be got at Ripon, and most
valuable it must be to any North-country fisherman.

But come, we must not waste our time in talk, for here is a cloud
over the sun, and plenty more coming up behind, before a ruffling
south-west breeze, as Shelley has it, –

Calling white clouds like flocks to feed in air.

Let us up and onward to that long still reach, which is now curling
up fast before the breeze; there are large fish to be taken, one or two
at least, even before the fly comes on. You need not change your
flies: the cast which you have on – governor, and black alder – will
take, if anything will. Only do not waste your time and muscle,
as you are beginning to do, by hurling your flies wildly into the
middle of the stream, on the chance of a fish being there. Fish
are there, no doubt, but not feeding ones. They are sailing about
and enjoying the warmth; but nothing more. If you want to find the
hungry fish and kill them, you must stand well back from the bank
– or kneel down, if you are really in earnest about sport; and throw
within a foot of the shore, above you and below, but if possible
above, with a line short enough to manage easily; by which I mean
short enough to enable you to lift your flies out of the water at each
throw without hooking them in the docks and comfrey which grow
along the brink. You must learn to raise your hand at the end of each
throw, and lift the flies clean over the land-weeds, or you will lose
time, and frighten all the fish, by crawling to the bank to unhook
them. Believe me, one of the commonest mistakes into which young
anglers fall is that of fishing in 'skip-jack broad;' in plain English, in
mid-stream, where few fish, and those little ones, are to be caught.
Those who wish for big fish work close under the banks, and seldom
take a mid-stream cast, unless they see a fish rise there.

The reason of this is simple. Walking up the Strand in search of a dinner, a reasonable man will keep to the trottoir, and look in at the windows close to him, instead of parading up the mid-street. And even so do all wise and ancient trout. The banks are their shops; and thither they go for their dinners, driving their poor little children tyrannously out into the mid-river to fare as hap may hap. Over these children the tyro wastes his time, flogging the stream across and across for weary hours, while the big papas and mammas are comfortably under the bank close at his feet, grubbing about the sides for water crickets, and not refusing at times a leech or a young crayfish, but perfectly ready to take a fly, if you offer one large and tempting enough. They do but act on experience. All the largest surface food – beetles, bees, and palmers – comes off the shore; and all the caperers and alders, after emerging from their pupa-cases, swim to the shore in order to change into the perfect insect in the open air. The perfect insects haunt sunny sedges and tree-stems – whence the one is often called the sedge, the other the alder-fly – and from thence drop into the trout's mouths; and within six inches of the bank will the good angler work, all the more sedulously and even hopefully if he sees no fish rising. I have known good men say that they had rather *not* see fish on the rise, if the day be good; that they can get surer sport, and are less troubled with small fish, by making them rise; and certain it is, that a day when the fish are rising all over the stream is generally one of disappointment. They are then picking at Ephemeræ, or small gnats, which rise up from their pupa-state pretty equally all over the stream, and which, as I have said before, no man can imitate – at least well enough to kill in anything but a strong stream or ripple. And even then it is a question whether the fish, which cover the surface with those fleeting rings of glass which Creswick alone knows how to paint, are really the large fish; and whether it is not wiser, instead of searching one's book through for some gnat which they will take perchance, to keep to the large standard flies and to the bank, save, of course, in those few glorious hours when the fly is up, and every man may do what is right in the sight of his own eyes.

Another advantage of bank fishing is, that the fish sees the fly only for a moment. He has no long gaze at it, as it comes to him across the water. It either drops exactly over his nose, or sweeps down the stream straight upon him. He expects it to escape on shore the next moment, and chops at it fiercely and hastily, instead of following and examining. Add to this the fact that when he is under the bank there is far less chance of his seeing you; and duly considering these things, you will throw away no more time in drawing, at least in chalk-streams, flies over the watery wastes, to be snapped at now and then by herring-sized pinkeens. In rocky streams, where the quantity of bank food is far smaller, this rule will perhaps not hold good; though who knows not that his best fish are generally taken under some tree from which the little caterpillars (having determined on slow and deliberate suicide) are letting themselves down gently by a silken thread into the mouth of the spotted monarch, who has but to sail about and about, and pick them up one by one as they touch the stream? – A sight which makes one think (as does a herd of swine crunching acorns, each one of which might have become a 'builder oak') how Nature is never more magnificent than in her waste.

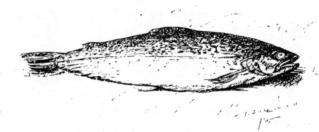

The next mistake, natural enough to the laziness of fallen man, is that of fishing down-stream, and not up. What Mr. Stewart says on this point should be read by every tyro. By fishing up-stream, even against the wind, he will on an average kill twice as many trout as when fishing down. If trout are out and feeding on the shallows, up or down will simply make the difference of fish or no fish; and even in deeps, where the difference in the chance of not being seen is not so great, many more fish will be hooked by the man who fishes up-stream, simply because when he strikes he pulls the hook into the trout's mouth instead of out of it. But he who would obey Mr. Stewart in fishing up-stream must obey him also in discarding his light London rod, which is in three cases out of four as weak and 'floppy' in the middle as a waggon whip, and get to himself a stiff and powerful rod, strong enough to spin a minnow; whereby he will obtain, after some weeks of aching muscles, two good things – a fore-arm fit for a sculptor's model,, and trout hooked and killed, instead of pricked and lost.

Killed, as well as hooked; for how large trout are to be killed in a weedy chalk-stream without a stiff rod which will take them down, is a question yet unsolved. Even the merest cockney will know, if he thinks, that weeds float with their points down-stream, and that therefore if a fish is to be brought through them without entangling, he must be 'combed' through them in the same direction. But how is this to be done, if a fish be hooked below you on a weak rod? With a strong rod indeed you can, at the chance of tearing out the hook, keep him by main force on the top of the water, till you have run past him and below him, shortening your line anyhow in loops – there is no time to wind it up with the reel – and then do what you might have done comfortably at first had you been fishing up, viz., bring him down-stream, and let the water run through his gills, and drown him. But with a weakrod – Alas for the tyro! He catches one glimpse of a silver side plunging into the depths; he finds his rod double in his hand; he finds fish and flies stop suddenly somewhere; he rushes down to the spot, sees weeds waving around his line, and guesses from what he feels and sees that the fish is grubbing up-stream through them, five feet under water. He tugs downwards and backwards, but too late; the drop-fly is fast wrapt in horse-tail and water-grass, callitriche and potamogeton, and half a dozen more horrid things with long names and longer stems; and what remains but the fate of Campbell's Lord Ullin? –

> The waters wild went o'er his child,
> And he was left lamenting.

Unless , in fact, large fish can be got rapidly down-stream, the chance of killing them is very small; and therefore the man who fishes a willow-fringed brook downward, is worthy of no crown but Ophelia's besides being likely enough, if he attempt to get down to his fish, to share her fate. The best fishermen, however, will come to shame in streams bordered by pollard willows, and among queer nooks, which can be only fished down-stream. I saw, but the other day, a fish hooked cleverly enough, by throwing to an inch where he ought to have been and indeed was, and from the only point whence the throw could be made. Out of the water he came, head and tail, the moment he felt the hook, and showed a fair side over two pounds weight . . . and then? Instead of running away, he ran right at the fisherman, for reasons which were but too patent. Between man and fish were ten yards of shallow, then a deep weedy bank, and then the hole which was his house. And for that weedy bank the spotted monarch made, knowing that there he could drag himself clear of the fly, as perhaps he had done more than once before.

What was to be done? Take him down-stream through the weed? Alas, on the man's left hand an old pollard leant into the water, barring all downward movement. Jump in and run round it? He had rather to run back from the bank, for fear of a loose line; the fish was coming at him so fast that there was no time to wind up. Safe into the weeds hurls fish; man, as soon as he finds fish stop, jumps in mid-leg deep and staggers up to him, in hopes of clearing; finds the dropper fast in the weeds, the stretcher, which had been in fish's mouth, wantoning somewhere in the depths – *Quid plura?* Let us draw a veil over that man's return to shore.

No mortal skill could have killed that fish. Mortal luck (which is sometimes, as the present Ministry know, very great) might have done it, if the fish had been irretrievably fast hooked; as, *per contra*, I once saw a fish of nearly four pounds hooked just above an alder bush, on the same bank as the angler. The stream was swift; there was a great weed-bed above; the man had but about ten feet square of swift water to kill the trout in. Not a foot down-stream could he take him; in fact, he had to pull him hard up-stream to keep him out of his hover in the alder roots. Three times that fish leapt into the air nearly a yard high; and yet, so merciful is luck, and so firmly was he hooked, in five breathless minutes he was in the landing-net; and when he was there and safe ashore, just of the shape and colour of a silver spoon, his captor lay down panting upon the bank, and with Sir Hugh Evans, manifested 'a great dispositions to cry.' But it was a beautiful sight. A sharper round between man and fish never saw I fought upon this side of Merry England.

I saw once, however, a cleverer, though not a more dashing feat. A handy little fellow (I wonder where he is now?) hooked a trout of nearly three pounds with his dropper and at the same moment a post with his stretcher. What was to be done? To keep the fish pulling on him, and not on the post. And that, being favoured by standing on a four-foot bank, he did so well that he tired out the fish in some six feet square of water, stopping him and turning him beautifully whenever he tried to run, till I could get in to him with the land-ing-net. That was twenty years since. If the little man has progressed in his fishing as he ought, he should be now one of the finest anglers in England.

★ ★ ★

So, Thanks to bank fishing, we have, you see, landed three or four more good fish in the last two hours.

And here we come to a strip of thick cover, part of our Squire's home preserves, which it is impossible to fish, so closely do the boughs cover the water. We will walk on through it toward the hall, and there get – what we begin sorely to need – something to eat. It will be of little use fishing for some time to come; for these hot hours of the afternoon, from three till six, are generally the 'deadest time' of the whole day.

And now, when we have struggled in imagination through the last bit of copse, and tumbled over the palings into the lawn, we will see a scene quite as lovely, if you will believe it, as any Alp on earth.

What shall we see as we look across the broad, still, clear river, where the great dark trout sail to and fro lazily in the sun? For having free-warren of our fancy and our paper, we may see what we choose.

White chalk-fields above, quivering hazy in the heat. A park full of merry haymakers; gay red and blue waggons, stalwart horses, switch-ing off the flies; dark avenues of tall elms; groups of abele, 'tossing their whispering silver to the sun;' and amid them the house – what manner of house shall it be? Tudor or Elizabethan, with oriels, mullioned window, gables, and turrets of strange shape? No: that is commonplace. Everybody builds Tudor houses now. Our house shall smack of Inigo Jones or Christopher Wren; a great square red-brick mass, made light and cheerful though, by coins and windows of white sarsdenstone; high-peaked French roofs, with louvers and dormers, haunted by a thousand swallows and starlings. Old walled gardens gay with flowers, shall stretch right and left. Clipt yew alleys shall wander away into mysterious glooms; and out of the black arches shall come tripping children, like white fairies, to laugh and talk with the fair girl who lies dreaming and reading in the hammock there, beneath the black velvet canopy of the great cedar-tree, like some fair Tropic flower hanging from its boughs. Then they shall wander down across the smooth-shorn lawn, where the purple rhododendrons hang double, bush and image, over the water's edge, and call to us across the stream, 'What sport?' and the old Squire shall beckon the keeper over the long stone bridge, and return with him bringing luncheon and good ale; and we will sit down and eat and drink among the burdock leaves, and then watch the quiet house, and lawn and flowers, and fair human creatures, and shining water, all sleeping breathless in the glorious light beneath the glorious blue, till we doze off, lulled by the murmur of a thousand insects, and the rich minstrelsy of nightingale and blackcap, thrush and dove.

Peaceful, graceful, complete English country life and country houses – everywhere finish and polish, neatness, Nature perfected by the wealth and art of peaceful centuries! Why should I exchange you, even for the sight of all the Alps, for bad food, bad washing, bad beds, and fleas, fleas, fleas?

Let that last thought be enough. There may be follies, there may be sorrows, there may be sins (though I know there are no very heavy ones), in that fine old house opposite; but, thanks to the genius of my native land, there are at least no fleas.

Think of that, wandering friend; and of this also, that you will find your warm bath ready when you go to bed to-night, and your cold one when you rise to-morrow morning; and in content and thankfulness, stay in England, and be clean.

★ ★ ★

Here, then let us lounge a full two hours, too comfortable and too tired to care for fishing, till the hall-bell rings for that dinner which we as good anglers will despise. Then we will make our way to the broad reaches above the house. The evening breeze should be ruffling it gallantly; and see, the fly is getting up. the countless thousands are rising off the grass and flickering to and fro above the stream. Stand still a moment, and you will hear the air full of the soft rustle of innumerable wings. Hundreds, even more delicate and gauzy, more are rising through the water and floating helplessly along the surface, as Aphrodite may have done when she rose in the Ægean, half-frightened at the sight of the new upper world. And see, the great trout are moving everywhere. Fish too large and well fed to care for the fly at any other season, who have been lounging among the weeds all day and snapping at passing minnows, have come to the surface and are feeding steadily, splashing five or six times in succession, and then going down awhile to bolt their mouthful of victims; while here and there a heavy silent swirl tells of a fly taken before it has reached the surface, slain untimely ere it has seen the day.

Now – put your May-fly on, and throw, regardless of bank-fishing or any other rule, wherever you see a fish rise. Do not work your flies in the least, but let them float down over the fish, or sink if they will; he is more likely to take them under water than on the top. And mind this rule: be patient with your fish, and do not fancy that because he does not rise to you the first or the tenth time, therefore he will not rise at all. He may have filled his mouth and gone down to gorge; and when he comes up again, if your fly be the first which he meets, he will probably seize it greedily, and all the more so if it be under water, so seeming drowned and helpless. Besides, a fish seldom rises twice exactly in the same place unless he be lying between two weeds, or in the corner of an eddy. His small wits, when feeding in the open, seem to hint to him that after having found a fly in one place he must move a foot or two on to find another; and therefore it may be some time before your turn comes, and your fly passes just over his nose; which if it do not do, he certainly will not, amid such an abundance, go out of his way for it. In the meanwhile your footlink will very probably have hit him over the back, or run foul of his nose, in which case you will not catch him at all. A painful fact for you but if you could catch every fish you saw, where would be the trout for next season?

So put on a dropper of some kind, say a caperer, as a second chance. I almost prefer the dark claret spinner, with which I have killed very large fish alternately with the greendrake, even when it was quite dark; and for your stretcher, of course a greendrake.

For a blustering evening like this your drake can hardly be too large or too rough; in brighter and stiller weather the fish often prefer a fly half the size of the natural one.

Only bear in mind that the most tempting forms among these millions of drakes is that one whose wings are very little coloured at all, of a pale greenish yellow; whose body is straw-coloured, and his head, thorax, and legs, spotted with dark brown – best represented by a pheasant or coch-a-bonddhu hackle.

The best imitation of this, or of say drake, which I have ever seen, is one by a Mr. Macgowan, whilome of Ballyshannon, now of 7, Bruton-street, Berkeley-square, whose drakes, known by a waxy body of some mysterious material, do surpass those of all other men, and should be known and honoured far and wide. But failing them, you may do well with a drake which is ribbed through the whole length with red hackle over a straw-coloured body. A North countryman would laugh at it, and ask us how we fancy that fish will mistake for that delicate waxy fly a great rough palmer, made heavier and rough by two thick tufts of yellow mallard wing: but if he will fish therewith, he will catch trout; and mighty ones they will be. I have found, again and again, this drake, in which the hackle is ribbed all down the body, beat a bare-bodied one in the ratio of three fish to one. The reason is difficult to guess. Perhaps the shining transparent hackle gives the fly more of the waxy look of the natural insect; or perhaps the 'buzzy' look of the fly causes the fish to mistake it for one half-emerged from its pupa case, fluttering, entangled and helpless. But whatever be the cause, I am sure of the fact. Now − silence and sport for the next three hours.

★ ★ ★

There! All things must end. It is so dark that I have been fishing for the last five minutes without any end fly; and we have lost our two last fish simply by not being able to guide them into the net. But what an evening's sport we have had. Beside several over a pound which I have thrown in (I trust you have been generous and done likewise), there are six fish averaging two pounds a-piece; and what is the weight of that monster with whom I saw you wrestling dimly through the dusk, your legs stuck knee-deep in a mudbank, your head embowered in nettles, while the keeper waltzed round you, roaring mere incoherencies? − four pounds, full. Now, is there any sherry left in the flask? No. Then we will give the keeper five shillings; he is well worth his pay; and then drag our weary limbs toward the hall to bath and bed, while you confess, I trust, that you may get noble sport, hard exercise, and lovely scenery, without going fifty miles from London town.

THE DIARIES OF
FRANCIS KILVERT

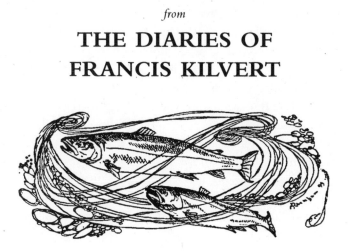

Francis Kilvert, like Charles Kingsley, was a parish priest, and from 1870 wrote a diary in which he recorded his love of the Welsh border country. He continued writing his diary up until the year before he died. Sadly, his widow destroyed much of what he wrote. In this brief extract he shows himself to be unpompous, observant and able to tell a good story – a man after my own heart.

Wednesday, 29 March

WENT down the meadows to Mrs. Tudor's. Handsome Tudor was working in his garden. By the door lay a salmon rod on the ground, so I knew the Squire was having luncheon in the cottage. I went round and there he was with old Harry Pritchard. He brought out his telescope and we had a look at Crichton and Mrs. Nicholl both wading in the river and fishing under the red cliff. I crossed the ditch, climbed the bank and went along the beautiful cliff walk on the edge of the cliff looking over the edge at Mrs. Nicholl standing on a rock fishing far below till I came to a steep path leading down the rocks to where Crichton was fishing. 'Henry,' called Mrs. Nicholl's voice faintly down the river. 'She has got a good fish,' said Crichton, winding up his line after looking at her a moment. We scrambled over the rocks to her, but she had landed her fish before we reached her. I was amazed to see Mrs. Nicholl coolly wading more than ankle deep in the river with her ordinary lady's boots on. She walked about in the river as if she were on dry land, jumped from rock to rock, slipped off the rocks into the river, scrambled out again, splashed about like a fish. March water is cold, Mrs. Nicholl must be an uncommonly plucky woman. Crichton says she rides to hounds and nothing stops her. She does not care what she does. He hooked a salmon the other day and his boy was clumsy in landing the fish, so Mrs. Nicholl plunged into the water on the edge of a deep hole, embraced the great fish round the body, and carried him out in her arms.

Saturday, 8 June

A pouring wet morning. Nevertheless my Father and I started in the rain for the Vale of Arrow, he riding the Vicarage pony sheltered by two mackintoshes and an umbrella and I on foot with an umbrella only. We plodded on doggedly through the wet for 6 miles, casting wistful glances at all the quarters of the heavens to catch any gleam of hope. Hope however there seemed to be none. The rain fell pitilessly. The Harbour below us in the Vale of Arrow was a welcome sight, a haven of refuge.

In spite of the wild weather on the open mountain we could not help noticing the beautiful effect produced upon the steep slopes by the vast sheets of brilliantly green young fern spreading amongst the old black heather. The mountain ashes were still in full blossom in the Fuallt fold and the meadows round the old farm house and the graceful trees were covered with the bunches of white bloom.

We reached the Harbour more like drowned rats than clergymen of the Established Church.

The boy took the pony to the stable and Mrs. Jones came to the door. And now here is a fine specimen of Radnorshire manners. She was in her working dress and in the midst of her Saturday cleaning but quite unconscious of herself and her dress she simply and naturally came forward at once and welcomed us to the Harbour with her grand courteous manner as if she had been a queen in disguise or in full purple and ermine. Then at the time when the work was done the mistress of the house took her place at the head of her table with all the natural grace and simple quiet dignity of a woman in the best society. Mrs. Irvine came down and Watkeys Jones, the master of the house, appeared like a wounded soldier with his head bound up in a red handkerchief. The good people were most kind to us, providing us with dry coats, hats and leggings and hot brandy and water and when the rain had a little abated we went down to the little river to fish under the guidance of the master of the house. The stream was too muddy for the fly and too clear for the worm. But the water was rising fast. We crossed a swampy meadow to the Glasnant above the meeting of the waters, a little stream flowing swiftly under alders. Then we followed the Glasnant down to its meeting with the Arrow. Some willows grew here and there was a likely hole with deep smooth still water under a bush sheltered by a sudden curve in the bank. Out came two trout. From the next pool four trout came out fast one after another. 'Well done, well done!' cried the good farmer with delight, clapping my Father on the back, 'I've never seen better work than that.'

My fishing diary cannot, of course, compare with Kilvert's but here is an entry from 1944. I was returning from a fishing trip through the Welsh valleys.

Coming up from Newport in the little local train, one climbs endlessly up the valley on the southern side of the Brecon Beacons, the rivers foul with black from the coal mines and the steel mills, the mountainsides scarred with slag heaps. On that first visit, we wondered what we were coming to. Then, suddenly, we reached the top on a glorious spring evening and sank down into Talyboat, past the reservoirs and the green trees and the unspoilt mountains of the northern side of the Brecon Beacons.

from

BEVIS: THE STORY
OF A YOUNG BOY

Richard Jefferies

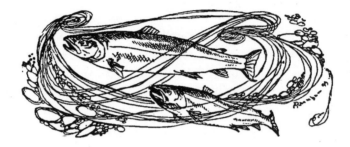

The writer and naturalist Richard Jefferies is best remembered for
Bevis: The Story of a Young Boy. *In it, he captures a country*
childhood for both adults and children. It is characteristic of all his
writing in that it combines his love of the natural world with his own
individual and poetic way of perceiving it. I am led to believe that
Jefferies relied heavily on 'field notebooks', meticulous observations of
the countryside. It must be this that gives this 'poetic' accuracy.

NEXT morning Bevis went out into the meadow to try and find a
plant whose leaves, or one of them, always pointed to the north, like
a green compass lying on the ground. There was one in the prairies
by which the hunters directed themselves across those oceans of grass
without a landmark as the mariners at sea. Why should there not
be one in the meadows here – in these prairies – by which to guide
himself from forest to forest, from hedge to hedge, where there was
no path? If there was a path it was not proper to follow it, nor ought
you to know your way; you ought to find it by sign.

He had 'blazed' ever so many boughs of the hedges with the
hatchet, or his knife if he had not got the hatchet with him, to
recognize his route through the woods. When he found a nest

begun or finished, and waiting for the egg, he used to cut a 'blaze' – that is, to peel off the bark – or make a notch, or cut a bough off about three yards from the place, so that he might easily return to it, though hidden with foliage. No doubt the grass had a secret of this kind, and could tell him which was the way, and which was the north and south if he searched long enough.

So the raft being an old story now, as he had had it a day, Bevis went out into the field, looking very carefully down into the grass. Just by the path there were many plantains, but their long narrow leaves did not point in any particular direction, no two plants had their leaves parallel. The blue scabious had no leaves to speak of, nor had the red knapweed, nor the yellow rattle, nor the white moon-daisies, nor golden buttercups, nor red sorrel. There were stalks and flowers, but the plants of the mowing-grass, in which he had no business to be walking, had very little leaf. He tried to see if the flowers turned more one way than the other, or bowed their heads to the north, as men seem to do, taking that pole as their guide, but none did so. They leaned in any direction, as the wind had left them, or as the sun happened to be when they burst their green bonds and came forth to the light.

The wind came past as he looked and stroked everything the way it went, shaking white pollen from the bluish tops of the tall grasses. The wind went on and left him and the grasses to themselves. 'How should I know which was the north or the south of the west from these?' Bevis asked himself, without framing any words to his question. There was no knowing. Then he walked to the hedge to see if the moss grew more on one side of the elms than the other, or if the bark was thicker and rougher.

After he had looked at twenty trees he could not see much differ-ence; those in the hedge had the moss thickest on the eastern side (he knew which was east very well himself, and wanted to see if the moss knew), and those in the land just through it had the moss thickest on their western side, which was clearly because of the shadow. The trees were really in a double row, running north and south, and the coolest shadow was in between them, and so the moss grew there most. Nor were the boughs any longer or bigger any side more than the other, it varied as the tree was closely surrounded with other trees, for each tree repelled its neighbour. None of the trees, nor the moss, nor grasses cared anything at all about north or south.

Bevis sat down in the mowing-grass, though he knew the Bailiff would have been angry at such a hole being made in it; and when he was sitting on the ground it rose as high as his head. He could see nothing but the sky, and while he sat there looking up he saw that the clouds all drifted one way, towards his house. Presently a starling came past, also flying straight for the house, and after a while another. Next three bees went over as straight as a line, all going one after another that way. The bees went because they had gathered as much honey as they could carry, and were hastening home without looking to the right or to the left. The starlings went because they had young in their nests in a hole of the roof by the chimney, and they had found some food for their fledglings. So now he could find his way home across the pathless prairie by going the same way as the clouds, the bees, and the starlings.

But when he had reached home he recollected that he ought to know the latitude, and that there were Arabs or some other people in Africa who found out the latitude of the place they were in by gazing at the sun through a tube. Bevis considered a little, and then went to the rick-yard, where there was a large elder bush, and cut a straight branch between the knots with his knife. He peeled it, and then forced out the pith, and thus made a tube. Next he took a thin board, and scratched a circle on it with the point of the compasses, and divided it into degrees. Round the tube he bent a piece of wire, and put the ends through a gimlet-hole in the centre of the board. The ends were opened apart, so as to fasten the tube to the board, allowing it to rotate round the circle. Two gimlet holes were bored at the top corners of the board, and string passed through so that the instrument could be attached to a tree or post.

He was tying it to one of the young walnut trees as an upright against which to work his astrolabe, when Mark arrived, and everything had to be explained to him. After they had glanced through the tube, and decided that the raft was at least ten degrees distant, it was clearly of no use to go to it to-day, as they could not reach it under a week's travel. The best thing, Mark thought, would be to continue their expedition in some other direction.

'Let's go round the Longpond,' said Bevis; 'we have never been quite round it.'

'So we will,' said Mark. 'But we shall not be back to dinner.'

'As if travellers ever thought of dinner! Of course we shall take our provisions with us.'

'Let's go and get our spears,' said Mark.

'Let's take Pan,' said Bevis

'Where is your old compass?' said Mark.

'Oh, I know – and I must make a map; wait a minute. We ought to have a medicine-chest; the savages will worry us for physic: and very likely we shall have dreadful fevers.'

'So we shall, of course; but perhaps there are wonderful plants to cure us, and we know them and the savages don't – there's sorrel.'

'Of course, and we can nibble some hawthorn leaf.'

'Or a stalk of wheat.'

'Or some watercress.'

'Or some nuts.'

'No, certainly not; they're not ripe,' said Bevis, 'and unripe fruit is very dangerous in tropical countries.'

'We ought to keep a diary,' said Mark. 'When we go to sleep who shall watch first, you or I?'

'We'll light a fire,' said Bevis. 'That will frighten the lions; they will glare at us, but they can't stand fire – you hit them on the head with a burning stick.'

So they went in, and loaded their pockets with huge double slices of bread-and-butter done up in paper, apples, and the leg of a roast duck from the pantry. Then came the compass, an old one in a brass case; Mark broke his nails opening the case, which was tarnished, and the card at once swung round to the north, pointing to the elms across the road from the window of the sitting-room. Bevis took the bow and three arrows, made of the young wands of hazel which grow straight, and Mark was armed with a spear, a long ash rod with sharpened end, which they thrust in the kitchen fire a few minutes to harden in the proper manner.

Besides which, there was Bevis's pocket-book for the diary, and a large sheet of brown paper for the map; you see travellers have not always everything at command, but must make use of what they have. Pan raced before them up the footpath; the gate that led to the Longpond was locked, and too high to be climbed easily, but they knew a gap, and crept through on hands and knees.

'Take care there are no cobras or rattlesnakes among those dead leaves,' said Mark, when they were halfway through, and quite over-arched and hidden under brambles.

'Stick your spear into them,' said Bevis, who was first, and Mark, putting his spear past him, stirred up the heap of leaves.

'All right,' said he. 'But look at that bough – is it a bough or a snake?'

There was an oak branch in the ditch, crooked and grey with lichen, half concealed by rushes; its curving shape and singular hue gave it some resemblance to a serpent. But when he stabbed at it with his spear it did not move; and they crept through without hurt. As they stood up in the field the other side they had an anxious consultation as to what piece of water it was they were going to discover; whether it was a lake in Central Africa, or one in America.

'I'm tired of lakes,' said Mark. 'They have found out such a lot of lakes, and the canoes are always upset, and there is such a lot of mud. Let's have a new sea altogether.'

'So we will,' said Bevis. 'That's capital – we will find a new sea where no one has ever been before. Look!' – for they had now advanced to where the gleam of the sunshine on the mere was visible through the hedge – 'look! there it is, is it not wonderful?'

'Yes,' said Mark, 'write it down in the diary; here's my pencil. Be quick; put 'Found a new sea' – be quick – there, come on – let's run – hurrah!'

They dashed open the gate, and ran down to the beach. It was a rough descent over large stones, but they reached the edge in a minute, and as they came there was a splashing in several places along the shore. Something was striving to escape, alarmed at their approach. Mark fell on his knees, and put his hand where two or three stones, half in and half out of water, formed a recess, and feeling about drew out two roach, one of which slipped from his fingers; the other he held. Bevis rushed at another splashing; but he was not quick enough, for it was difficult to scramble over the stones, and the fish swam away just as he got there. Mark's fish was covered with tiny slippery specks. The roach had come up to leave their eggs under the stones. When they had looked at the fish they put it back in the water, and with a kind of shake it dived down and made off. As they watched it swim out they now saw that three or four yards from the shore there were crowds upon crowds of fish travelling to and fro, following the line of the land.

They were so many, that the water seemed thick with them, and some were quite large for roach. These had finished putting their eggs under the stones, and were now swimming up and down. Every now and then, as they silently watched the roach – for they had never before seen such countless multitudes of fish – they could hear splashings further along the stones, where those that were up in the recesses were suddenly seized with panic fear without cause, and struggled to get out, impeding each other, and jammed together in the narrow entrances. For they could not forget their cruel enemies the jacks, and dreaded lest they should be pounced upon while unable even to turn.

A black cat came down the bank some way off, and they saw her swiftly dart her paw into the water, and snatch out a fish. The scales shone silver white, and reflected the sunshine into their eyes like polished metal as the fish quivered and leaped under the claw. Then the cat quietly, and pausing over each morsel, ate the living creature. When she had finished she crept towards the water to get another.

'What a horrid thing!' said Mark. 'She ate the fish alive – cruel wretch! Let's kill her.'

'Kill her,' said Bevis; and before he could fit an arrow to his bow Mark picked up a stone, and flung it with such a good aim and with such force that although it did not hit the cat, it struck a stone and split into fragments, which flew all about her like a shell.

The cat raced up the bank, followed by a second stone, and at the top met Pan, who did not usually chase cats, having been beaten for it, but seeing in an instant that she was in disgrace, he snapped at her and drove her wild with terror up a pine tree. They called Pan off, for it was no use his yapping at a tree, and walked along the shore, climbing over stones, but the crowds of roach were everywhere; till presently they came to a place where the stones ceased, and there was a shallow bank of sand shelving into the water and forming a point.

There the fish turned round and went back. Thousands kept coming up and returning, and while they stayed here watching, gazing into the clear water, which was still and illuminated to the bottom by the sunlight, they saw two great fish come side by side up from the depths beyond and move slowly, very slowly, just over the sand. They were two huge tench, five or six pounds a-piece, roaming idly away from the muddy holes they lie in. But they do not stay in such holes always, and once now and then you may see them like this as in a glass tank. The pair did not go far; they floated slowly rather than swam, first a few yards one way and then a few yards the other. Bevis and Mark were breathless with eagerness.

'Go and fetch my fishing-rod' whispered Bevis, unable to speak loud; he was so excited.

'No, you go,' said Mark; ' I'll stay and watch them.'

'I shan't,' said Bevis sharply, 'you ought to go.'

'I shan't,' said Mark.

Just then the tench, having surveyed the bottom there, turned and faded away into the darker deep water.

'There,' said Bevis, ' if you had run quick!'

'I won't fetch everything,' said Mark.

'Then you're no use,' said Bevis. 'Suppose I was shooting an elephant, and you did not hand me another gun quick, or another arrow; and suppose —'

'But *I* might be shooting the elephant,' interrupted Mark, 'and you could hand me the gun.'

'Impossible,' said Bevis; 'I never heard anything so absurd. Of course it's the captain who always does everything; and if there was only one biscuit left, of course you would let me eat it, and lie down and die under a tree, so that I might go on and reach the settlement.'

'I *hate* dying under a tree,' said Mark, 'and you always want everything.'

Bevis said nothing, but marched on very upright and very angry, and Mark followed, putting his feet into the marks Bevis left as he strode over the yielding sand. Neither spoke a word. The shore trended in again after the point, and the indentation was full of weeds, whose broad brownish leaves floated on the surface. Pan worked about and sniffed among the willow bushes on their left, which, when the lake was full, were in the water, but now that it had shrunk under the summer heat were several yards from the edge.

Bevis, leading the way, came to a place where the strand, till then so low and shelving, suddenly became steep, where a slight rise of the ground was cut as it were through by the water, which had worn a cliff eight or ten feet above his head. The water came to the bottom of the cliff, and there did not seem any way past it except by going away from the edge into the field, and so round it. Mark at once went round, hastening as fast as he could to get in front, and he came down to the water on the other side of the cliff in half a minute, looked at Bevis, and then went on with Pan.

Bevis, with a frown on his forehead, stood looking at the cliff, having determined that he would not go round, and yet he could not get past because the water, which was dark and deep, going straight down, came to the bank, which rose from it like a wall. First he took out his pocket-knife and thought he would cut steps in the sand, and he did cut one large enough to put his toe in; but then he recollected that he should have nothing to hold to. He had half a mind to go back home and get some big nails and drive into the hard sand to catch hold of, only by that time Mark would be so far ahead he could not overtake him and would boast that he had explored the new sea first. Already he was fifty yards in front, and walking as fast as he could. How he wished he had his raft, and then that he could swim! He would have jumped into the water and swum round the cliff in a minute.

He saw Mark climbing over some railings that went down to the water to divide the fields. He looked up again at the cliff, and almost felt inclined to leave it and run round and overtake Mark. When he looked down again Mark was out of sight, hidden by hawthorn bushes and the branches of trees. Bevis was exceedingly angry, and he walked up and down and gazed round in his rage. But as he turned once more to the cliff, suddenly Pan appeared at an opening in the furze and bramble about halfway up. The bushes grew at the side, and the spaniel, finding Bevis did not follow Mark, had come back and was waiting for him. Bevis, without thinking, pushed into the furze, and immediately he saw him coming, Pan, eager to go forward again, ran along the face of the cliff about four feet from the top. He seemed to run on nothing, and Bevis was curious to see how he had got by.

The bushes becoming thicker, Bevis had at last to go on hands and knees under them, and found a hollow space, where there was a great rabbit-bury, big enough at the mouth for Pan to creep in. When he stood on the sand thrown out from it he could see how Pan had done it; there was a narrow ledge, not above four inches wide, on the face of the cliff. It was only just wide enough for a footing, and the cliff fell sheer down to the water; but Bevis, seeing that he could touch the top of the cliff, and so steady himself, never hesitated a moment.

He stepped on the ledge, right foot first, the other close behind it, and held lightly to the grass at the edge of the field above, only lightly lest he should pull it out by the roots. Then he put his right foot forward again, and drew his left up to it, and so along, keeping the right first (he could not walk properly, the ledge being so narrow), he worked himself along. It was quite easy, though it seemed a long way down to the water (it always looked very much farther down than it does up), and as he glanced down he saw a perch rise from the depths, and it occurred to him in the moment what a capital place it would be for perch-fishing.

He could see al over that part of the lake, and noticed two moorhens feeding in the weeds on the other side, when puff! the wind came over the field, and reminded him, as he involuntarily grasped the grass tighter, that he must not stay in such a place where he might lose his balance. So he went on, and a dragonfly flew past out a little way over the water and then back to the field, but Bevis was not to be tempted to watch his antics; he kept steadily on, a foot at a time, till he reached a willow on the other side, and had a bough to hold. Then he shouted, and Pan, who was already far ahead, stopped and looked back at the well-known sound of triumph.

Running down the easy slope, Bevis quickly reached the railings and climbed over. On the other side a meadow came down to the edge, and he raced through the grass and was already halfway to the next rails when someone called 'Bevis!' and there was Mark coming out from behind an oak in the field. Bevis stopped, half-pleased, half-angry.

'I waited for you,' said Mark.

'I came across the cliff,' said Bevis.

'I saw you,' said Mark.

'But you ran away from me.' said Bevis.

'But I am not running now.'

'It is very wrong when we are on an expedition,' said Bevis. 'People must do as the captain tells them.'

'I won't do it again,' said Mark.

'You ought to be punished,' said Bevis, 'you ought to be put on half-rations. Are you quite sure you will never do it again?'

'Never.'

'Well then, this once you are pardoned. Now, mind in future, as you are lieutenant, you set a good example. There's a summer snipe.'

Out flew a little bird from the shore, startled as Pan came near, with a piping whistle, and, describing a semicircle, returned to the hard mud fifty yards farther on. It was a summer snipe, and when they approached, after getting over the next railings, it flew out again over the water, and making another half-circle passed back to where they had first seen it. Here the strand was hard mud, dried by the sun, and broken up into innumerable holes by the hoofs of cattle and horses which had come down to drink from the pasture, and had to go through the mud into which they sank when it was soft. Three or four yards from the edge there was a narrow strip of weeds, showing that a bank followed the line of the shore there. It was so unpleasant walking over this hard mud, that they went up into the field, which rose high, so that from the top they had a view of the lake.

★ ★ ★

'Do you see any canoes?' said Mark.

'No,' said Bevis. 'Can you? Look very carefully.'

They gazed across the broad water over the gleaming ripples far away, for the light wind did not raise them by the shore, and traced the edge of the willows and the weeds.

'The savages are in hiding,' said Bevis, after a pause. 'Perhaps they're having a feast.'

'Or gone somewhere to war.'

'Are they cannibals?' said Mark. 'I should not like to be gnawn.'

'Very likely,' said Bevis. 'No one has ever been here before, so they are nearly sure to be; they always are where no one has been. This would be a good place to begin the map as we can see so far. Let's sit down.'

'Let's get behind a tree, then,' said Mark; 'else if we stay still long perhaps we shall be seen.'

So they went a little farther to an ash, and sat down by it. Bevis spread out his sheet of brown paper.

'Give me an apple,' said Mark, 'while you draw.' Bevis did so, and then, lying on the ground at full length, began to trace out the course of the shore; Mark lay down too, and held one side of the paper that the wind might not lift it. First Bevis made a semicircle to represent the stony bay where they found the roach, then an angular point for the sandy bar, then a straight line for the shelving shore.

'There ought to be names,' said Mark. 'What shall we call this?' putting his finger on the bay.

'Don't splutter over the map,' said Bevis; 'take that apple-pip off it. Of course there will be names when I have drawn the outline. Here's the cliff.' He put a slight projection where the cliff jutted out a little way, then a gentle curve for the shore of the meadow, and began another trending away to the left for the place where they were.

'That's not long enough,' said Mark.

'It's not finished,' said Bevis. 'How can I finish it when we have only got as far as this? How do I know, you stupid, how far this bay goes into the land? Perhaps there's another sea round there,' point-ing over the field. 'Instead of saying silly things, just find out some names, now.'

'What sea it it?' said Mark thoughtfully.

'I can't tell,' said Bevis. 'It is most extraordinary to find a new sea. And such an enormous big one. Why how many days' journey have we come already?'

'Thirty,' said Mark. 'Put it down in the diary, thirty days' journey. There, that's right. Now, what sea is it? Is it the Atlantic?'

'No; it's not the Atlantic, nor the Pacific, nor the South Sea; it's bigger than all those.'

'It's much more difficult to find a name than a sea,' said Mark.

'Much,' said Bevis. They stared at each other for awhile. 'I know,' said Bevis.

'Well, what is it?' said Mark excitedly, raising himself on his knees to hear the name.

'I know,' said Bevis. 'I'll lie down and shut my eyes, and you take a piece of grass and tickle me; then I can think. I can't think unless I'm tickled.'

He disposed himself very comfortably on his back with his knees up, and tilted his straw hat so as to shade that side of his face towards the sun. Mark pulled a bennet.

'Not *too* ticklish,' said Bevis, 'else that won't do: don't touch my lips.'

'All right.'

Mark held the bending bennet (the spike of the grass) bending with the weight of its tip, and drew it very gently across Bevis's forehead. Then he let it just touch his cheek, and afterwards put the tip very daintily on his eyelid. From there he let it wander like a fly over his forehead again, and close by, but not in the ear (as too ticklish), leaving little specks of pollen on the skin, and so to the neck, and next up again to the hair, and on the other cheek under the straw hat. Bevis, with his eyes shut, kept quite still under this luxurious tickling for some time, till Mark, getting tired, put the bennet delicately on his lip, when he started and rubbed his mouth.

'Now, how stupid you are, Mark; I was just thinking. Now, do it again.'

Mark did it again.

'Are you thinking?' he asked presently.

'Yes,' whispered Bevis. They were so silent they heard the grasshoppers singing in the grass, and the swallows twittering as they flew over, and the loud midsummer hum in the sky.

'Are you thinking?' asked Mark again. Bevis did not answer – he was asleep. Mark bent over him, and went on tickling, half dreamy himself, till he nodded, and his hat fell on Bevis, who sat up directly.

'I know.'

'What is it?'

'It is not one sea,' said Bevis; 'it is a lot of seas. That's the Blue Sea, there,' pointing to the stony bay where the water was still and blue under the sky. 'That's the Yellow Sea, there,' pointing to the low muddy shore where the summer snipe flew up, and where, as it was so shallow and so often disturbed by cattle, the water was thick for some yards out.

'And what is that out there?' said Mark, pointing southward to the broader open water where the ripples were sparkling bright in the sunshine.

'That is the Golden Sea,' said Bevis. 'It is like butterflies flapping their wings' – he meant the flickering wavelets.

'And this round here?' where the land trended to the left, and there was a deep inlet.

'It is the Gulf,' said Bevis; 'Fir Tree Gulf,' as he noticed the tops of fir trees.

'And that up at the top yonder, right away as far as you can see beyond the Golden Sea?'

'That's the Indian Ocean' said Bevis; 'and that island on the left side there is Serendib.'

'Where Sinbad went?'

'Yes; and that one by it is the Unknown Island, and a magician lives there in a long white robe, and he has a serpent a hundred feet long coiled up in a cave under a bramble bush, and the most wonderful things in the world.'

'Let's go there,' said Mark.

'So we will,' said Bevis, 'directly we have got a ship.'

'Write the names down,' said Mark. 'Put them on the map before we forget them.'

Bevis wrote them on the map, and then they started again upon their journey. Where the gulf began they found a slight promontory, or jutting point, defended by blocks of stone; for here the waves, when the wind blew west or south, came rolling with all their might over the long broad Golden Sea from the Indian Ocean. Pan left them while they stood here, to hunt among the thistles in an old sand-quarry behind. He started a rabbit, and chased it up the quarry, so that when they looked back they saw him high up the side, peering into the bury. Sand-martins were flying in and out of their round holes. At one place there was only a narrow strip of land between the ocean and the quarry, so that it seemed as if its billows might at any time force their way in.

They left the shore awhile, and went into the quarry, and winding in and out the beds of nettles and thistles climbed up a slope, where they sank at every step ankle deep in sand. It led to a broad platform of sand, above which the precipice rose straight to the roots of the grass above, which marked the top of the cliff with brown, and where humble-bees were buzzing along the edge, and, bending the flowers down on which they alighted, were thus suspended in space. In the cool recesses of the firs at the head of Fir Tree Gulf a dove was cooing, and a great aspen rustled gently.

They took out their knives and pecked at the sand. It was hard, but could be pecked, and grooves cut in it. The surface was almost green from exposure to the weather, but under that white. When they looked round over the ocean they were quite alone: there was no one in sight either way, as far as they could see; nothing but the wall of sand behind, and the wide gleaming water in front.

'What a long way we are from other people,' said Mark.

'Thousands of miles,' said Bevis.

'Is it quite safe?'

'I don't know,' doubtfully.

'Are there not strange creatures in these deserted places?'

'Sometimes,' said Bevis. 'Sometimes there are things with wings, which have spikes on them, and they have eyes that burn you.'

Mark grasped his knife and spear, and looked into the beds of thistles and nettles, which would conceal anything underneath.

'Let's call Pan,' he whispered.

Bevis shouted 'Pan!' 'Pan!' came back in an echo from another part of the quarry. 'Pan!' shouted Bevis and Mark together. Pan did not come. They called again and whistled; but he did not come.

'Perhaps something has eaten him,' said Mark.

'Very likely,' said Bevis. 'We ought to have a charm. Don't forget next time we come to bring a talisman, so that none of these things can touch us.'

'I know,' said Mark. 'I know.' He took his spear and drew a circle on the platform of sand. 'Come inside this. There, that's it. Now stand still here. A circle is magic, you know.'

'So it is,' said Bevis. 'Pan!' 'Pan!'

Pan did not come.

'What's in those holes?' said Mark, pointing to some large rabbit-burrows on the right side of the quarry.

'Mummies,' said Bevis. 'You may be sure there are mummies there, and very likely magic writings in their hands. I wish we could get a magic writing. Then we could do anything, and we could know all the secrets.'

'What secrets?'

'Why, all these things have secrets.'

'All?'

'All,' said Bevis, looking round and pointing with an arrow in his hand. 'All the trees, and all the stones, and all the flowers –'

'And these?' said Mark, picking up a shell.

'Yes, once; but can't you see it is dead, and the secret, of course, is gone. If we had a magic writing.'

'Let's buy a book,' said Mark.

'They are not books; they are rolls, and you unroll them very slowly, and see curious things, pictures that move over the paper –'

Boom!

They started. Mark lifted his spear, Bevis his bow. A deep, low, and slow sound, like thunder, toned from it many mutterings to a mighty sob, filled their ears for a moment. It might have been very distant thunder, or a cannon in the forts far away. It was one of those mysterious sounds that are heard in summer when the sky is clear and the wind soft, and the midsummer hum is loud. They listened, but it did not come again.

'What was that?' said Mark at last.

'I don't know; of course it was something magic.'

'Perhaps they don't like us coming into these magic places,' said Mark. 'Perhaps it is to tell us to go away. No doubt Pan is eaten.'

'I shall not go away,' said Bevis, as the boom did not come again. 'I shall fight first;' and he fitted his arrow to the string. 'What's that!' and in his start he let the arrow fly down among the thistles.

It was Pan looking down upon them from the edge above, where he had been waiting ever since they first called him, and wondering why they did not see him. Bevis, chancing to glance up defiantly as he fitted his arrow to shoot the genie of the boom, had caught sight of the spaniel's face peering over the edge. Angry with Pan for making him start, Bevis picked up a stone and flung it at him, but the spaniel slipped back and escaped it.

'Fetch my arrow,' said Bevis, stamping his foot.

Mark went down and got it. As he came up the sandy slope he looked back.

'There's a canoe,' he said.

'So it is.'

A long way off there was a black mark as it were among the

glittering wavelets of the Golden Sea. They could not see it properly for the dazzling gleam.

'The cannibals have seen us,' said Mark. 'They can see miles. We shall be gnawn. Let's run out of sight before they come too near.'

They ran down the slope into the quarry, and then across to the fir trees. Then they stopped and watched the punt, but it did not come towards them. They had not been seen. They followed the path through the firs, and crossed the head of the gulf.

A slow stream entered the lake there, and they went down to the shore, where it opened to the larger water. Under a great willow, whose tops rose as high as the firs, and an alder or two, it was so cool and pleasant, that Mark, as he played with the water with his spear, pushing it this way and that, and raising bubbles, and a splashing as a whip sings in the air, thought he should like to dabble in it. He sat down on a root and took off his shoes and stockings, while Bevis, going a little way up the stream, flung a dead stick into it, and then walked beside it as it floated gently down. But he walked much faster than the stick floated, there was so little current.

'Mark,' said he, suddenly stopping, and taking up some of the water in the hollow of his hand, 'Mark!'

'Yes. What is it?'

'This is fresh water. Isn't it lucky?'

'Why?'

'Why, you silly, of course we should have died of thirst. *That's* the sea' (pointing out). 'That will save our lives.'

'So it will,' said Mark, putting one foot into the water and then the other. Then looking back, as he stood half up his ankles, 'We can call here for fresh water when we have our ship – when we go to the Unknown Island.'

'So we can,' said Bevis. 'We must have a barrel and fill it. But I wonder what river this is,' and he walked back again beside it.

Mark walked further out till it was over his ankles, and then till it was half as deep as his knee. He jumped up both feet together, and splashed as he came down, and shouted. Bevis shouted to him from the river. Next they both shouted together and a dove flew out of the firs and went off.

'What river is this?' Bevis called presently.

'Oh!' cried Mark suddenly; and Bevis glancing round saw him stumble, and, in his endeavour to save himself, plunge his spear into the water as if it had been the ground, to steady himself; but the spear, though long, touched nothing up to his hand. He bent over. Bevis held his breath, thinking he must topple and fall headlong; but somehow he just saved himself, swung round and immediately he could, ran out upon the shore. Bevis rushed back.

'What was it?' he asked.

'It's a hole,' said Mark, whose cheeks had turned white, and now became red, as the blood came back. 'An awful deep hole – the spear won't touch the bottom.'

As he waded out at first on shelving sand he laughed, and shouted, and jumped, and suddenly, as he stepped, his foot went over the edge of the deep hole; his spear, as he tried to save himself with it, touched nothing, so that it was only by good fortune that he recovered his balance. Once now and then in the autumn, when the water was very low, dried up by the long summer heats, this hole was visible and nearly empty, and the stream fell over a cataract into it, boiling and bubbling, and digging it deeper. But now, as the water had only just begun to recede, it was full, so that the stream ran slow, held back and checked by their sea.

This hollow was quite ten feet deep, sheer descent, but you could not see it, for the shore seemed to slope as shallow as possible.

Mark was much frightened, and sat down on the root to put on his shoes and stockings. Bevis took the spear, and going to the edge, and leaning over and feeling the bottom with it, he could find the hole, where the spear slipped and touched nothing, about two yards out.

'It's a horrid place,' he said. 'How should I have got you out? I wish we could swim.'

'So do I,' said Mark. 'And they will never let us go out in a boat by ourselves – I mean in a ship to the Unknown Island – till we can.'

'No; that they won't,' said Bevis. 'We must begin to swim directly. My papa will show me, and I will show you. But how should I have got you out if you had fallen? Let me see; there's a gate up there.'

'It is so heavy,' said Mark. 'You could not drag it down, and fling it in quick enough. If we had the raft up here.'

'Ah, yes. There is a pole loose there – that would have done.' He pointed to some railings that crossed the stream. The rails were nailed, but there was a pole at the side, only thrust into the bushes. 'I could have pulled that out and held it to you.'

Mark had now got his shoes on, and they started again, looking for a bridge to cross the stream, and continue their journey round the New Sea. As they could not see any they determined to cross by the railings, which they did without much trouble, holding to the top bar, and putting their feet on the second, which was about three inches over the water. The stream ran deep and slow; it was dark, because it was in shadow, for the trees hung over from each side. Bevis, who was first, stopped in the middle and looked up it. There was a thick hedge and trees each side, and a great deal of fern on the banks. It was straight for a good way, so that they could see some distance till the boughs hid the rest.

'I should like to go up there,' said Mark. 'Some day, if we can get a boat under these rails, let us go up it.'

'So we will,' said Bevis. 'It is proper to explore a river. But what river is this?'

'Is it the Congo?' said Mark.

'Oh! no. The Congo is not near this sea at all. Perhaps it's the Amazon.'

'It can't be the Mississippi,' said Mark. 'That's a long way off now. I know — see, it runs slow, and it's not clear, and we don't know where it comes from. It's the Nile.'

'So it is,' said Bevis. 'It is the Nile, and some day we will go up to the source.'

'What's that swimming across up there?' said Mark.

'It is too far; I can't tell. Most likely a crocodile. How fortunate you did not fall in.'

When they had crossed, they whistled for Pan, who had been busy among the fern on the bank, sniffing after the rabbits which had holes there. Pan came and swam over to them in a minute. They travelled on some way and found the ground almost level and so thick with sedges and grass and rushes that they walked in a forest of green up to their waists. The water was a long way off beyond the weeds. They tried to go down to it, but the ground got very soft and their feet sank into it; it was covered with horsetails there, acres and acres of them, and after these shallow water hidden under floating weeds. Some coots were swimming about the edge of the weeds too far to fear them. So they returned to the firm ground and walked on among the sedges and rushes. There was a rough path, though not much marked, which wound about so as to get the firmest footing, but every now and then they had to jump over a wet place.

'What immense swamps,' said Mark; 'I wonder wherever we shall get to.'

Underfoot there was a layer of the dead sedges of last year which gave beneath their weight, and the ground itself was formed of the roots of sedges and other plants. The water had not long since covered the place where they were, and the surface was still damp, for the sunshine could not dry it, having to pass through the thick growth above and the matted stalks below. A few scattered willow bushes showed how high the water had been by the fibres on the stems which had once flourished in it and were now almost dried up by the heat. A faint malarious odour rose from the earth, drawn from the rotting stalks by the hot sun. There was no shadow, and after a while they wearied of stepping through the sedges, sinking a little at every step, which much increases the labour of walking.

The monotony, too, was oppressive, nothing but sedges, flags, and rushes, sedges and horsetails, and they did not seem to get much farther after all their walking. First they were silent: labour makes us quiet; then they stopped and looked back. The perfect level caused the distance to appear more than it really was, because there was a thin invisible haze hovering over the swamp. Beyond the swamp was the gulf they had gone round, and across it the yellow sand-quarry facing them. It looked a very long way off.

During my early teens on Dartmoor I couldn't be kept away from the water but made this pathetic note in my diary:

Easter 1931

Rather a poor holiday as far as fishing is concerned. Margaret somehow got round Major H. for me and I had every Tuesday on his water during April and only got two keepable fish the whole time. The stream itself (the Bovey) is meant to be one of the best in Britain but the Major thinks of little but his pheasants, which he very closely resembles!

from

ANGLING ADVENTURES OF
AN ARTIST
John Shirley-Fox

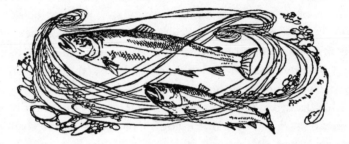

I leave it to John Shirley-Fox himself to introduce the next two extracts.

'The following sketches are mostly of incidents which have occurred to me during my own fairly long fishing career. They are not so much records of the capture of big fish or of the making of heavy bags as descriptions of various adventures which have provided pleasant memories and left behind them clear and well-defined pictures on the mind. Some, indeed, are of fish which were never caught at all, but as the late Joseph Choate once remarked at a Fly Fishers' Club dinner, "If the fish we catch leave happy recollections, what of those we do not catch? to these there is no limit; either in shape, size, or colour." This was, I fear, a sly hit at the doubts so often entertained of the ordinary fisherman's veracity, but there was perhaps more in what he said than the witty orator quite realised.' Introduction to Angling Adventures.

TWO LUCKY CAPTURES

ALTHOUGH it so often happens that a big fish gets away, after having been apparently well within our grasp, most of us hesitate to speak of these things lest we provide the scoffer with an opportunity of letting off at our expense the threadbare joke from which all anglers have suffered in their time. But just occasionally it is the contrary which occurs, and the big fish, which had apparently every opportunity to make good its escape, by some lucky chance in no way due to skill on the part of its captor, eventually ends its career in the landing net. Such an incident has found a lasting place in my memory.

I was once sitting with my brother on the flat bank below a good-sized hatch-hole on the upper waters of a chalk stream. To our left was the pool, immediately opposite a row of willows, the overhanging boughs of which swept down to the water, and just below us on our own bank was a stunted willow which had been converted with the aid of posts and barbed wire into a place for the cattle to drink. We had already hooked and played for some time a good trout, which had eventually rushed under the willows opposite and got away. This disturbance had effectually scared every other fish within sight, so we sat down to wait for confidence to be restored and hope that some other fish might in time start feeding within reach. Gradually a few smaller trout began to take up their positions in the openings between the weeds, but for a long while nothing appeared that seemed worth trying for. At last, after a long wait, there came out from the depths of the pool a magnificent trout, apparently about 2 lbs. in weight, thick, bronzed, and in splendid condition. After cruising about for some time in the clear shallow water at the tail of the pool where we could observe him as in an aquarium, he eventually sailed slowly down under the protecting willow boughs, and took up a position almost opposite us. There he lay, the spots on his broad back clearly visible, a most tempting looking object in the morning sunshine. At last he rose, and soon after yet again. The time had come to begin the attack, so without moving more than was absolutely necessary, I got out line and dispatched towards him the medium olive which happened at the time to be attached to my cast. There was just one narrow opening in the willow boughs into which the fly must be delivered if it was to be floated fairly over the trout, and to do this was not so easy. It was, however, accomplished at last, and the trout acknowledged the attention by coming up to the fly and giving it a careful scrutiny. Our pulses quickened! Would he take it? No! Something did not please him. Either there was a bit of a drag, or he saw the gut or something. Anyhow, he let the fly pass and returned unperturbed to his former position.

We kept up the attack at intervals for quite a long time, trying all sorts of flies, including a big alder and a large red palmer. In the two last he was keenly interested, and once even opened his mouth at the palmer, but at the last moment thought better of it. It really seemed that there was no chance of getting him to take, and we were already considering giving up the game, when my brother suggested as a last resource to try him with a 'Hassam.' This was the name we always used for a most minute fly tied by a friend of that name, dressed on an iron so frail that to try and land so big a fish upon one seemed absurd, especially as two patches of weed like feather-beds lay between us and our quarry, to say nothing of the willow boughs beyond and barbed wire below. However, I agreed to make the attempt, and having put on an extra fine point suitable to the minute object that was to be attached to it, managed by a lucky shot to get the fly nicely over the fish at the first attempt. Presumably its small size disarmed suspicion, for as it passed he put up his head and took it in. The light strike which followed caused him to do no more than shake his head irritably, he was not in the least alarmed, and made no immediate effort to leave his position. Presently he started off on a cruise downstream under the opposite bank. Having lately proved the futility of trying to hold a large trout out by force from the tangle of roots and other obstacles beneath the willow trees, I let the fish with which I was now in contact go absolutely as he wished, putting on no strain whatever, and keeping the rod point almost in the water so as to prevent the line fouling the overhanging branches. Quite slowly he reached the bottom of the run, and then of his own accord came back again and entered the pool, where for some time he swam quietly about in the deep water. I then put on some strain and got him out on the shallows once more, and this time he started on a downstream journey under our own bank, passing quite close to us as we sat motionless; evidently quite unaware of our presence. He was now approaching the barbed wire enclosure, and into it at last he went. Now we thought, 'all is over! he has but to go right through and out into the stream beyond and all chance of recovering him is gone.' But no! after a short stay and inspection of the small pool formed by treading of the cattle, he came out the way he had gone in, and was soon once more in open water. All this time he had obviously no conception of what was the matter but as he was now to some extent exhausted, and no dangerous hazards were within easy reach, I began to put on pressure, and it was then only a matter of patience getting him to the net. But during the whole of the struggle neither of us had moved from our seats, and to the last I do not believe the trout had the least idea that we were there. Had we shown ourselves earlier in the game I am convinced that this fish would have had to be added to the long list of big fish hooked and lost.

Another trout that ought to have got away and didn't was a fine fish of 3½ lbs. that once lived in a mill-head on the lower Kennet. I had gone one day in early May-fly time to a fine broad reach of water some distance above the mill full of hopeful expectations; but, as so often happens, these were not realised. No flies were hatching, and in consequence no trout were to be seen, so having promised to be back at one o'clock without fail, I started soon past noon to walk slowly downstream in a homeward direction. Nothing in the way of a likely looking rise was visible until I came to a place where the stream had been narrowed up by an artificial bank to form the mill-head. At one point the soil had worked away from the camp-sheathing supporting the bank, leaving several strong, solid piles sticking up some 2 feet out in the stream, which just there flowed strong and deep under my own bank. As I approached the place, there was a small rise inside one of the piles. It did not look much, and seemed quite likely to have been caused by one of the large dace which often frequented the spot, so without bothering to get below and fish up in the approved manner, I let out a long line and cast it along with plenty of slack under the bank, the fly well cocked going on ahead. The strong stream carried the line nicely, and the fly at last arrived without the least drag at the exact place where the rise had occurred. Immediately the fly disappeared, and I struck. There was a heavy boil in the water, and a big fish turned over and then all in one action plunged straight down among the piles. After this there was no sensation of movement whatever. It had all happened in a few seconds, and this seemed, so far as one could see, likely to be the end of the adventure.

Gradually reeling in I eventually reached the spot where my line went down into the water, and standing immediately over the point where it was fast, saw to my horror that it went straight into a large accumulation of weed that was caught up round the piles. There seemed nothing to be done except haul on the stout May-fly cast until something broke, but one always puts off as long as possible such desperate measure. A vigorous course of handling brought no result whatever, the fly might have been stuck in one of the posts for any sensation of 'give' it produced, so letting the line go quite slack with the forlorn hope that the fish might come out, I spiked my rod and looked round to see if some sort of pole or stake could be found with which to try and dislodge the submerged mass of weeds. Having at last discovered a very weak and inefficient stick, I was just about to begin operations, when suddenly in midstream there leaped into the air a splendid trout. It did not occur to me at first that this was in any way connected with the fish I supposed to be skulking at the bottom of the piles, but a violent twitch at the rod caused me to seize it with alacrity, when to my intense delight and surprise, I discovered that the fish was my fish, and what was more, that he was free of all obstacles and in clear open water. A good strong cast and May-fly hook soon brought him to the net, and I knocked him on the head still marvelling at the glorious uncertainty of fishing. There was a trout, apparently absolutely master of the situation, and yet he must in some extraordinary way disengage himself from what appeared to be a hopeless entanglement, and swim off into clear water in the most ridiculous manner!

I was so pleased with the success of this downstream drift that on approaching a little bay in the bank almost down by the mill, I again dispatched my fly as before, and sure enough, as the current took it well round into the little opening, a trout came up and took the fly. This time it was a two-pounder, and as no obstacles in the way of piles and weeds were available, the fish was soon disposed of. Thus in a very short space of time, two fine trout found their way into my bag, and transformed what looked like a blank morning into quite a successful little outing. But one must have a bit of luck sometimes!

from Angling Adventures of an Artist
THE OLD STONE TROUT

CARVED on a stone forming part of the inner wall of an old mill in Hampshire may yet be seen the somewhat worn presentment of a fine trout over 24 inches in length. Time has softened its outlines considerably, as it is over fifty years since the fish it represents was caught, and there are very few living who know the story of its capture. But it may be of interest to record, even now, how this noble trout came to be thus permanently recorded in stone. The stream upon which the mill is situated is a tributary of the Test and is within easy reach of a cheery little market town. In this town once dwelt a doctor and a lawyer, excellent friends in most respects, but both rather inclined to rivalry where their fishing interests were concerned.

In the early days of one particular season, each of them had in turn become aware of the existence in the mill-head of a very large trout, greatly exceeding in size any big fish that either of them had ever known to inhabit the river. Needless to say, neither imparted to the other the knowledge he had acquired, and each sought to keep from the other the secret of the big trout's whereabouts. If, as sometimes happened, one of the rivals was on the watch near the fish's haunt, and the other chanced to appear in the distance, the first comer would hurriedly remove himself from the spot, devoutly hoping that he had not been observed and the reason for his presence there not suspected. In course of time, however, it became clear to both anglers that the secret was a secret no longer, and although when they occasionally met by the river they discussed politely all manner of questions concerning flies and trout and the method of their capture, they studiously avoided all reference to big fish in general, and the one known to both of them in particular.

From this time onwards their fishing operations developed into a matter of tactics, each seeking to out-manœuvre the other, and in this game the doctor had a slight advantage, as he could often arrange his morning round so as to allow himself a spare half-hour at the mill, and sometimes his work would take him in the same direction later in the day. On the other hand, the wily lawyer managed somehow to be the more often successful in securing the coveted position for the evening rise. So matters went on for weeks, but beyond the occasional sight of a big wave, as the trout roused at last by the too persistent attention of an artificial fly swam off across the shallow bit of water near his home and sought shelter in the weedy depths beyond, no attention was paid to the efforts of either aspirant.

At length came the summer holidays, and with them the return home of the parson's eldest boy, a fishing enthusiast whose energy knew no bounds but whose experience had been so far mostly limited to float-fishing in the neighbouring ponds. But the recent birthday gift of a fly-rod and line now afforded him the opportunity to realise a long-cherished ambition and become a fly fisherman. So on the morning following his return home, he at once betook himself to the shop of the local barber, where fishing tackle could be procured, and there purchased what was then known as a gut 'collar' and a penny fly. The pattern he selected was a large-sized coachman. What induced him to choose this variety we can never know, possibly he thought the white wings would show up well and be more likely to attract the attention of fish, anyhow having now secured the requisite fishing equipment the next thing was to use it; so, in spite of the threatening look of the weather, he hurried off to the mill, where in common with most applicants for permission to fish, he was made welcome by the kindly miller. As the boy reached the mill, the heavens opened, and the long-threatening downpour began. For a time he exercised his patience and remained pottering about within the shelter of the mill, always a delightful place in which to while away spare time, but as the rain showed no signs of abating, the young angler could at last endure inactivity no longer, and having procured a garment of sorts to throw over his shoulders, sallied forth into the pelting rain. He had already some small knowledge of how to work a fly (there was no talk of dry flies in those days!), and as the wind was blowing sharply off his own bank he had little difficulty in getting his line to go well out.

Yard by yard he fished his way up the mill-head, dragging his fly through the water in what he conceived to be the proper manner. For some time nothing happened, but there was no hurry; he had sandwiches with him, and was out for the day. As he got about half-way up the mill-head, there was a boil in the water near where he conceived his fly to be, followed by a slight check as he drew it in towards him, and the next moment his line was running steadily off the reel in a most perplexing manner. His experience with tench and other fish in ponds fortunately prevented him from trying to stop its revolutions, and when at last it slowed down, he had wit enough to get his rod well up and keep in touch with the unseen force which was so persistently tugging at the other end of his line. That he had hooked a big fish he soon realised, but how it was to be got out was quite another matter. The miller's man was just then passing along the road close by, driving a cart towards the mill, and to him the boy shouted, but the other, wishing to get rid of his load and not realising that his presence was so urgently required, continued his way without paying any special attention to the youngster on the bank. Some quarter of an hour later, having deposited his sacks in the mill, the man passed again with his empty cart. To his surprise the boy was still in the same place, and at frequent intervals shouting for help. The carter's curiosity was aroused, so he stopped his horse, got down from the cart, and walked across the withy bed to where the boy stood, clinging desperately to a bending rod, and evidently fast in a very heavy fish. The carter quickly realised that the boy had on one of unusual size, and that to secure it some sort of landing net was essential, so leaving his cart to look after itself, he hurried off to the mill and shortly returned with a long-handled wire 'dipper' that was sometimes used to remove foreign bodies from the eel trap. The trout was by this time fairly played out, and was soon brought within reach and safely lifted out of the water. It was borne in triumph to the mill, where the scales recorded its weight as well over 5 lbs.; and one of the mill hands, who was a clever stone worker, was so impressed by its fine size and condition, that he traced it off on to the wall, and in his spare time carved out a fine portrait of the fish.

What were the feelings of the two other anglers when they heard the fate which had overtaken the object of their desire can only be imagined. But their common loss must to some extent have softened the feeling of rivalry which existed between them, for it was noted that henceforth they were often seen fishing together in friendly fashion, when they no doubt discussed again the time-worn theme of beginners' ridiculous good luck. Gone now are they both, the jovial miller too, and the head of he who carved the trout will never ache again. But the old stone trout is with us still, and looks good for many a year to come. Some day, if you are wandering in Hampshire, you may come across him unawares, in which case you will perhaps be interested to know how he came to be there!

FAR AWAY AND LONG AGO
W. H. Hudson

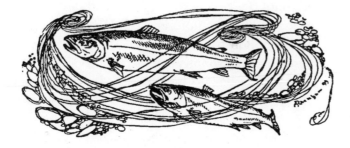

W. H. Hudson, the author of Green Mansions, *a magnificent novel of jungle romance, was a naturalist who also wrote vividly about the British countryside. However, he was born in Argentina where this tale is set.*

ONE day I witnessed a very strange thing, the action of a dog, by the waterside. It was evening and the beach was forsaken; cartmen, fishermen, boatmen all gone, and I was the only idler left on the rocks; but the tide was coming in, rolling quite big waves on to the rocks, and the novel sight of the waves, the freshness, the joy of it, kept me at that spot, standing on one of the outermost rocks not yet washed over by the water. By and by a gentleman, followed by a big dog, came down on to the beach and stood at a distance of forty or fifty yards from me, while the dog bounded forward over the flat, slippery rocks and through pools of water until he came to my side, and sitting on the edge of the rock began gazing intently down at the water. He was a big, shaggy, round-headed animal, with a greyish coat with some patches of light reddish colour on it; what his breed was I cannot say, but he looked somewhat like a sheep-dog or an otter-hound. Suddenly he plunged in, quite disappearing from sight, but quickly reappeared with a big shad of about three and a half or four pounds weight in his jaws. Climbing on to the rock he dropped the fish, which he did not appear to have injured much, as it began floundering about in an exceedingly lively manner. I was astonished and looked back at the dog's master; but there he stood in the same place, smoking and paying no attention to what his animal was doing. Again the dog plunged in and brought out a second big fish and dropped it on the flat rock, and again and again he dived, until there were five big shads all floundering about on the wet rock and likely soon to be washed back into the water.

The shad is a common fish in the Plata and the best to eat of all its fishes, resembling the salmon in its rich flavour, and is eagerly watched for when it comes up from the sea by the Buenos Ayres fishermen, just as our fishermen watch for mackerel on our coasts. But on this evening the beach was deserted by every one, watchers included, and the fish came and swarmed along the rocks, and there was no one to catch them – not even some poor hungry idler to pounce upon and carry off the five fishes the dog had captured. One by one I saw them washed back into the water, and presently the dog, hearing his master whistling to him, bounded away.

For many years after this incident I failed to find any one who had even seen or heard of a dog catching fish. Eventually, in reading I met with an account of fishing-dogs in Newfoundland and other countries.

from

THREE MEN IN A BOAT
Jerome K. Jerome

As a fellow actor, no collection of fishing stories would be complete without an extract from Three Men in a Boat, *the story of three young men who take a rowing holiday on the Thames.*

I KNEW a young man once, he was a most conscientious fellow and, when he took to fly-fishing, he determined never to exaggerate his hauls by more than twenty-five per cent.

'When I have caught forty fish,' said he, 'then I will tell people that I have caught fifty, and so on. But I will not lie any more than that, because it is sinful to lie.'

But the twenty-five per cent plan did not work well at all. He never was able to use it. The greatest number of fish he ever caught in one day was three, and you can't add twenty-five per cent to three – at least, not in fish.

So he increased his percentage to thirty-three and a third, but that, again, was awkward, when he had only caught one or two; so, to simplify matters, he made up his mind to just double the quantity.

He stuck to this arrangement for a couple of months, and then he grew dissatisfied with it. Nobody believed him when he told them that he only doubled, and he, therefore, gained no credit that way whatever, while his moderation put him at a disadvantage among the other anglers. When he had really caught three small fish, and said he had caught six, it used to make him quite jealous to hear a man, whom he knew for a fact had only caught one, going about telling people he had landed two dozen.

So, eventually he made one final arrangement with himself, which he has religiously held to ever since, and that was to count each fish that he caught as ten, and to assume ten to begin with. For example, if he did not catch any fish at all, then he said he had caught ten fish – you could never catch less than ten fish by his system; that was the foundation of it. Then, if by any chance he really did catch one fish, he called it twenty, while two fish would count thirty, three forty, and so on.

It is a simple and easily worked plan, and there has been some talk lately of its being made use of by the angling fraternity in general. Indeed, the Committee of the Thames Anglers' Association did recommend its adoption about two years ago, but some of the older members opposed it. They said they would consider the idea if the number were doubled, and each fish counted as twenty.

If ever you have an evening to spare, up the river, I should advise you to drop into one of the little village inns, and take a seat in the tap-room. You will be nearly sure to meet one or two old rod-men, sipping their toddy there, and they will tell you enough fishy stories in half an hour to give you indigestion for a month.

George and I – I don't know what had become of Harris; he had gone out and had a shave, early in the afternoon, and had then come back and spent full forty minutes in pipe-claying his shoes, we had not seen him since – George and I, therefore, and the dog, left to ourselves, went for a walk to Wallingford on the second evening, and, coming home, we called in at a little riverside inn, for a rest, and other things.

We went into the parlour and sat down. There was an old fellow there, smoking a long clay pipe, and we naturally began chatting.

He told us that it had been a fine day today and we told him that it had been a fine day yesterday, and then we all told each other that we thought it would be a fine day tomorrow; and George said the crops seemed to be coming up nicely.

After that it came out, somehow or other, that we were strangers in the neighbourhood, and that we were going away the next morning.

Then a pause ensued in the conversation, during which our eyes wandered round the room. They finally rested upon a dusty old glass-case, fixed very high up above the chimney-piece, and containing a trout. It rather fascinated me, that trout; it was such a monstrous fish. In fact, at first glance, I thought it was a cod.

'Ah!' said the old gentleman, following the direction of my gaze, 'fine fellow that, ain't he?'

'Quite uncommon,' I murmured; and George asked the old man how much he thought it weighed.

'Eighteen pounds six ounces,' said our friend, rising and taking down his coat. 'Yes,' he continued, 'it wur sixteen year ago, come the third o' next month, that I landed him. I caught him just below the bridge with a minnow. They told me he wur in the river, and I said I'd have him, and so I did. You don't see many fish that size about here now, I'm thinking. Good night, gentlemen, good night.'

And out he went, and left us alone.

We could not take our eyes off the fish after that. It really was a remarkably fine fish. We were still looking at it, when the local carrier, who had just stopped at the inn, came to the door of the room with a pot of beer in his hand, and he also looked at the fish.

'Good-sized trout, that,' said George, turning round to him.

'Ah! you may well say that, sir,' replied the man; and then, after a pull at his beer, he added, 'Maybe you wasn't here, sir, when that fish was caught?'

'No,' we told him. We were strangers in the neighbourhood.

'Ah!' said the carrier, 'then of course, how should you? It was nearly five years ago that I caught that trout.'

'Oh! Was it you who caught it, then?' said I.

'Yes, sir,' replied the genial old fellow. 'I caught him just below the lock – leastways, what was the lock then – one Friday afternoon; and the remarkable thing about it is that I caught him with a fly. I'd gone out pike fishing, bless you, never thinking of a trout, and when I saw that whopper on the end of my line, blest if it didn't quite take be aback. Well, you see, he weighed twenty-six pound. Good night, gentlemen, good night.'

Five minutes afterwards a third man came in, and described how *he* had caught it early one morning, with bleak; and then he left, and a stolid, solemn-looking, middle-aged individual came in, and sat down over by the window.

None of us spoke for a while; but, at length, George turned to the new-comer, and said:

'I beg your pardon, I hope you will forgive the liberty that we – perfect strangers in the neighbourhood - are taking, but my friend here and myself would be so much obliged if you would tell us how you caught that trout up there.'

'Why, who told you I caught that trout!' was the surprised query.

We said that nobody had told us so, but somehow or other we felt instinctively that it was he who had done it.

'Well, it's a most remarkable thing – most remarkable,' answered the stolid stranger, laughing; 'because, as a matter of fact, you are quite right. I did catch it. But fancy your guessing it like that. Dear me, it's really a most remarkable thing.'

And then he went on, and told us how it had taken him half an hour to land it, and how it had broken his rod. He said he had weighed it carefully when he reached home, and it had turned the scale at thirty-four pounds.

He went in his turn, and when he was gone, the landlord came in to us. We told him the various histories we had heard about his trout, and he was immensely amused, and we all laughed very heartily.

'Fancy Jim Bates and Joe Muggles and Mr Jones and old Billy Maunders all telling you that they had caught it. Ha! ha! ha! Well, that is good,' said the honest old fellow, laughing heartily. 'Yes, they are the sort to give it *me*, to put up in *my* parlour, if *they* had caught it, they are! Ha! ha! ha!'

And then he told us the real history of the fish. It seemed that he had caught it himself, years ago, when he was quite a lad; not by any art or skill, but by that unaccountable luck that appears to always wait upon a boy when he plays the wag from school, and goes out fishing on a sunny afternoon, with a bit of string tied on to the end of a tree.

He said that bringing home that trout had saved him from a whacking, and that even his schoolmaster had said it was worth the rule-of-three and practice put together.

He was called out of the room at this point, and George and I turned our gaze upon the fish.

It really was a most astonishing trout. The more we looked at it, the more we marvelled at it.

It excited George so much that he climbed upon the back of a chair to get a better view of it.

And then the chair slipped, and George clutched wildly at the trout-case to save himself, and down it came with a crash, George and the chair on top of it.

'You haven't injured the fish, have you?' I cried in alarm, rushing up.

'I hope not,' said George, rising cautiously and looking about.

But he had. That trout lay shattered into a thousand fragments – I say a thousand, but they may have only been nine hundred. I did not count them.

We thought it strange and unaccountable that a stuffed trout should break up into little pieces like that.

And so it would have been strange and unaccountable, if it had been a stuffed trout, but it was not.

That trout was plaster of Paris.

from

FLY FISHING
Edward Grey

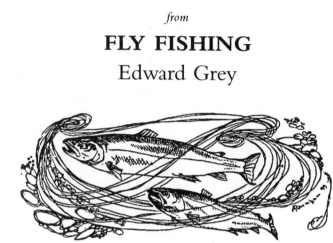

Edward Grey, Viscount Fallodon, was British Foreign Secretary at the outbreak of World War I but, apart from being a great states- man, he was devoted to fishing and ornithology. If only modern politicians had his sense of priorities! His great book, Fly Fishing, *was published in 1899 and is one of my most treasured fishing books.*

IT IS WITH much diffidence that any attempt can be made to describe the delights of dry fly fishing. Those who know and prac- tise the art best are the epicures amongst anglers; they have carried both the skill and pleasure of angling to a height of exquisite refine- ment, and to them I fear that any detailed account of a day's dry fly fishing must seem inadequate. There are, however, other less fortunate anglers whom circumstances have prevented from becom- ing acquainted with the use of the dry fly on those rivers which are most perfectly suited for it, and as these anglers are not only many in number, but are probably a very large majority of anglers, I will endeavour to describe some of the days, the events, the places, the rivers, the seasons, which are to me typical of dry fly angling, in the hope of finding readers to whom these things are not already too familiar. If the written words can convey to them even a little of what dry fly angling means to us on the Test and the Itchen, of the affection we feel for these rivers and their water meadows, my object will be gained and my hope fulfilled.

First, let us take the season. Every season has its claim upon the attention of men whose recreations are in the country and in open air, but in the case of the dry fly angler this claim is paramount, for the season which is the very best for the use of the dry fly is also the very best of the whole year. It consists of the months of May and June, when Nature does her utmost on a scale that is magnificent, and with a variety that seems infinite, to persuade us that we live in a beautiful world. The extent to which this appeal, which Nature makes to us, is admitted or felt by different persons, varies within very wide limits. A large number of people leave their homes, and make considerable pecuniary sacrifices, in order apparently to spend the best part of the spring and early summer in London and out of the country. There are others, on the contrary, to whom it is a calamity to be shut up in a town for the whole of the months of May and June; and whom no purely self-regarding misfortune, except perhaps the complete loss of liberty or of health, could make more wretched than this. It is, however, not only the season of the year, but the places for dry fly angling, that add to the attractions of the sport. It would be arrogant to say that the valleys of the Test and Itchen are better than any other part of the country in May and June, but I do say that no part is better than they are. The angler who is fishing in one of these rivers at this time of year, is seeing the most beautiful season at its best. This is the time of blossom and promise, everywhere there should be visible growth responding to increasing warmth, a sense of luxuriant and abundant young life all around us. All this is assured every year in the valleys of such rivers as the Test and the Itchen. There may be, and too often is, a spring drought in other countries, and on the great downs of Hampshire itself. Other rivers may shrink, and leave their banks dry, but the Hampshire chalk streams run brim full,[1] and their valleys are all of water meadows, intersected by streams and runnels and channels and cuts of all sorts and sizes carrying over the land the bounty of water. Hence it is, that on the way to our river we have no thought of what order it will be in, or of what rain there has been lately. The river is sure to be found

---

[1]Undoubtedly this is generally the case, but an exception must be made in regard to the angling season of 1898. The upper Test, for instance, was far lower in April 1898 than in the June of the preceding year, when it was gloriously full. – Eds.

full and clear. North country rivers are fed by constant tributaries. Down every glen comes a burn, and after heavy rain there is a rush of surface water, which swells them all. A true chalk stream has few tributaries. The valleys on the higher ground near it have no streams; the rain falls upon the great expanse of high exposed downs, and sinks silently into the chalk, till somewhere in a large low valley it rises in constant springs, and a full river starts from them towards the sea. There is always something mysterious to me in looking at these rivers, so little affected by the weather of the moment, fed continually by secret springs, flowing with a sort of swiftness, but for the most part (except close to mills and large hatches) silently, and with water which looks too pure and clear for that of a river of common life.

And now let the season be somewhere about the middle of May, and let there be a holiday and the angler be at the Test or the Itchen, and let us consider a day's fishing, which shall be typical of many days in this month. The wind shall be south-west, a perceptible breeze, but with no squalls or rough manners; and there shall be light clouds moving before it between which gleams of sunshine fall upon the young leaves and woods – for there are many fine woods by the sides of water meadows. Granted these first two conditions, it will follow that the day is warm, with a temperature reaching 62° in the shade, the mean temperature for midsummer, but a very suitable maximum for a day in May. It is almost certain that there will be a rise of trout at some time during the day, and it is all important to know at what hour it will begin. The chances in my experience are something as follows: It is not certain that there will be no rise before ten o'clock, but it is very improbable that there will be any. After ten o'clock the rise may begin at any time. The most likely time for it is between eleven and twelve, but there need be no dis-appointment if it does not begin till twelve o'clock. On a day such as this I do, however, become anxious if at one o'clock there is still no rise. Taking then these chances into consideration, desiring earnestly not to miss a minute of the rise, and leaving a fair margin for uncertainties, the angler will probably be at the water by 9.30.

If this forecast of the time of the rise proves correct, and there is at first neither fly nor fish to be seen, the angler has at any rate the satisfaction of feeling that the day is all before him, and that he has so far missed nothing. If he is very impatient to have an outlet at once for his energy, he may put on a medium-sized hackle fly and use it wet in the rough water of hatch-holes, but he can do no good – and perhaps he may do some harm – by attempting to fish the river at large. Even in the hatch-holes he will probably prick more fish than he hooks, and if one or two are landed they will either be small trout, or large ones in inferior condition. The fact is, that attempts to anticipate success in a chalk stream before the proper rise begins are unsatisfactory; however resolutely the angler may have made up his mind to expect nothing from these attempts, yet if he labours at them, some sense of disappointment will insensibly steal over him, and take just a little off the edge of his keenness. In my opinion, it is better to keep this unimpaired till the rise begins. It is not hard to wait for an hour or two on such a day; one need only watch and listen to the life about the river. To read a book at this time is not so easy, for the eyes are continually being lifted to the water. On the other hand, there is not much to be gained by wandering up and down, and the best plan is for the angler to go to the lowest part of the water he means to fish, and there sit down to watch some particular bit of it, which is known to be a good place for free rising trout. The first sign of the coming rise will be a few flies upon the water, either olive duns or some near relations of theirs. These are generally noticed by the angler before the fish begin to take them, but sometimes it is a trout which first notices a fly, and then a rise is the first sign seen. When this is so, the angler becomes alert at once. The pleasure of the day began for him, let us hope, hours ago, when he woke to the consciousness of what sort of day it was; but now there is suddenly added to his happiness the delight of endeavour and excitement, suspense ends, action begins, and hope is raised to the height of expectation. He does not, however, cast at once, but gets quietly within reach, kneeling if necessary to be out of sight, and waiting for the fish to rise again. This first trout should at any rate be risen, if it is in a convenient place where the fly does not drag. In a little time it may have made up its mind not to take any flies on the surface, or its appetite may have become less keen, or its sense of what all natural flies look like more exact; but just at first, at the very beginning of the rise, there is most probability of finding it hungry and off its guard. By the time the first fish is done with, it should be easy to find others rising, and if there is a free rise and plenty of fly, the angler will in May get the best conditioned fish

in comparatively quick running water in the main stream. The first
half-hour will decide what kind of rise there is to be, whether it
is to be a good taking one or not: if it is a good one, the angler
should feel for the next two hours that there is at any rate a fair
chance of his having a rise whenever he can succeed in floating his
fly satisfactorily and accurately over a rising trout. Should the rise
last as much as four hours, it is a long one and ought to result in an
exceptionally heavy basket. I have generally found, however, that
in the last hour or so of the rise the trout become very fastidious and
particular. Sometimes they can be seen still in their feeding places,
keeping close to the surface of the water, but only taking a fly occasionally, and the angler may, till he is weary, float his own fly over
them continually and get no response whatever. As a rule, on a fairly
warm day the rise of fly will be over by three or four o'clock. The
trout will by then have disappeared, and the angler may leave off.
Bad luck or good luck may have made the difference of one or two
brace to his basket, but ten pounds' weight of trout should make him
content, fifteen pounds may be considered very good, and twenty
pounds and upwards exceptional.

The number of trout in different parts of the Itchen and Test is in
inverse proportion to their weight; but in the parts of these rivers
where the trout are not overcrowded and average from a pound and
a half to two pounds, they rise freely and their appearance in a good
season is splendid. The extraordinary fatness to which they attain,
and the brilliancy of their colour and condition in May, June and
July, surpass anything it has been my good fortune to see amongst
river trout, and anything I could have believed, if I had fished only
in north country rivers. On the other hand, the chalk stream
trout do not fight so strongly in proportion to their size as the trout
in rocky or swifter rivers with rougher water and no weeds. It is not
that the southern trout is less strong, but it thinks too much of
the weeds: it is always trying to hide itself instead of trying to get
free by wild desperate rushes, for which indeed the presence of the
weeds and the gentleness of the water make these rivers less suited.
Sometimes the first rush of a chalk stream trout when hooked is
as sudden and wild and strong as that of a fish of the same size in
any other river; but in my experience this generally happens with a
south country trout when its feeding place is far down on a shallow
or in a long mill-tail, and its home is in the hatch-hole or under the

mill above. In such places I have known a trout of one and a half pounds leave very few yards of line upon the reel before its first rush could be checked, and the line to be run out as swiftly and as straight as any one could wish. Twice during the last season did it happen to me to have fine experiences of this kind. In the first case the trout had something over twenty yards to go for safety, and nearly succeeded. Had the distance been two or three yards less it would have been accomplished in the first rush, but in the last few yards the trout had to collect his strength for a second effort. There was a moment's break in the impetus of the rush, and a struggle began in which at first the trout gained ground, but very slowly, while every foot was contested with the utmost pressure that I dared put upon the gut: then there ceased to be progress, and at last within close sight of his home the trout had to turn his head. The rest was easy, the mill–tail being fairly clear of weeds, and both time and stream being against the fish.

In the second case the result was different. I was wading in a shallow where I could see the trout, which, as it turned out, was never to be mine. It was a light–coloured fish feeding actively and recklessly on the flies, which were coming down freely, and it took my fly at once with perfect confidence. It sometimes happens, however, that these active, reckless, easily hooked trout are more surprised and desperate when hooked than any others. I never saw anything more mad and sudden than the rush of this trout. It gained a pool below some hatches, where no doubt it lived, and took the line under the rough main stream into a fine whirling back-water: then I felt the confusion of having lost touch with the fish, for there was nothing but the dull sodden strain of a line hopelessly drowned in the contending currents of the hatch-hole. The trout jumped high in the middle of the pool, and showed me that, if under two pounds, he was certainly very thick and strong; I dropped the point of the rod without being able to give the least relief to the fine gut at the end, and the stream swept downwards a useless length of submerged line without a fly.

Those anglers, who are used to thinking that a day's fishing means fishing all day, may ask whether it does not make the pleasure less when the actual fishing is concentrated into a space of sometimes only two, and at most four or five hours, as is the case on a chalk stream in the month of May. The answer is, that the pleasure and excitement are highly concentrated too, and that the work while it lasts is very hard. To be amongst plenty of large trout, with a small fly and fine gut, when there is a good rise, is a glorious experience. Before it is over the angler will have had thrilling and exciting incidents, enough to provide much reflection, and let us hope satisfaction too, and if the rise lasted all day we should be apt to miss much of the glory of the month.

There is so much to be seen and heard in May. There are the separate and successive greens of the fresh young leaves of different trees, perhaps the most tender and the most transient of all the colours that leaves or flowers give to any season. Then there are the great blossoms of May, of which I especially value six, all so conspicuous in colour as to compel one's attention, and three of them wonderful in perfume. They are the lilac, hawthorn, gorse, horse-chestnut, laburnum and brook. Not to spend time in the country while all these things are at their best, is to lead a dull life indeed; and yet, if we are not to miss some of them, we must spend a part at least of every week of May in going about the country with attention free and eyes afield. Dry fly fishing leaves many hours free for this. The first half of May, too, is the most favourable time for making discovery of birds. The summer birds have nearly all arrived, and all birds are singing; but the leaves are not thick yet, and both in brushwood and in trees it is comparatively easy to see the different species. They are active with the business and excitement of the breeding season, and it is just at this time that they most attract the notice of eye and ear. A little later on the air will still be full of sound and song, but it will be much more difficult owing to the leaves to get a good sight of any bird that has attracted attention or raised a doubt of its identity by its song.

May is a good month on a chalk stream, but to my mind the perfection of dry fly fishing is to be had on a good day in mid-June, on water where the May-fly never appears, first to excite the trout and the anglers, and then to leave the fish without appetite and the angler too often discontented. The May-fly is a fine institution, and where it comes in enormous quantities, as it does on some rivers such as the Kennet, it provides a fortnight of most glorious fishing; but elsewhere it interrupts the season, and unless the trout are very large, or there is a great lack of duns and small flies, I would not attempt to reintroduce the May-fly where it has ceased to exist in any numbers.

And now let the pleasure of this June day be heightened by the contrast of work and life in London. This is not the place in which to write of the deep human interests of London, of what great affairs have their centre and of what issues are discussed and decided there. All that follows is written without any thought of denying or minimising the attraction of these things for men's minds; but there is an aspect of London which is inevitable and becomes most oppressive in hot June days. There is the aggressive stiffness of the buildings, the brutal hardness of the pavement, the smell of the streets festering in the sun, the glare of the light all day striking upon hard substances, and the stuffiness of the heat from which there is no relief at night – for no coolness comes with the evening air, and bedroom windows seem to open into ovens; add to these hardships what is worse than all, the sense of being deprived of the country at this time and shut off from it. Perhaps you own a distant garden, which you know by heart, and from which occasionally leaves and flowers are sent to you in London; you unpack these and spread them out and look at them, spelling out from them and recalling to memory what the garden is like at this time. There were the young beech leaves and the sprays of double flowering cherry in May, and now there come the first out-of-door roses and the first of other things, perhaps the flower of some special iris lately planted. You see these things, you know the very trees, bushes, and places from which they were taken; you know the very form and aspect which the beauty

of the season is taking in your garden, and you have the knowledge
that it is passing away, that you are missing for all this year things
which are dear to you, both for the delight of seeing them afresh
each season and for many old associations of other years. At such
moments there surges within you a spirit of resentment and indignation, kept in abeyance during the actual hours of hard work, but
asserting itself at all other times, and you pass through the streets
feeling like an unknown alien, who has no part in the bustle and
life of London, and cannot in the place of his exile share what seem
to others to be pleasures. Work alone, however interesting, cannot
neutralise all this, because it is only partly by the mind that we live.
Mental effort is enough for some of the satisfaction of life; but we
live also by the affections, and where out-of-door things make to
these the irresistible appeal, which they do make to some natures,
it is impossible to live in London without great sacrifice. Happily it
is possible to go away, if not to home, at any rate to some country
retreat at the end of the week, and to combine the best of dry fly
fishing with this on Saturday. Where this can be done, the prospect
of the escape on Saturday till Monday is a great consolation in all
moments of leisure during the week. It is borne about with us like
a happy secret; it draws the thoughts towards it continually, as
Ruskin says that the luminous distance in a picture attracts the eye,
or as the gleam of water attracts it in a landscape.

   If our work will let us escape on Friday evening, it is luxury; but
even if we belong only to those in the middle state of happiness, who
work till midnight or later on Friday, and can have the whole of

Saturday and Sunday in the country, we may still be splendidly well off, provided that we are careful to miss nothing. The earliest trains leave Waterloo, the usual place of departure for the Itchen or Test, either at or just before six o'clock in the morning. To leave London it is possible once a week, even after late hours, to get up in time for these early trains, and if you have no luggage (and you need have none if you go to the same place week after week), you will not find it difficult to get to the station. There are places where hansoms can be found even at these hours of the morning; they are not numerous, and they seem quite different from the hansoms that are abroad at more lively hours, but they can be found if you will look for them at certain places. The best plan, however, is to live within a walk of Waterloo, and as you cross the river in the early summer morning, you may feel more reconciled to London than at any other time, and understand Wordsworth's tribute to the sight from Westminster Bridge. I pass over the scene at Waterloo station, which at this hour is very different from the usual one, and the journey on which perhaps one sleeps a little, though I have found that, while it is very easy to sleep sitting up in the late hours of the evening, it is necessary to lie down, if one wishes to sleep in the early hours of the morning. At some time between eight and nine o'clock, you step out of the train, and are in a few minutes amongst all the long-desired things. Every sense is alert and excited, every scent and everything seen or heard is noted with delight. You are grateful for the grass on which you walk, even for the soft country dust about your feet.

Let me again be free to choose the day, and let it be bright and cloudless without wind this time. A warm day with a maximum temperature of 75° in the shade; rather trying weather for a wet fly angler, but not at all bad for dry fly fishing at this season, and the sooner the angler can satisfy himself with breakfast and be by the water the better. On such a day in mid-June some fish should be found rising at any time after eight o'clock, and this is said without prejudice to what may happen before eight o'clock, of which I have no experience. There are thirteen hours of daylight after eight o'clock in the morning, and that is enough for a full day's fishing. But the rise will probably be quite different in character to the rise in May. It will be much more prolonged, but more quiet, and the beginning and end of it will not be so clearly defined. You may expect the fish to take best, and to find most fish rising between ten o'clock and two o'clock in the day; but both before and after these hours, there should be some trout feeding. The rise of fish corresponds of course to the rise of fly, and there will probably be some duns upon the water all day, but at no time in such quantities as during the few hours into which the hatching is concentrated earlier in the season and in colder weather. This is what makes June such a good month: the fishing is spread over a much longer period of the day. It is true that the trout are not so greedy, but on the other hand, partly for this very reason and partly because the flies are less numerous at any one time, they are not so likely to do nothing but rush about after *larvae*, and it is better to be casting over the most fastidious trout which is taking flies on the surface, than over the hungriest one that is 'bulging.' On a bright warm day such as this, the angler will go very quietly, watching the water, always expecting to see a rise, but knowing that a trout may be well on the feed and yet rising slowly at comparatively long intervals of time. The little light coloured places with a gentle swirl of water immediately below a patch of weed are very favourite spots, and in these it is often possible to see a fish very clearly. On a bright day, the angler should therefore not only look for a rise, but look also for the fish, and many a trout will be discovered lying on the watch for flies before it is actually seen to take one. There is not much difficulty in telling by its attitude in the water, whether a trout is worth trying for. Between the appearance of a trout that is resting motionless and dull upon the bottom, and one that is poised in the water near the surface, there is all the difference in the world; the very attitude of the latter, still as it may be for the moment, seems to have something watchful and lively about it.

In June the trout should be at their very best and strongest, and the angler should be ambitious and go to the water, where he knows there are large ones, to match his skill and his fine gut against them in bright weather. Many a big trout will be seen, risen, and hooked, but the weeds as well as the fish are strong now, and where two-pounders are common and taking well, there are sure to be catastrophes in a long day's fishing. On the other hand, except on very unlucky days, what triumphs there are! what moments of suspense as the fly is floating to the place where one feels sure, either from the sight of the rise or of the very fish itself, that a great trout is feeding! Often in the case of these large trout my rod trembles visibly as the fly comes to the spot, perhaps after all not to be taken. I cannot say which is the more exciting, to have seen only the rise, or to be watching the movement of the fish. The crisis of the rise at one's own fly comes more suddenly when the body of the trout is unseen, but when the fish itself is visible there is a tremendous instant of expectation, as he is seen to prepare to take the fly. The next feeling with me is generally one of downright fear as to where the first rush of the fish will end. This rush may have nothing deliberate about it, in which case all may go well, and in a few seconds the angler may be on equal terms with the fish, and before a minute is over fighting with the odds on his side. On the other hand, there may be in the first rush a horrible set purpose, on the part of the trout, to gain some root under the bank, or to plunge far into a thick bed of weeds, in which case the angler is likely to have the worst of it, for during the first few seconds after being hooked any good conditioned trout of two pounds or upwards can be the master

of fine gut. Nor is fine gut the only difficulty: there is another risk owing to the smallness of the hook. It may be possible to succeed with a fairly large imitation of an olive dun on dark days early in the season, but on these days in June a rather small red quill will be the best fly. A small fly, if it is to float well must be tied on a small hook, and a small hook, unless it should fasten in an extra tough part of the mouth, can have but a weak hold of the fish. The angler must therefore be prepared to lose a large fish every now and then – oftener probably than he thinks quite consistent with good luck – by the hook losing its hold. In this matter of losing fish we are more at the mercy of luck in June than in May, and there are times when the luck seems so bad as to turn what promises to be a record day into a comparatively poor one. Sometimes this luck comes in runs. I remember on one day in the height of the summer having, with small red quills and fine gut, the best and the worst luck combined. There were not great numbers of fish feeding, and the trout that were rising were not rising fast. It took a little patience to find a rising fish, and then more patience to fix its exact position by waiting for its next rise. When these things were discovered, however, each fish took my fly confidently, and it seemed as if only the biggest and fattest trout were rising. With each of the first seven fish hooked there was a moment when a catastrophe seemed imminent, and yet all were landed. They averaged just over two pounds apiece, and after each one the sense of triumph and success mounted higher, till it produced a feeling of confidence in my own skill and luck, which I knew was not justified, but which was irresistible. Then everything changed and one disaster succeeded another. I lost more than seven large trout successively. Some broke my tackle, in the case of others the small hook lost its hold unexpectedly, whilst others again went into weeds and there freed themselves from the hook. Indeed I had a very bad time all round. At the end of the rise my basket was heavy, but I had a sense of being much chastened, and I could have wished that the luck had been more evenly distributed.

After two o'clock on this June day the angler will probably find that it becomes increasingly difficult to find a rising trout, and that when one is found, it is not nearly so ready to take his fly. By working hard all the afternoon he may add a brace more to his basket, and he must decide for himself whether this extra brace is worth two or three hours of watching and walking and crawling and kneeling and effort. If he has done pretty well by two o'clock, and if the rise has then become very slack, he may find it more pleasant to leave off for a few hours and arrange the rest of his day so as to come fresh and strong and keen to the evening rise. One difficulty about the evening rise is to settle the time for dining. After various experiments I have found it best to have dinner, if possible, between five and six. Two conditions are essential for this, one is, that there should be some place near the river where dinner can be had, and the other, that the angler should not have eaten much luncheon. The latter of these conditions is not only always possible, but easy out of doors:

the former one is generally present on the Itchen or Test, where numerous villages with inns are to be found all along the river valleys. Having dined, the angler can call the whole of the long June evening his own, and may enjoy that sense of perfect freedom, strength and patience which is so valuable, and which in fishing is destroyed by hunger or the thought of a fixed dinner hour ahead.

I must own that I do not appreciate the evening rise so well as that in the morning; and there are various reasons for this. In the first place, there is a more definite limit to the end of the evening rise. It is often nearly eight o'clock when it begins, and you know then that the light cannot last for more than an hour. Now part of the charm of the morning rise is the prospect of indefinite length. It may only last a short time, but it may go on for hours, and you feel at the beginning that its possibilities are unknown. There is nothing of this with a late evening rise. On the contrary, you feel in a hurry because the time must be short. If a rising trout will not take your fly, you begin to fidget as to whether it will be better to stick to that fish or to try another, and if half-an-hour passes without any success, the threat of an absolutely blank evening makes itself felt. There is a story of a thrifty and anxious housewife, who used to call her household early on Monday mornings in terms like these, 'Get up! get up at once! to-day's Monday, to-morrow's Tuesday, next day's Wednesday, here's half the week gone and no work done!' It is some such fidgety anxiety that comes over me, if I do not get a fish soon in the evening rise. I seem to have the anticipation of complete failure. The time is so short; the beginning and the end of the rise are so near together, that failure in the first part seems a presage of failure in the whole.

The *look* of the evening rise is so often the best of it. Numbers of trout appear to be rising frequently and steadily and confidently, but when the angler puts them to the test, they disappoint him. On some evenings the trout cease to rise after an artificial fly has once been floated over them; on others they continue to rise freely, but will take nothing artificial, and the angler exhausts himself in efforts and changes of fly, working harder and more rapidly as he becomes conscious of the approaching end of the day.

But all evenings are not alike disappointing, and on a warm still evening in June we may expect some success. A few fish may be found rising very quietly and unobtrusively at any time after six o'clock. The angler will probably find that these trout are not feeding in the same way as they fed in the morning. They may be the same fish, but their manners and behaviour are different. They are apparently taking some very small insect, are much more easily scared, and are apt to rise very short, if they rise at all to an artificial fly; still they are feeding, and are worth trying for. If the angler can get one or two of these fish before eight o'clock he will have done well. Soon after eight the evening rise proper should have begun. More rises will be seen than at any previous time of the day, and as the light fades the easier it is to get near the fish, and the more chance is there of hooking them. Yet in my experience it is comparatively seldom that one has a really successful evening, and feels that everything has gone well. Now and then one gets two or three brace, or even more, of good trout, but more often, either because the trout rise short, or because too much time is spent unsuccessfully over a stubborn fish, the angler seems to be always on the point of great success without attaining it.

Anglers differ as to how late the evening fishing should be prolonged. Night fishing with a large wet fly should not be allowed on good dry fly water. It is poor fun to haul out of the river by main force in the dark, on thick gut, a trout that might give good sport in daylight. Before it gets dark, however, there is a half-hour in which it is just possible to see where a fish is rising, but just not possible to see one's fly. It needs both skill and judgment to put an artificial fly properly over a fish in these condition, but during this half-hour a skilful angler may expect to get a brace of good trout with a floating sedge fly. This is perfectly fair fishing, but it has not the same interest as the finer fishing in better light; it needs skill, and yet it is comparatively clumsy work. The angler strikes at sight of a rise without being sure whether it is to his fly or not. He can, and indeed must, use stronger gut, because, when a trout is hooked, he cannot tell accurately what it is doing, or follow its movements adjusting the strain carefully to the need of each moment as he would do in daylight. In short a great part of all that happens, both before and after he hooks a trout, is hidden from him, and he has in the end to rely more upon force, and less upon skill to land the fish. All this takes away much of the pleasure, and if the day has been a fairly good one, I would rather forego the last brace than kill them under inferior conditions. On the other hand, if luck has been very bad, or the trout have been particularly exasperating and successful in defeating the angler, or have

refused to rise all day, then the sedge fly in the last half-hour of perceptible twilight gives a very satisfactory opportunity of trying to get
even with them. After a fair day, however, it seems to me better to
leave off when I cease to be able to see a medium-sized quill gnat upon
the water at a reasonable distance.

Very pleasant the evening is after a successful day in hot, bright
weather in June. Let us suppose that the angler has caught some three
brace of trout in the day, and a brace and a half in the evening on
good water. He will then have had plenty of interest and excitement,
moments of anxiety and even of disappointment, but all contribut-
ing at the end to give a delightful satisfactory feeling of successful
effort. Some great events, some angling crisis there will have been
during the day, to which his thoughts will recur often involuntarily.
Some incidents will seem to have been photographed upon his
mind, so that he can recall clearly not only the particular things done
or seen, but his own sensation at the time. What he thinks about in
the evening will not be only of angling, but of the scenes in which
he has spent the day. I am often ashamed to think how much passes
unnoticed in the actual excitement of angling, but the general
impression of light and colour, and surroundings is not lost; some is
noted at the time, and some sinks into one's mind unconsciously and
is found there at the end of the day, like a blessing given by great
bounty to one who was too careless at the time to deserve it. May
is the month of fresh leaves and bright shrubs, but June is the month
in which the water meadows themselves are brightest. The common
yellow iris, ragged robin and forget-me-not make rough damp places
gay, and the clear water in the little runnels amongst the grass sparkle
in the sun. Of wild shrubs which flower in June, there are two so
common that they seem to possess the month and meet the eye
everywhere. One is the wild rose, and the other is the elder, and
great is the contrast between them. The commonest sort of wild rose
is surely the most delicate of all shrubs in spite of its thorns. It is
exquisitely delicate in the scent, colour, form and character of its
flowers, and there is nothing more graceful in nature than the way
in which a long spray of wild rose in full blossom offers its beauty
to be admired. I am not so fond of the elder; when one is close to
it there is a certain stiff thickness about the bush, and a deadness of
colour both of leaves and flowers, and the scent is heavy and spirit-
less. But masses of elder flower at a distance have a fine foamy

appearance, and I always feel that they are doing their best to honour the season. Though the sun may be as hot as midsummer, everything in the first half of June seems young and fresh and active. Birds are singing still, and for a week or two it seems as if the best of spring and summer, warmth and songs, luxuriance and freshness, were spread abroad so abundantly that it is almost too much. The cup of happiness is full and runs over. Such may be one's last thoughts in the quiet of approaching night after sounds have ceased, and in the perfect enjoyment of 'that still spirit shed from evening air.'

As June draws to a close, and during the whole of July, the rise during the day becomes more uncertain and feeble. There are many days in July when the dry fly angler spends more time in watching and waiting than in active fishing. His best chance before the evening will be between ten and one o'clock, and though he must be prepared for very light baskets, yet there are mornings in July when trout are to be found feeding slowly and quietly here and there, and when they will take a red quill gnat if it is put to them attractively. I have known days in July, when the result of a morning's fishing has been unexpectedly good, equal in total weight to that of the very best days in other months, and equal also in regard to the size and condition of the individual fish.

In August I have only once had a morning's fishing which could fairly be compared, as regards the total weight of trout landed, with the good days of earlier months, and it always seems to me that the condition of the trout in this month ceases to be quite first-rate. Of September, on dry fly rivers, I have had no experience. Anglers who write of it agree in saying that the trout rise better, but that their condition has fallen off, and that an unduly large proportion of female fish are killed.

from

WHERE THE BRIGHT WATERS MEET
H. Plunket Greene

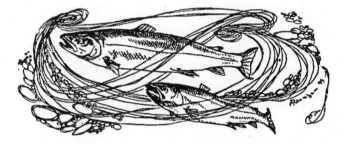

Harry Plunket Greene was a famous singer and passionate fisher-man. I don't think there is another writer who quite catches nature for me as he does. The Bourne is constantly alive in Where the Bright Waters Meet.

I LOVED the Bourne for her preference for a hot day. There used every now and then to be a phenomenal rise of fly in a north-easter, but as a rule the hotter the day the better the rise. A still, sweltering day on the chalk stream for me! To wake up in the morning and see the sun through the river mist and the trees dead still, and to know that the day is yours and that you will be hot the whole of it! I often lie awake and go over the old places in my mind. I come round the bend and see the fairy boats sailing down, and the great head-and-tailers, black against the white-blue water light, crossing and re-crossing, lazy and infinitely graceful. They are to me the very embodiment of 'style,' the perfection of motion with the greatest ease, the economy of visible effort which is the secret of all style whatever it be, in singing, or swimming or playing golf; in a Kreisler, a John Roberts, a kestrel, or a school of porpoises.

I do not know anything more beautiful in nature than the head-and-tailing trout. Why does not some enterprising cinema-nature-picture man give us the evening rise upon the 'movies'? It would hold its own against the cuckoo or the golden eagle. He would have to choose his day, when the evening light was pink upon the water and the black duns were sailing down thick, when the wave from each great shoulder rolled away in purple velvet and the widening rings overlapped and spent themselves. Let him first give us that perfect picture of evening peace among the poplars and the sedges and the golden mimulus; and then, if he will, bring man upon the scene to spoil it all, and show us the whole battle of wits – the crawling to position, the casting of the little dun, the big nose coming up, the slow strike, the wild rush, the wearing-down, the netting, and the two-pounder on the bank.

I would infinitely rather fish to the rise than to visible fish. I love looking into the light on the water, watching for the rise, and seeing my fly float down into the ring, and never knowing till it comes to him whether he will take it or not. This is the chief charm of the evening rise at Stockbridge. You fish to the right, and the tense excitement of watching it enter the circle and waiting for the strike is, for me, far greater than that of seeing any fish, however big, come to your fly. That was the only excitement, apart from the weather, that I missed on the Bourne, where, as I have before said, you could see your fish every time, watch every move he made, and almost follow the reasoning processes of trout in general as well as of your adversary in particular.

The Bourne taught me one thing which has been of infinite service to me whenever trout are visible, and that is, that you need never despair either of getting any rising fish that you do not actually put down, or – in shallow water – of bringing up a fish that apparently is not on the rise already.

The first of these is common enough. Everybody knows the insults he showers upon you, rushing to your fly, looking at it, and returning to the real article, sometimes coldly, sometimes with a flaunt of his tail; sailing up to it with a smile, and bumping it with his nose, knowing that he is making your heart jump into your mouth and your hand give a convulsive twitch; or opening his mouth at it and then suddenly turning round with a swirl as he spits it out; or, worst of all, following it right down to have a good look at it, while you grovel with your stomach on the ground and your head in the nettles and let the line go hang; and when at last you venture to look up, you find that he has deserted you long ago and is back again feeding at his old post. As long as he goes back again to the same spot and stays on top of the water, you are as likely to get him as not. It sometimes means a few minutes' rest and a change of fly, but as often as not you can wear down his patience without a change of any sort. There comes a moment, sooner or later, when he is either off his guard – generally immediately after taking the real fly – and takes yours in his stride, or when he will snap at it in sheer impatience as though he could not be bothered with the infernal thing any more.

There was a Longparish Common three-pounder who was a case in point. I was standing in the middle of the river directly behind him and could follow his temperamental impulses. I had risen him and missed him three times running, and he sulked at last; but I knew he was a wearing-down case, and I stuck to him for nearly an hour without a change of fly. I decided finally to give him fifty more casts before leaving him – we deal in big figures in this process – and I got him on the fiftieth. I do not expect this to be believed.

But if you can wear a rising fish down you can also bring a non-rising fish up – by creating an artificial rise and persuading him that the duns have started in for the day. I have done it on the Bourne dozens of times, and was able once to demonstrate it to 'Corrigeen' of the *Field*, who, though sceptical at first, accepted it at once when he saw it in performance. He has, I understand, practised it since himself with great success. Two things are necessary to bring it off – you must see your fish, and your sixth sense must tell you that he will rise if it is made worth his while. He may be lying motionless on the bottom, sullen and asleep to look at, he may not have a wag in his tail, he may, in fact, look hopeless for your purpose; but if you know in your bones, as you do in some queer way, that he would be glad of a dun or two for breakfast, you can try for him with perfect confidence. One thing is sure – he is perfectly comfortable where he is, and is not going to trouble to come up unless it is really going to be a good thing – in other words, unless he is convinced that a rise has come on and is well set. What you have got to do is to persuade him that the river has never provided such a rise of dun in its existence, and that if he does not come up for them he will have missed the meal of a lifetime.

You keep pegging your fly above him, sometimes in front of his nose, sometimes close to his right, sometimes to his left, sometimes far out in the circle and sometimes at the back of his head. In fact, you must cover the whole field of vision. There is no need to change the fly; the same one does for all. You may do it a couple of hundred times before he will take any notice. Then you will see an almost imperceptible undulation of his body; at the next cast his tail will wag very slightly; then he rises about two inches off the bottom and settles back again; then he either rushes at the fly and takes it with a snap or, much oftener, sails slowly up to it and starts quietly in on his meal, fully believing that there is a good hour's feed ahead of him. (The millionaire can, of course, send his chauffeur up to the bridge above, with a box of flies, and instructions to drop them one by one into the various ripples. Why make a toil of a pleasure?)

It is an almost invariable experience when duns begin to come up after a long blank, that only the small fish take them for the first few minutes. There is evidently a reluctance on the part of their elders to bestir themselves unless it means real business. The 'artificial' rise is simply a matter of patience and keeping out of sight, and if the fish is worth it so is the patience, and the watching of the progress of the plot is as good as any 'shocker.'

I once had a visible encounter with a salmon. I was fishing for bass in an estuary in Devonshire and was standing on a rock which commanded a clear view downstream, and was presently aware of a long dark form following my sand-eel up towards me. As it came near I saw it was a salmon. No salmon ever received such affectionate attention. I joggled the bait in front of his eyes, I tickled his ribs with it, I blobbed it suddenly up against his nose, I swished it along his back and finally I tried to stroke-haul him. Anyhow, he sailed majestically up-river under my very feet, leaving me in a fury of self-recrimination at having somehow missed an obvious certainty.

A friend of mine had better luck. I was shooting in Scotland with the late Albert Vickers, and his son Billy, then a boy at Eton, got up early one morning and took a gun with him on the chance of a shot at a rabbit or some other beast in or out of season. The only thing he came across was a salmon sunning himself near the surface of a pool, and he promptly shot it. (The statute of limitations presumably holding good, I can give him away now.) When he produced it at breakfast his father gave him a sovereign for his early rising, casting, catching, and tailing, and Billy pocketed it, having miserably failed in the momentary struggle to tell the truth for once in his life. It was put right, however, in the evening, when his father broke one of his teeth on a pellet of shot.

I had an experience with a trout on the Kennet, which I always associate, quite undeservedly, with 'snatching.' It was in 1922, and I was staying with the late Mr. Giveen, who had taken the Mill fishing from Colonel Grove-Hills for the latter half of the season. His brother Charles and I had often stood on the bridge at the top, where the water falls down from the lake of Ramsbury Manor, and hungrily objurgated the great fat three-pounders which laughed at us from beneath. These were rovers by profession, and never stayed long enough in one place to be fished for individually from below, and were up to every trick from above. They would lie with their noses on the ledge immediately underneath us, and dreamily watch the smoke from our pipes ascending to the blue; but the moment the top of a rod appeared over the edge, off they went. We tried concerted action many times, but as soon as ever one of the watchers disappeared from the bridge the pool was abandoned to two-year-olds. On this occasion I was passing by the sluice which forms a small side-carrier to the main fall and I put my head casually over the side, expecting nothing, and there, right below me, was a big golden trout tucked up under the boards, with his head down-stream and his tail up against the cracks where the water spurted through. He was doing no good there, so I felt it was my duty to get him.

It was an awful prospect. Immediately below him two planks ran across the sluice at intervals of about eight feet, and below them again in the fairway there was a veritable barricade of posts sticking up out of the stream in ragged profusion. There were three on the near side and two on the far side and a gaunt rubbing-post in the middle acting as a buoy, round which every sporting fish was in honour bound to double. Below these again there was another pole running right across the stream only four inches above the water, which swirled under it at a great pace. A more hopeless barbed-wire entanglement it would be hard to imagine to try and fish a fish out of, even if one hooked him. However, he was a beauty, and the fact that he was practically ungetable made it all the more exciting. I had up the ordinary tackle; by all the laws of caution

I should have put up a ginger-quill with a No.1 hook and a Mayfly cast, but I reflected that if he got tangled up in the barriers a steel hawser would not hold him, and that if by some amazing fluke he ever came through, the fine tackle would be as good as anything else. Moreover, I should be able to swagger to the others about 4X casts and 000 hooks even more insupportably than before; so I stuck to what I had.

I stood well back where I could just see the tip of his nose, and he could not see me, reeled in the line to within six inches of the cast, and gently dropped the fly on to him. It was at once carried out by the stream. I thought it was going to be hopeless, when to my intense delight the back eddy swirled it round at exactly the right moment and brought it over him again. It was then seized once more by the stream and carried off afresh. The process was repeated automatically without my having to do a thing, and there went my fly playing 'last across' with him, rushing up the backwater, tweaking his nose and dashing off down-stream before he could say a word. I was so delighted and laughing so hard that I could not help crawling up to see the fun, and I put my head over to have a look. He was intently absorbed in the game and never saw me. He appeared to take no notice at first and treated it all with dignified unconcern, but as the impudent little beast dashed past him smothering him with insults he began to get impatient, and I saw his tail detach itself from the sluice-board and begin to wag. Then be began to shake his head and bunch himself to attack. But nothing happened for a long time, and I was just going to give it up, as my arm was getting tired from the unnatural position, when I had a wonderful bit of luck. There was a twig sticking out from the wall on the far side over the back eddy, and the gut caught over it, and, before I knew it, there was the fly bobbing up and down in the water, right in front of him. This was too much. His enemy was delivered into his hands.

He leaped at it, seized it, knew in a moment what had happened, and dashed off down-stream under the planks and through the posts and out into the pool at the bottom. There I had to leave him for a long time to settle himself, with my rod bent double under the first plank. Then the fun began. I cautiously passed it under this with one hand and retrieved it with the other, and did the same with the second plank. All idea of keeping the line taut was perforce abandoned. I still had the six upright posts and the flat pole beyond to negotiate. If he once got tangled up in these it would be all over. He was near the top of the pool now, and I lay flat on the ground with the point of the rod out in the space between me and the centre post, terrified lest he should swim up on the near side of A post, catch sight of me, and dash down on the far side or pay a visit to X, Y or Z post. I clung to Mother Earth like a tiger-skin on a polished oak floor. Sure enough, up he came. He swam through the near channel and roamed about under my eyes (or the corner of one of them) for about a fortnight apparently, and then swam slowly back to the pool the same way he had come!

It was almost too good to be true! But the crux was still to be faced – there was still the flat pole to get under. It ran across the top of the pool, with a space of about four inches between it and the water. It was a bare two inches thick and it was quite rotten. I had to get the rod under it somehow (for I could never risk letting him out of the pool again), and I could only just reach it with my hand by holding on to the bank above with my toes and descending apoplectically towards the water. It crackled loudly the moment I touched it. I had to lean hard on the horrible thing with my right hand, pass the rod under with my left, scrabble it out again somehow with my right on the other side, change hands and work myself back up the bank. It groaned and shivered its timbers and fired off shots like a machine-gun – but the little iron-blue had squared it and it held. It was not all over even then, for if the fish had caught sight of me he would have dashed up through the uprights again; so I backed slowly out of sight into a withy-bed and stayed there till there was not a kick left in him. As a matter of fact, he had done it all for my by returning through the posts the same way he had come. The only credit I can take is for keeping out of sight and performing gymnastics with an almost superhuman skill for one of my size and weight. He weighed 2¼ lbs.

from

JOHN MACNAB
John Buchan

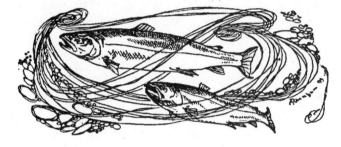

John Buchan is, of course, the author of The Thirty-Nine Steps *and other splendid 'shockers', as he called them. One of his most popular light novels is* John Macnab, *published in 1925. Three 'great men' take a rest from their public duties and – a familiar Buchan theme – try to get back in touch with the real world in strenuous physical activity. Using the* nom de guerre *John Macnab, they challenge three landowners to prevent them, on a certain day, shooting a stag or fishing a salmon on their property. Buchan was a master at describing his beloved Scottish Highlands and here he captures the pure excitement of poaching.*

THE dining-room at Strathlarrig was a remnant of the old house which had been enveloped in the immense sheath of the new. It had eighteenth-century panelling unchanged since the days when Jacobite chiefs in lace and tartan had passed their claret-glasses over the water, and the pictures were all of forbidding progenitors. But the ancient narrow windows had been widened, and Sir Archie, from where he sat, had a prospect of half a mile of the river, including Lady Maisie's Pool, bathed in the clear amber of twilight. He was on his host's left hand, opposite the Professor, with Agatha Raden next to him; then came Junius: while Janet was between Johnson Claybody and the guest of the occasion.

Mr. Claybody still brooded over John Macnab.

'I call the whole thing infernal impertinence,' he said in his loud, assured voice. 'I confess I have ceased to admire undergraduate "rags." He threatens to visit us, and my father intends to put the matter into the hands of the police.'

'That would be very kind,' said Janet sweetly, 'You see, John Macnab won't have the slightest trouble in beating the police.'

'It's the principle of the thing, Miss Raden. Here is an impudent attack on private property, and if we treat it as a joke it will only encourage other scoundrels. If the man is a gentleman, as you say he is, it makes it more scandalous.'

'Come, come, Mr. Claybody, you're taking it too seriously,' Colonel Raden could be emphatic enough on the rights of property, but no Highlander can ever grow excited about trespass. ' The fellow has made a sporting offer and is willing to risk a pretty handsome stake. I rather admire what you call his impudence. I might have done the same thing as a young man, if I had the wits to think of it.'

Mr. Claybody was quick to recognise an unsympathetic audience. 'Oh, I don't mean that we're actually going to make a fuss. We'll give him a warm reception if he comes – that's all. But I don't like the spirit. It's too dangerous in these unsettled times. Once let the masses get into their heads that landed property is a thing to play tricks with, and you take the pin out of the whole system. You must agree with me, Roylance?'

Sir Archie, remembering his part, answered with guile. 'Rather! Rotten game for a gentleman, I think. All the same, the chap seems rather a sportsman, so I'm in favour of letting the law alone and dealing with him ourselves. I expect he won't have much of a look-in on Haripol.'

'I can promise you he won't,' said Mr. Claybody shortly.

Professor Babwater observed that it would be difficult for a descendant of Harald Blacktooth to be too hard on one who followed in Harald's steps. 'The Celt,' he said, 'has always sought his adventures in a fairy world. The Northman was a realist, and looked to tangible things like land and cattle. Therefore he was a conqueror and a discoverer on the terrestrial globe, while the Celt explored the mysteries of the spirit. 'Those who, like you, sir' – he bowed to Colonel Raden – 'have both strains in their ancestry, should have successes in both worlds.'

'They don't mix well,' said the Colonel sadly. 'There was my grandfather, who believed in Macpherson's Ossian and ruined the family fortunes in hunting for Gaelic manuscripts on the continent of Europe. And his father was in India with Clive, and thought about nothing except blackmailing native chiefs till he made the place too hot to hold him. Look at my daughters, too. Agatha is mad about poetry and such-like, and Janet is a bandit. She'd have made a dashed good soldier, though.'

'Thank you, Papa,' said the lady. She might have objected to the description had she not seen that Sir Archie accepted it with admiring assent.

'I suppose,' said old Mr Bandicott reflectively, 'that the War was bound to leave a good deal of unsettlement. Junius missed it through being too young — never got out of a training camp — but I have noticed that those who fought in France find it difficult to discover a groove. They are energetic enough, but they won't "stay put," as we say. Perhaps this Macnab is one of the uprooted. In your country, where everybody was soldiering, the case must be far more common.'

Mr. Claybody announced that he was sick of hearing the War blamed for the average man's deficiencies. 'Every waster,' he said, 'makes an excuse of being shell-shocked. I'm very clear that the War twisted nothing in a man that wasn't twisted before.'

Sir Archie demurred. 'I don't know. I've seen some pretty bad cases of fellows who used to be as sane as a judge, and came home all shot to bits in their mind.'

'There are exceptions, of course. I'm speaking of the general rule. I turn away unemployables every day — good soldiers, maybe, but unemployable — and I doubt if they were ever anything else.'

Something in his tone annoyed Janet.

'You saw a lot of service, didn't you?' she asked meekly.

'No — worse luck! They made me stick at home and slave fourteen hours a day at controlling cotton. It would have been a holiday for me to get into the trenches. But what I say is, a sane man usually remained sane. Look at Sir Archibald. We all know what a hectic time he had, and he hasn't turned a hair.'

'I'd like you to give me that in writing,' Sir Archie grinned. 'I've known people who thought I was rather cracked.'

'Anyhow, it made no difference to your nerves,' said Colonel Raden.

'I hope not. I expect that was because I enjoyed the beastly thing. Perhaps I'm naturally a bit of a bandit – like Miss Janet.'

'Perhaps you're John Macnab,' said the lady.

'Well, you've seen him and can judge.'

'No. I'll be a witness for the defence if you're ever accused. But you mustn't be offended at the idea. I suppose poor John Macnab is now crawling round Strathlarrig trying to find a gap between the gillies to cast a fly.'

'That's about the size of it,' Junius laughed. 'And there's twenty special correspondents in the neighbourhood cursing his name. If they get hold of him, they'll be savager than old Angus.'

Mr. Bandicott, after calling his guests' attention to the merits of a hock which he had just acquired – it was a Johannisberg with the blue label – declared that in his belief the War would do good to English life, when the first ferment had died away.

'As a profound admirer of British institutions,' he said, 'I have sometimes thought that they needed a little shaking up and loosening. In America our classes are fluid. The rich man of to-day began life in a shack, and the next generation may return to it. It is the same with our professions. The man who starts in the law may pass to railway management, and end as the proprietor of a department store.

'Our belief is that it doesn't matter how often you change your trade before you're fifty. But an Englishman, once he settles in a profession, is fixed to it till the Day of Judgment, and in a few years he gets the mark of it so deep that he'd be a fish out of water in anything else. You can't imagine one of your big barristers doing anything else. No fresh fields and pastures new for them. It would be a crime against Magna Charta to break loose and try company-promoting or cornering the meat trade for a little change.'

Professor Babwater observed that in England they sometimes – in his view to the country's detriment – became politicians.

'That's the narrowest groove of all,' said Mr. Bandicott with conviction. 'In this country, once you start in on politics you're fixed in a class and members of a hierarchy, and you've got to go on, however unfitted you may be for the job, because it's a sort of high treason to weaken. In America a man tries politics as he tries other things, and if he finds the air of Washington uncongenial he quits, and tries newspapers, or Wall Street, or oil.'

'Or the penitentiary,' said Junius.

'And why not?' asked his father. 'I deplore criminal tendencies in any public man, but the possibility of such a downfall keeps the life human. It is very different in England. The respectability of your politicians is so awful that, when one of them backslides, every man of you combines to hush it up. There would be a revolution if the people got to suspect. Can you imagine a Cabinet Minister in the police court on a common vulgar charge?'

Professor Babwater said he could well imagine it − it was where most of them should be; but Colonel Raden agreed that the decencies had somehow to be preserved, even at the cost of a certain amount of humbug. 'But, excuse me,' he added, 'if I fail to see what good an occasional sentence of six months' hard would do to public life?'

'I don't want it to happen,' said his host, who was inspired by his own Johannisberg, 'but I'd like to think it *could* happen. The permanent possibility of it would supple the minds of your legislators. It would do this old country a power of good if now and then a Cabinet Minister took to brawling and went to gaol.'

It was a topic which naturally interested Sir Archie, but the theories of Mr. Bandicott passed by him unheeded. For his seat at the table gave him a view of the darkening glen, and he was aware that on that stage a stirring drama was being enacted. His host could see nothing, for it was behind him; the Professor would have had to screw his head round; to Sir Archie alone was vouchsafed a clear prospect. Janet saw that he was gazing abstractedly out of the window, but she did not realise that his eyes were strained and every nerve in him excitedly alive. . . .

For suddenly into his field of vision had darted a man. He was on the far side of the Larrig, running hard, and behind him, at a distance of some forty yards, followed another. At first he thought it was Leithen, but even in the dusk it was plain that it was a shorter man − younger, too he looked, and of a notable activity. He was gaining on his pursuers, when the chase went out of sight. . . . Then Sir Archie heard a far-away whistling, and would have given much to fling open the window and look out. . . .

Five minutes passed and again the runner appeared − this time dripping wet and on the near side. Clearly not Leithen, for he wore a white sweater, which was a garment unknown to the Crask wardrobe. He must have been headed off upstream, and had doubled back. That way danger lay, and Sir Archie longed to warn him, for his route would bring him close to the peopled appendages of Strathlarrig House. . . . Even as he stared he saw what must mean the end, for two figures appeared for one second on the extreme left of his range of vision, and in front of the fugitive. He was running into their arms!

Sir Archie seized his glass of the blue-labelled Johannisberg, swallowed the wine the wrong way, and promptly choked.

★ ★ ★

When the Hispana crossed the Bridge of Larrig, His Majesty's late Attorney-General was modestly concealed in a bush of broom on the Crask side, from which he could watch the sullen stretches of the Lang Whang. He was carefully dressed for the part in a pair of Wattie Lithgow's old trousers much too short for him, a waistcoat and jacket which belonged to Sime the butler and which had been made about the year 1890, and a vulgar flannel shirt borrowed from Shapp. He was innocent of a collar, he had not shaved for two days, and as he had forgotten to have his hair cut before leaving London his locks were of a disreputable length. Last, he had a shocking old hat of Sir Archie's from which the lining had long since gone. His hands were sunburnt and grubby, and he had removed his signet-ring. A light ten-foot greenheart rod lay beside him, already put up, and to the tapered line was fixed a tapered cast ending in a strange little cocked fly. As he waited, he was busy oiling fly and line.

His glass showed him an empty haugh, save for the figure of Jimsie at the far end close to the Wood of Larrigmore. The sun-warmed waters of the river drowsed in the long dead stretches, curled at rare intervals by the faintest western breeze. The banks were crisp green turf, scarcely broken by a boulder, but five yards from them the moss began – a wilderness of hags and tussocks. Somewhere in its depths he knew that Benjie lay coiled like an adder, waiting on events.

Leithen's plan, like all great strategy, was simple. Everything depended on having Jimsie out of sight of the Lang Whang for half an hour. Given that, he believed he might kill a salmon. He had marked out a pool where in the evening fish were usually stirring, one of those irrational haunts which no piscatorial psychologist has ever explained. If he could fish fine and far, he might cover it from a spot below a high bank where only the top of his rod would be visible to watchers at a distance. Unfortunately, that spot was on the other side of the stream. With such tackle, landing a salmon would be a critical business, but there was one chance in ten that it might be accomplished; Benjie would be at hand to conceal the fish, and he himself would disappear silently into the Crask thickets. But every step bristled with horrid dangers. Jimsie might be faithful to his post – in which case it was hopeless; he might find the salmon dour, or a fish might break him in the landing, or Jimsie might return to find him brazenly tethered to forbidden game. It was no good thinking about it. On one thing he was decided: if he were caught, he would not try to escape. That would mean retreat in the direction of Crask, and an exploration of the Crask covers would assuredly reveal what must at all costs be concealed. No. He would go quietly into cap-tivity, and trust to his base appearance to be let off with a drubbing.

As he waited, watching the pools turn from gold to bronze, as the sun sank behind the Glenraden peaks, he suffered the inevitable reaction. The absurdities seemed huge as mountains, the difficulties innumerable as the waves of the sea. There remained less than an hour in which there would be sufficient light to fish – Jimsie was immovable (he had just lit his pipe and was sitting in meditation on a big stone) – every moment the Larrig waters were cooling with the chill of evening. Leithen consulted his watch, and found it half-past eight. He had lost his wrist-watch, and had brought his hunter, attached to a thin gold chain. That was foolish, so he slipped the chain from his buttonhole and drew it through the arm-hole of his waistcoat.

Suddenly he rose to his feet, for things were happening at the far end of the haugh. Jimsie stood in an attitude of expectation – he seemed to be hearing something far upstream. Leithen heard it too, the cry of excited men. . . . Jimsie stood on one foot for a moment in doubt, then he turned and doubled towards the Wood of Larrigmore. . . . The gallant Crossby had got to business and was playing hare to the hounds inside the park wall. If human nature had not changed, Leithen thought, the whole force would presently join in the chase – Angus and Lennox and Jimsie and Davie and doubt-less many volunteers. Heaven send fleetness and wind to the South London Harrier, for it was his duty to occupy the interest of every

male in Strathlarrig till such time as he subsided with angry expos-
tulations into captivity.

The road was empty, the valley was deserted, when Leithen raced
across the bridge and up the south side of the river. It was not two
hundred yards to his chosen stand, a spit of gravel below a high bank
at the tail of a long pool. Close to the other bank, nearly thirty yards
off, was the shelf where fish lay of an evening. He tested the water
with his hand, and its temperature was at least sixty degrees. His
theory, which he had learned long ago from the aged Bostonian, was
that under such conditions some subconscious memory revived in
salmon of their early days as parr when they fed on surface insects,
and that they could be made to take a dry fly.

He got out his line to the required length with half a dozen casts
in the air, and then put his fly three feet above the spot where a
salmon was wont to lie. It was a curious type of cast, which he had
been practising lately in the early morning, for by an adroit check
he made the fly alight in a curl, so that it floated for a second or two
with the leader in a straight line away from it. In this way he believed
that the most suspicious fish would see nothing to alarm him, nothing but a hapless insect derelict on the water.

Sir Archie had spoken truth in describing Leithen to Wattie
Lithgow as an artist. His long, straight, delicate casts were art indeed.
Like thistledown the fly dropped, like thistledown it floated over the
head of the salmon, but like thistledown it was disregarded. There
was, indeed, a faint stirring of curiosity. From where he stood
Leithen could see that slight ruffling of the surface which means
an observant fish. . . . Already ten minutes had been spent in this
barren art. The crisis craved other measures.

His new policy meant a short line, so with infinite stealth and care Leithen waded up the side of the water, sometimes treading precarious ledges of peat, sometimes waist-deep in mud and pond-weed, till he was within twenty feet of the fishing-ground. Here he had not the high bank for a shelter, and would have been sadly conspicuous to Jimsie, had that sentinel remained at his post. He crouched low and cast as before with the same curl just ahead of the chosen spot.

But now his tactics were different. So soon as the fly had floated past where he believed the fish to be, he sank it by a dexterous twist of the rod-point, possible only with a short line. The fly was no longer a winged thing; drawn away under water, it roused in the salmon early memories of succulent nymphs. . . . At first cast there was a slight swirl which meant that a fish near the surface had turned to follow the lure. The second cast the line straightened and moved swiftly upstream.

Leithen had killed in his day many hundreds of salmon – once in Norway a notable beast of fifty-five pounds. But no salmon he had ever hooked had stirred in his breast such excitement as this modest fellow of eight pounds. '"'Tis not so wide as a church-door,"' he reflected with Mercutio, '"but 'twill suffice" – if I can only land him.' But a dry-fly cast and a ten-foot rod are a frail wherewithal for killing a fish against time. With his ordinary fifteen-footer and gut of moderate strength he could have brought the little salmon to grass in five minutes, but now there was immense risk of a break, and a break would mean that the whole enterprise had failed. He dared not exert pressure; on the other hand, he could not follow the fish except by making himself conspicuous on the greensward. Worst of all, he had at the best ten minutes for the job.

Thirty yards off an otter slid into the water. Leithen wished he was King of the Otters, as in the Highland tale, to summon the brute to his aid.

The ten minutes had lengthened to fifteen – nine hundred seconds of heart-disease – when, wet to the waist, he got his pocket gaff into the salmon's side and drew it on to the spit of gravel where he had started fishing. A dozen times he thought he had lost, and once when the fish ran straight up the pool his line was carried out to its last yard of backing. He gave thanks to high Heaven, when, as he landed it, he observed that the fly had all but lost its hold and in another minute would have been free. By such narrow margins are great deeds accomplished.

He snapped the cast from the line and buried it in mud. Then cautiously he raised his head above the high bank. The gloaming was gathering fast, and so far as he could see the haugh was still empty. Pushing his rod along the ground he scrambled on to the turf.

Then he had a grievous shock. Jimsie had reappeared, and he was in full view of him. Moreover, there were two men on bicycles coming up the road, who, with the deplorable instinct of human nature, would be certain to join in any pursuit. He was on turf as short as a lawn, cumbered with a telltale rod and a poached salmon. The friendly hags were a dozen yards off, and before he could reach them his damning baggage would be noted.

At this supreme moment he had an inspiration, derived from the memory of the otter. To get out his knife, cut a ragged wedge from the fish, and roll it in his handkerchief was the work of three seconds. To tilt the rod over the bank so that it lay in the deep shadow was the work of three more . . . Jimsie had seen him, for a wild cry came down the stream, a cry which brought the cyclists off their machines and set them staring in his direction. Leithen dropped his gaff after the rod, and began running towards the Larrig Bridge – slowly, limpingly, like a frightened man with no resolute purpose of escape. And as he ran he prayed that Benjie from the deeps of the moss had seen what had been done and drawn the proper inference.

It was a bold bluff, for he had decided to make the salmon evidence for, not against, him. He hobbled down the bank, looking over his shoulder often as if in terror, and almost ran into the arms of the cyclists, who, warned by Jimsie's yells, were waiting to intercept him. He dodged them, however, and cut across to the road, for he had seen that Jimsie had paused and had noted the salmon lying blatantly on the sward, a silver splash in the twilight. Leithen doubled up the road as if going towards Strathlarrig, and Jimsie, the fleet of foot, did not catch up with him till almost on the edge of the Wood of Larrigmore. The cyclists, who had remounted, arrived at the same moment to find a wretched muddy tramp in the grip of a stalwart but breathless gillie.

'I tell ye I was daein' nae harm,' the tramp whined. 'I was walkin' up the water-side — there's nae law to keep a body frae walkin' up the waterside when there's nae fence — and I seen an auld otter killin' a saumon. The fish is there still to prove I'm no leein'.'

'There is a fush, but you wass thinkin' to steal the fush, and you would have had it in your breeks if I hadna seen you. That is poachin', ma man, and you will come up to Strathlarrig. The master said that any one goin near the watter was to be lockit up, and you will be lockit up. You can tell all the lees you like in the morning.'

Then a thought struck Jimsie. He wanted the salmon, for the subject of otters in the Larrig had long been a matter of dispute between him and Angus, and here was evidence for his own view.

'Would you two gentlemen oblige me by watchin' this man while I rin back and get the fush? Bash him on the head if he offers to rin.'

The cyclists, who were journalists out to enjoy the evening air, willingly agreed, but Leithen showed no wish to escape. He begged a fag in a beggar's whine, and, since he seemed peaceable, the two kept a good distance for fear of infection. He stood making damp streaks in the dusty road, a pitiable specimen of humanity, for his original get-up was not improved by the liquefaction of his clothes and a generous legacy of slimy peat. He seemed to be nervous, which, indeed, he was, for if Benjie had not seized his chance he was utterly done, and if Jimsie should light upon his rod he was gravely compromised.

But when Jimsie returned in a matter of ten minutes it was empty-handed.

'I never kenned the like,' he proclaimed. 'That otter has come back and gotten the fush. Ach, the maleecious brute!'

The rest of Leithen's progress was not triumphant. He was con-
ducted to the Strathlarrig lodge, where Angus, whose temper and
wind had alike been ruined by the pursuit of Crossby, laid savage
hands upon him, and frog-marched him to the back premises. The
head keeper scarcely heeded Jimsie's tale. 'Ach, ye poachin'
va-agabond. It is the jyle ye'll get,' he roared, for Angus was in a
mood which could only be relieved by violence of speech and
action. Rumbling Gaelic imprecations, he hustled his prisoner into
an outhouse, which had once been a larder and was now a supple-
mentary garage, slammed and locked the door, and, as a final warn-
ing, kicked it viciously with his foot, as if to signify what awaited
the culprit when the time came to sit on his case.

★ ★ ★

Sir Archie, if not a skeleton at the feast, was no better than a
shadow. The fragment of drama which he had witnessed had rudely
divorced his mind from the intelligent conversation of Mr.
Bandicott, he was no longer slightly irritated by Mr. Claybody, he
forgot even the attractions of Janet. What was going on in that twilit
vale? Lady Maisie's pool had still a shimmer of gold, but the woods
were now purple and the waterside turf a dim amethyst, the colour
of the darkening sky. All sound had ceased, except the rare cry of a
bird from the hill, and the hoot of a wandering owl. . . . Crossby had
beyond doubt been taken, but where was Leithen?

He was recalled to his surroundings by Janet's announcement that
Mr. Bandicott proposed to take them all in his car to the meeting at
Muirtown.

'Oh, I say,' he pleaded, 'I'd much rather you didn't. I haven't a
notion how to speak – no experience, you see – only about the third
time I've opened my mouth in public. I'll make an awful ass of
myself, and I'd much rather my friends didn't see it. If I know you're
in the audience, Miss Janet, I won't be able to get a word out.'

Mr. Bandicott was sympathetic. 'Take my advice, and do not
attempt to write a speech and get it by heart. Fill yourself with your
subject, but do not prepare anything except the first sentence and
the last. You'll find the words come easily when you once begin –
if you have something you really want to say.'

'That's the trouble – I haven't. I'm goin' to speak about foreign
policy, and I'm dashed if I can remember which treaty is which, and

what the French are making a fuss about, or why the old Boche can't pay. And I keep on mixin' up Poincaré and Mussolini . . . I'm goin' to write it all down, and if I'm stuck I'll fish out the paper and read it. I'm told there are fellows in the Cabinet who do that.'

'Don't stick too close to the paper,' the Colonel advised. 'The Highlander objects to sermons read to him, and he may not like a "read" speech.'

'Whatever he does I'm sure Sir Archibald will be most enlightening,' Mr. Bandicott said politely. 'Also I want to hear Lord Lamancha. We think rather well of that young man in America. How do you rate him here?'

Mr. Claybody, as an inhabitant of the great world, replied: 'Very high – in his own line. He's the old-fashioned type of British statesman, and people trust him. The trouble about him and his kind is that they're a little too far removed from the ordinary man – they've been too cosseted and set on a pedestal all their lives. They don't quite know how to handle democracy. You can't imagine Lamancha rubbing shoulders with Tom, Dick, and Harry.'

'Oh, come!' Sir Archie broke in. 'In the War he started as a captain in a yeomanry regiment, and he commanded a pretty rough Australian push in Palestine. His men fairly swore by him.'

'I dare say,' said the other coldly. 'The War doesn't count for my argument, and Australians are not quite what I mean.'

The butler, who was offering liqueurs, was seen to speak confidentially to Junius, who looked towards his father, made as if to speak, and thought better of it. The older Mr. Bandicott was once more holding the table.

'My archæological studies,' he said, 'and my son's devotion to sport are apt to circumscribe the interest of my visits to this country. I do not spend more than a couple of days in London, and when I am there the place is empty. Sometimes I regret that I have not attempted to see more of English society in recent years, for there are many figures in it I would like to meet. There are some acquaintances, too, that I should be delighted to revive. Do you know Sir Edward Leithen, Mr. Claybody? He was recently, I think, the British Attorney-General.'

Mr. Claybody nodded. 'I know him very well. We have just briefed him in a big case.'

'Sir Edward Leithen visited us two years ago as the guest of our Bar

Association. His address was one of the most remarkable I have ever listened to. It was on John Marshall – the finest tribute ever paid to that great man, and one which I venture to say no American could have equalled. I had very little talk with him, but what I had impressed me profoundly with the breadth of his outlook and the powers of his mind. Yes, I should like to meet Sir Edward Leithen again.'

The company had risen and were moving towards the drawing-room.

'Now I wonder,' Mr. Claybody was saying. 'I heard that Leithen was somewhere in Scotland. I wonder if I could get him up for a few days to Haripol. Then I could bring him over here.'

An awful joy fell upon Sir Archie's soul. He realised anew the unplumbed preposterousness of life.

Ere they reached the drawing-room, Junius took Agatha aside.

'Look here, Miss Agatha, I want you to help me. The gillies have been a little too active. they've gathered in some wretched hobo they found looking at the river, and they've annexed a journalist who stuck his nose inside the gates. It's the journalist that's worrying me. From his card he seems to be rather a swell in his way – represents the 'Monitor' and writes for my father's New York paper. He gave the gillies a fine race for their money, and now he's sitting cursing in the garage and vowing every kind of revenge. It won't do to antagonise the Press, so we'd better let him out and grovel to him, if he wants apologies. . . . The fact is we're not in a very strong position, fending off the newspapers from Harald Blacktooth because of this ridiculous John Macnab. If you could let the fellow out it would be casting oil on the troubled waters You could smooth him down far better than me.'

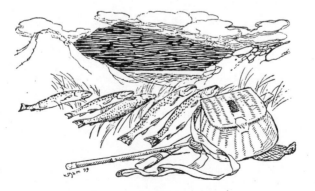

'But what about the other? A hobo, you say! That's a tramp, isn't it?'

'Oh, tell Angus to let him out too. Here are the keys of both garages. I don't want to turn this place into a lock-up. Angus won't be pleased, but we have to keep a sharp watch for John Macnab to-morrow and it's bad tactics in a campaign to cumber yourself with prisoners.'

The two threaded mysterious passages and came out into a moon-lit stable-yard. Junius handed the girl a great electric torch. 'Tell the fellow we eat dirt for our servants' officiousness. Offer him supper, and – I tell you what – ask him to lunch the day after to-morrow. No, that's the Muirtown day. Find out his address and say we'll write to him and give him first chop at the Viking. Blame it all on the gillies.'

Agatha unlocked the door of the big garage and to her surprise found it brilliantly lit with electric light. Mr. Crossby was sitting in the driver's seat of a large motor-car, smoking a pipe and compos-ing a story for his paper. At the sight of Agatha he descended hastily.

'We're so sorry,' said the girl. 'It's all been a stupid mistake. But, you know, you shouldn't have run away. Mr. Bandicott had to make rules to keep off poachers, and you ought to have stopped and explained who you were.'

To this charming lady in the grass-green gown Mr. Crossby's manner was debonair and reassuring.

'No apology is needed. It wasn't in the least the gillies' blame. I wanted some exercise, and I had my fun with them. One of the young ones has a pretty turn of speed. But I oughtn't to have done it – I quite see that – with everybody here on edge about this John Macnab. Have I your permission to go?'

'Indeed you have. Mr. Bandicott asked me to apologise most humbly. You're quite free unless – unless you'd like to have supper before you go.'

Mr. Crossby excused himself, and did not stay upon the order of his going. He knew nothing of the fate of his colleague, and hoped that he might pick up news from Benjie in the neighbourhood of the Wood of Larrigmore.

The other garage stood retired in the lee of a clump of pines – a rude, old-fashioned place, which generally housed the station lorry. Agatha, rather than face the disappointed Angus, decided to complete the task of gaol-delivery herself. She had trouble with the lock, and when the door opened she looked into a pit of darkness scarcely lightened by the outer glow of moonshine. She flashed the torch into the interior and saw, seated on a stack of petrol tins, the figure of the tramp.

Leithen, who had been wondering how he was to find a bed in that stony place, beheld the apparition with amazement. He guessed that it was one of the Miss Radens, for he knew that they were dining at Strathlarrig. As he stood sheepishly before her, his wits suffered a dislocation which drove out of his head the remembrance of the part he had assumed.

'Mr. Bandicott sent me to tell you that you can go away,' the girl said nervously.

'Thank you very much,' said Leithen in his ordinary voice.

Now in the scramble up the river-bank and in the rough handling of Angus his garments had become disarranged, and his watch had swung out of his pocket. In adjusting it in the garage he had put it back in its normal place, so that the chain showed on Sime's ancient waistcoat. From it depended one of those squat little gold shields which are the badge of athletic prowess at a famous school. As he stood in the light of her torch, Agatha noted this shield, and knew what it signified. Also his tone when he spoke had startled her.

'Oh!' she cried, 'you were at Eton?'

Leithen was for a moment nonplussed. He thought of a dozen lies and then decided on qualified truth.

'Yes,' he murmured shamefacedly. 'Long ago I was at Eton.'

The girl flushed with embarrassed sympathy.

'What — what brought you to this?' she murmured.

'Folly,' said Leithen recovering himself. 'Drink and such-like. I have had a lot of bad luck, but I've mostly myself to blame.'

'You're only a tramp now?' Angels might have envied the melting sadness of her voice.

'At present. Sometimes I get a job, but I can't hold it down.' Leithen was warming to his work, and his tones were a subtle study in dilapidated gentility.

'Can't anything be done?' Agatha asked, twining her pretty hands.

'Nothing,' was the dismal answer. 'I'm past helping. Let me go, please, and forget you ever saw me.'

'But can't Papa . . . won't you tell me your name or where we can find you?'

'My present name is not my own. Forget about me, my dear young lady. The life isn't so bad. . . . I'm as happy as I deserve to be. I want to be off, for I don't like to stumble upon gentlefolks.'

She stood aside to let him pass, noting the ruin of his clothes, his dirty unshaven face, the shameless old hat that he raised to her. Then, melancholy and reflective, she returned to Junius. She could not give away one of her own class, so, when Junius asked her about the tramp, she only shrugged her white shoulders. 'A miserable creature. I hope Angus wasn't too rough with him. He looked as if a puff of wind would blow him to pieces.'

Ten minutes later Leithen, having unobtrusively climbed the park wall and so escaped the attention of Mactavish at the lodge, was trotting at a remarkable pace for a tramp down the road to the Larrig Bridge. Once on the Crask side, he stopped to reconnoitre. Crossby called softly to him from the covert and with Crossby was Benjie.

'I've gotten the saumon,' said the latter, 'and your rod and gaff too. Hae ye the bit you howkit out o' the fush?'

Leithen produced his bloody handkerchief.

'Now for supper, Benjie my lad,' he cried. 'Come along, Crossby, and we'll drink the health of John Macnab.'

The journalist shook his head. 'I'm off to finish my story. The triumphant return of Harald Blacktooth is going to convulse these islands to-morrow.'

In September 1931 I recorded two examples of a Scottish 'ghillie's' pawky humour. I was explaining to Angus how I had been delayed by a talkative old lady. 'Och,' says he, 'but it's a good thing. A silent woman is like a rocky pool!' Angus was also responsible for a description of bad casting which I still cherish: 'He cast like a hane (hen).'

THE FISH
Rupert Brooke

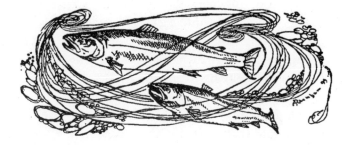

Rupert Brooke was not only a great poet of World War I, but also a true countryman. In this poem written in 1911, one of my favourite fish poems, he distils the essence of 'fishiness'.

In a cool curving world he lies
And ripples with dark ecstasies.
The kind luxurious lapse and steal
Shapes all his universe to feel
And know and be; the clinging stream
Closes his memory, glooms his dream,
Who lips the roots o' the shore, and glides
Superb on unreturning tides.
Those silent waters weave for him
A fluctuant mutable world and dim,
Where wave ring masses bulge and gape
Mysterious and shape to shape
Dies momently through whorl and hollow,
And form and line and solid follow
Solid and line and form to dream
Fantastic down the eternal stream;
An obscure world, a shifting world,
Bulbous, or pulled to thin, or curled,

Or serpentine, or driving arrows,
Or serene sliding, or March narrows.
There slipping wave and shore are one,
And weed and mud. No ray of sun,
But glow to glow fades down the deep
(As dream to unknown dream in sleep);
Shaken translucency illumes
The hyaline of drifting glooms;
The strange soft-handed depth subdues
Drowned colour there, but black to hues,
As death to living, decomposes –
Red darkness of the heart of roses,
Blue brilliant from dead starless skies,
And gold that lies behind the eyes,
The unknown unnameable sightless white
That is the essential flame of night,
Lustreless purple, hooded green,
The myriad hues that lie between
Darkness and darkness!. . .

                         And all's one,
Gentle, embracing, quiet, dun,
The world he rests in, world he knows,
Perpetual curving. Only – grows
An eddy in that ordered falling,
A knowledge from the gloom, a calling
Weed in the wave, gleam in the mud –
The dark fire leaps along his blood;
Dateless and deathless, blind and still,
The intricate purpose works its will;
His woven world drops back; and he,
Sans providence, sans memory,
Unconscious and directly driven,
Fades to some dank sufficient heaven.

O world of lips, O world of laughter,
Where hope is fleet and thought flies after,
Of lights in the clear night, of cries
That drift along the wave and rise

Thin to the glittering stars above,
You know the hands, the eyes of love!
The strife of limbs, the sightless clinging,
The infinite distance, and the singing,
Blown by the wind, a flame of sound,
The gleam, the flowers, the vast around
The horizon, and the heights above –
You know the sigh, the song of love!

But there the night is close, and there
Darkness is cold and strange and bare;
And the secret deeps are whisperless;
And rhythm is all deliciousness;
And joy is in the throbbing tide,
Whose intricate fingers beat and glide
In felt bewildering harmonies
Of trembling touch; and music is
The exquisite knocking of the blood.
Space is no more, under the mud;
His bliss is older than the sun.
Silent and straight the waters run.
The lights, the cries, the willows dim,
And the dark tide are one with him.

from

THE MAKING OF A
TROUT STREAM
Eric Taverner

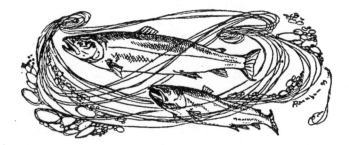

Trout and salmon are 'my' fish. I not long ago filmed George Eliot's
Middlemarch for the BBC and found that she firmly understood
the merits of the trout stream as this extract from her romantic novel
proves:

'"I hear what you are talking about", said the wife, "But you will
make no impression on Humphrey. As long as the fish rise to his bait,
everybody is what he ought to be. Bless you, Casaubon has got a
trout-stream, and does not care about fishing in it himself: could there
be a better fellow?"

"Well, there is something in that," said the Rector, with his quiet
inward laugh. "It's a very good quality in a man to have a trout
stream."'

Eric Taverner wrote a host of excellent fishing books but my
favourite is his account of the making of a trout stream written as a
series of 'letters'.

MERRIMENT PARVA
October the First

DEAR JASPER,

And so you have at long last secured the lease of a stretch of river –
a thing you've been wanting all these years – and have had your first
season on it. Not a particularly good one for you, I feel. You appear
to have found the trout, what there were of them very difficult and
not always in the best of condition at a time when they should have
been. You say that the water generally was in good order in your
part of the country; and that other rods in the neighbourhood
enjoyed sport at least as high in quality as rivers similar in type normally afford. And yet Doctor Marryat had some of the best bags he's
had for years and very few blank days. Glad to hear he's still got that
length three miles below you. He's a really good fellow and incur-
ably generous. You know already what I mean by that, I expect.

Most of your river I know very well indeed and, also, how much
the owners and tenants, especially that excellent man, the doctor,
have done in the past, to improve the angling-potentialities of the
water as well as to increase their own capabilities as anglers. They
put a great deal of work into schemes to augment the stock of trout
and have trained themselves, in season and out, to become better
fishermen. Before I relinquished my lease of that choice stretch just
below the doctor's length, he had already graduated into an artist of
such class, that he passed for a wizard in discovering and often catching trout in places, where other men would not have suspected their
existence. But what a delectable river it is!

You mention the yield of fish as though it were the only test of a
river's worth, which I think wrong. Don't you consider it far better
to judge by the quality as well as, perhaps more than, by the head of
fish the water holds? And there's the manner in which they are to
be caught and the pleasure, apart from that derived from angling,
afforded by the river itself. Quite as much of the joy of angling lives
in the heart as lies in the creel, so much so that a day some men
write off as blank need very rarely be so.

Playing by the riverside can be as fascinating as flower-gardening,
for a stream soon becomes for those dwelling beside it a living thing.
And a trout-stream, such as yours, with its changing moods - none
of them evil or threatening as those of a great salmon-river can be –
has, for the most part, the solid placidity of a tried friend, to whom

one can turn in moments of the most acute distress of mind and spirit.

You and I are fortunate in having, each of us, a length of river we can think of as our own, the character of which we can to some extent mould or modify more or less as we desire. We are more fortunate than those whose opportunities of angling are restricted to the week-ends of the season. They can only become aware of a season developing in stages. We are privileged to watch it grow and can afford to devote many hours to the observation of trout and riverside insect and, also to the work of repair and to experiments designed to improve the water. They fish feverishly and with one eye on the clock, grudging every minute not devoted to fishing. We are able without passion to consider the calendar, so that fishing is transformed for us into a leisurely way of life, full of chances of learning the habits and eccentricities of fish. Thus the trout that has outwitted us one day may in its turn be outwitted on the morrow. And there is value beyond all calculation in continuity.

Your letter raises so many interesting problems, that I believe the best method of answering it is by sending you a detailed description of the way in which the length of Merriment I am now renting was gradually moulded and encouraged to become the pleasant fishing it is to-day. I propose to extract the somewhat disjointed and matter-of-fact entries in the River-Journal and throw them together into rough literary shape. You will thus, I hope find them more enter-taining; and I am adding a few of the comments and stray thoughts that have insinuated themselves into its pages. The story of our labours by the river will take some time to work out, so I will write to you as the winter firelight inspires me and as the demands of a busy life allow.

★ ★ ★

Merriment is a stream that has been well described as a happy combination of the excellent, if somewhat querulous, virtues of Upper Wharfe or a Welsh Border stream and the quiet solidity of Gloucestershire Coln. That is more or less true of Merriment at the present time; although my latest improvements have much modified the whole of the faster part of the stretch I am renting. This has now become a series of lively pools, which are far more closely tenanted than the original, thin stickles and shallow glides, in which trout

used to pick up only a precarious living and were very slow in coming back into condition after they had spawned. The oxygenation
of the water has not thereby been reduced. What has been lost of
atmospheric oxygen has been replaced by dissolved oxygen derived
from aquatic plants, which are now able to maintain themselves
where they have been set.

Although the head-waters of Merriment are situated on high
ground, less damage is caused by spates than hitherto, largely because
a more stable environment has been created for weeds and the
animal-population. The main force of the swollen stream passes over
as a mass of water instead of rushing uncontrolled through the river-
channel and scouring out everything but the living rock and the very
large boulders.

We are certainly very fortunate in the chemical quality of the
water. Merriment runs over beds of limestone in the reaches above
us and is always alkaline, a property which encourages vegetable-
growth. Small rivulets enter the main from one side that are pro-
nouncedly acid, a character they acquire from the low bogland.
Acid-loving flowers and vegetation thrive in that region. So insignificant, however, is the volume of these tiny feeders, that the water of
the main is unaltered in character, even just below the point of entry.

The first thing I decided, when, after much haggling with old
Lord Mulberry's lawyers and encouragement from him and after
much signing of documents, I became for a long term of years master of the fishing and the narrow meadows through which the river
runs, was to enunciate a principle that has guided me ever since. To
increase the pleasure of angling it is not enough to try and increase

the head of trout to be caught. So much more can be achieved by trying to improve the quality as well as the quantity of the fish, by adapting the river to this end and, also, by training oneself towards becoming a more accomplished angler. In fact, an angler placed as you and I are to-day ought to consider equally the river, the fish and his own technique.

My work on the length was made much easier, because I had secured the tenancy of both banks throughout; otherwise I could hardly have made any radical alterations or experiments without obtaining at least the agreement of those who would have been fishing opposite me. It would be unreasonable to expect to find the owners of two opposite banks having like views on improvements. Each side of a river invites a different approach. The interests of the owners may be diametrically opposed. The projecting branch that hinders casting from one bank may in some mysterious way give essential cover to a trout easily accessible from the far side. If you are master of both banks, you will set yourself to discover how to satisfy the claims of each. Some measure of control of a water, either ownership or a long lease, is thus obviously essential. If a fisherman does not possess one or other of these, all his efforts may well be a waste of time or of money – probably of both.

The terms upon which a man holds a fishing ought to be clear and unequivocal and such as to render subsequent recourse to law or to its documents quite unnecessary. There are, of course, fellow-anglers renting fishing downstream of our stretch and two millers, all of whom I felt I had to consult and to whom I gave a vague promise not to spoil their sport nor to trespass on water-rights, respectively. Rights or no rights, it was well worth while taking that trouble. They have all been very friendly and helpful ever since.

When I first took over the fishing, about the middle of July, there had been a drought for about ten weeks; and the river had so shrunk, that the weed-beds stood out above the surface of the water like large green islands. These had already been adopted as permanent breeding-grounds by ever-trustful waterhens, which normally seem to occupy the entire summer in the business of producing broods of chicks and of attending to their education. The upper part of the length consisted merely of attenuated stickles and very slack, shallow glides making a way past rather than between large, grey boulders. The watercourse appeared to be in the grip of the dank green fingers of blanket-weed, here and there set with the belated white flowers of water-ranunculus.

I do not for one moment suppose that any alterations I subsequently made could have affected the river under those extreme conditions, which so far have not recurred. But it was the sight of the river-bed, almost uncovered by water, that made me realize in a flash that an opportunity was being presented me to build throughout the upper portion a series of dams. A wonderful chance had been handed to me of making a close study of river bed, a chance which, whenever given me on a salmon-river, I have used to memorize the position of snags and awkward stones along my accustomed wading-course.

Heavy work, indeed! No man, single-handed, could encompass the work I proposed to myself. I prayed for some gift from heaven and it arrived, sent straight by the saint who watches over anglers' interests, in the person of an old sailor, Purves, forenamed Peter. Perhaps, it would be more correct to call him a *ci-devant* sailor, for he bore no signs of age and had lost none of his mastery of knots and splices or of his deftness in handling and thinking out the innumerable problems that confronted us in the early years of our association.

Peter was his name, but he was invariably spoken of as Highland Tom, a sobriquet acquired, he once told me from being a son of a pipe-major of Boer War days. But he has never explained why he came ashore from a sea-faring life, one which was short but apparently pretty full. When you come and stay with us in our little cottage, I'll get him to tell you some of his quite unbelievable fo'-castle yarns. But that's by the way.

When I first knew Tom, he was in his late fifties and appeared to have functioned as under river-keeper and odd man up and down the countryside ever since he deserted the sea. Deserted is, I believe, the right expression, for there have been moments when I have divined that the spiritual cord binding sailor and sea has never been cut and that at times it is drawn more tautly than at others. If you think these details of Tom's life are uncalled for, you must forgive until you have met him and have had an opportunity of understanding.

He and I first met in the bar-parlour of the inn where I was staying during the first summer of my tenancy of the fishing, which goes

to show that a good inn is an asset to an angler and a factor not to
be neglected. And certainly no inn is more comfortable than 'The
Polecat' with its centuries-old fabric and its deeply-cellared ale.

It was on the second evening of my stay there that Tom walked
in, just after my return from surveying the river. At once he attracted
my attention by his unusual height, his strong hands and a voice
remarkably soft and tempered for so large a man. From his ears
descended thin gold rings, a relict custom from the main current of
life and not an affectation impersonating tradition. There is nothing
obsequious about Tom.

We fell almost at once into deep conversation about sailing-ships,
for which he had a passion; but I had just seen the light through the
bottom of my second tankard, when he suddenly proffered his services
in any capacity on the river. I suppose a townsman would have been
surprised, might even have asked him how he knew help such as he
could give was needed just then. But you and I have lived too long in
the country to harbour any illusions about the probability of our most
secret plans being other than village-property.

'It's going to be tough work at first', I remarked. Then without
giving him a chance to back out, I quickly added, 'Right, we'll start
tomorrow, if the drought holds. Meet me here at half-past nine.
We'll have another half-and-half on that.'

Time and again, Tom has been worth what little I can afford to
pay him – and he's still with me. If – which I seriously doubt – you
ever come across another Peter Purves, don't scruple for one instant
to kidnap him – almost I was going to write, to shanghai him – in
order to persuade him to enter your service. Then make him not
only your helper at the riverside, but your constant friend.
Unfortunately, my resources do not allow me to employ him on full
time. I give him so much for a day's work and during the close season a weekly retainer; but, when his hands are not working for me,
his ears are. All of this, further, goes to prove that, if there's an
angling problem to be solved, the proper court of appeal is that of
Saint Peter.

from

ROD AND LINE
Arthur Ransome

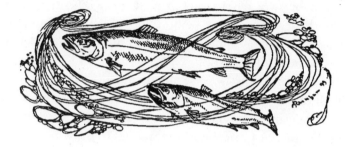

Arthur Ransome is not just my favourite writer on fish but my favourite writer full stop. I discovered him when I was seventeen. In my diary for 12 August 1929, I wrote:

'P & C.D have just given me Rod and Line *by Arthur Ransome, truly quite the best fishing book I've read, it's so amusing and yet full of really good advice and well written, the author really appreciates the sort of fishing that poor anglers like myself can only get. It's rather significant that more really good books are written on the art of fishing than any other of our English sports.'*

It was a great relief to know that I was not the only fisherman who talked to himself!

I WONDER whether all fishermen, without knowing it, talk to their fish. When with a companion they seem in talking to him to find relief from an excitement that must otherwise come out in monologue. A gillie I know, says that all the men he has carried a gaff for, swear all the time they have a fish on, with the exception of two parsons. One of these grunts and the other 'talks mush in such a way that if you did not know him you would think he was using bad language'. I have heard a small boy adjuring his float to 'Bob, you brute!' and a small girl who did not like taking fish off the hooks, apologizing to a perch for snatching away the bait which he was visibly on the point of taking. Pike, certainly, are seldom caught in silence. The language used to them is not polite. They look for hostility and are met with it. Many an angler more than half believes that he has heard them answer back. When a pike comes up out of the water, opens his great white mouth and shakes his head, it is hard to believe that he does not actually bark.

A month or two ago I was fortunate in overhearing nearly the whole of the catching of a salmon. I was eating my sandwiches behind a rock when a salmon fisher who did not know I was there came to the head of the pool. There was no one else in sight, and I was startled by hearing him say, not at all below his breath, 'Just by the rock's the place'. He began casting at once and at the second or third cast I heard 'Ha! Looked at it did you? Wondered what museum I'd stolen it from and why I wanted to show it to you? Well, take another look at it. It'll be coming to you in a moment. Now where are you? Hurry up or the gates'll be closed. Last chance of seeing the celebrated Johannes Scotus. . . . There you are. . . . But why not take the beastly thing? Not good enough for you? Rubbish. Now all the wise men say that I ought to offer you a smaller one of the same. But you and I know better. You want to see this one again. And you shall. Now then. Out of the smooth and into the stream. Are you waiting for it or have you gone off to lament your lack of appetite. Ha. . . . Ha. . . . One to be ready. Two to be steady. Three to decide that even if he takes it striking is a mug's game and four to . . . tighten . . . ra. . . . ther . . . FIRMLY.'

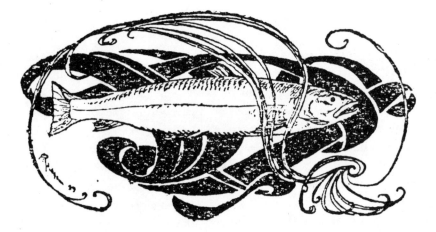

At this point the fisherman came down through the shallows at the head of the pool with his rod point well up, his reel screaming and his line taut to something moving rapidly far down the pool. The fisherman hurried over the boulders. 'Would you? Would you?' I heard him ejaculate defiantly, evidently attributing to the fish responsibility for an awkward stumble. He got below his fish and I could see from his lips that he was talking continuously, though I could hear nothing but the stream. I picked up my gaff and, keeping well away from the river went down and took up a position not far from the fisherman, but well out of his way so that I could act as gillie for him if he wanted one. I suppose he must have heard the noise of my arrival, for he looked for half a second in my direction, but he was far too much engrossed in his contest with the fish not to forget my presence almost instantly. He and the fish were alone together.. There was no one else in their world.

'Yes, my dear,' I heard him say, 'you are perfectly right. That big stone is the place to make for. Get the line round that and we part company. But I lost a relation of yours round that stone and just for that very reason . . . steady now . . . I am not going to lose you. No, no, my lad. You're on the wrong side. You should have gone on the other side and got the gut on the sharp edge. What? You think you'll settle down there, do you? Tire me out, eh? We'll see about that . . . Now then. This way with your head, my friend. Just feel the current on your cheek. So. Out you come. Up-stream? De . . . lighted. As far as you want to go. Nothing keeping you. There's sixty yards of backing on this reel. Oh. So you don't want to go any further after all. Well, my dear, you'll have to work hard to keep where you are. There's good strong water coming down there. What? dropping already. You might have had the decency to drop this side of the stream. You can't think that I'm going to lug you across. Now this little backwater here would be just the place to land you. If you won't see it, I can't make you. But . . . look here, if you go much further, you'll have to take a nasty toss into the pool below and I shall have to get down before you. Disobliging brute. Another two yards and there'll be no stopping yourself. Now then, easy, easy. . . .'

The fisherman slid down over the rocks just in time to keep the line clear as the fish rolled through the fall into the low pool. Few things are more astonishing than the gymnastics of which even an elderly man finds himself capable when he has a good fish at the end of his line. The fisherman went down over those rocks like a boy and, with the fish still on, was moving steadily down the low pool before I had had time to make up my mind to follow him. I had no fish to give wings to my feet and took a minute or two to climb down.

I found the conversation still proceeding, though its tone was much less friendly, 'Tired are you, now? No more tricks of that kind. You've spoilt two pools for me. Couldn't you stick to the ring and fight it out handsomely in one. Turning the best pool of the river into a circus. It'll be a couple of hours before it is worth fishing. No, enough of that. You wouldn't come into that backwater. Try this one. So. Another yard. Another foot. What? Not tired yet? Saw the gaff, did you? Didn't like the look of my face. I shouldn't have thought you had that much run left in you. Coming down again now. Turning over. Keep your head up-stream. Round again. Thank you. Inshore with you. Over it. Now, my beauty . . .' The fisherman lifted out his fish and carried it up the shingle.

He turned to me. He was very hot and rather breathless. 'He's not a bad fish,' he said, 'Twelve or fourteen pounds. Not more.' He spoke in quiet appraisement. I am sure that if I had told him that he had been talking aloud to that same fish for the last ten minutes, he would not have believed me. I wonder, is it so with us all?

from

BIG TWO-HEARTED RIVER
Ernest Hemingway

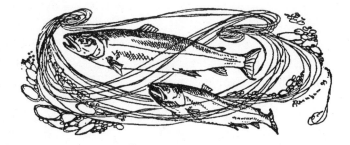

Hemingway may be rather out of fashion but nobody captures as vividly as he does what it is like to do battle with nature. This beautiful story sums up perfectly what it means to have a passion for fishing.

Part I

THE train went on up the track out of sight, around one of the hills of burnt timber. Nick sat down on the bundle of canvas and bedding the baggage man had pitched out of the door of the baggage car. There was no town, nothing but the rails and the burned-over country. The thirteen saloons that had lined the one street of Seney had not left a trace. The foundations of the Mansion House hotel stuck up above the ground. The stone was chipped and split by the fire. It was all that was left of the town of Seney. Even the surface had been burned off the ground.

Nick looked at the burned-over stretch of hillside, where he had expected to find the scattered houses of the town and then walked down the railroad track to the bridge over the river. The river was there. It swirled against the log piles of the bridge. Nick looked down into the clear, brown water, coloured from the pebbly bottom, and watched the trout keeping themselves steady in the current with wavering fins. As he watched them they changed their positions by quick angles, only to hold steady in the fast water again. Nick watched them a long time.

He watched them holding themselves with their noses into the current, many trout in deep, fast moving water, slightly distorted as he watched far down through the glassy convex surface of the pool, its surface pushing and swelling smooth against the resistance of the log-driven piles of the bridge. At the bottom of the pool were the big trout. Nick did not see them at first. Then he saw them at the bottom of the pool, big trout looking to hold themselves on the gravel bottom in a varying mist of gravel and sand, raised in spurts by the current.

Nick looked down into the pool from the bridge. It was a hot day. A kingfisher flew up the stream. It was a long time since Nick had looked into a stream and seen trout. They were very satisfactory. As the shadow of the kingfisher moved up the stream, a big trout shot upstream in a long angle, only his shadow marking the angle, then lost his shadow as he came through the surface of the water, caught the sun, and then, as he went back into the stream under the surface, his shadow seemed to float down the stream with the current, unresisting, to his post under the bridge where he tightened facing up into the current.

Nick's heart tightened as the trout moved. He felt all the old feeling.

He turned and looked down the stream. It stretched away, pebbly-bottomed with shallows and big boulders and a deep pool as it curved away around the foot of a bluff.

Nick walked back up the ties to where his pack lay in the cinders beside the railway track. He was happy. He adjusted the pack harness around the bundle, pulling straps tight, slung the pack on his back, got his arms through the shoulder straps and took some of the pull off his shoulders by leaning his forehead against the wide band of the tump-line. Still, it was too heavy. It was much too heavy. He had his leather rod-case in his hand and leaning forward to keep the weight of the pack high on his shoulders he walked along the road that paralleled the railway track, leaving the burned town behind in the heat, and then turned off around a hill with a high, fire-scarred hill on either side on to a road that went back into the country. He walked along the road feeling the ache from the pull of the heavy pack. The road climbed steadily. It was hard work walking up-hill. His muscles ached and the day was hot, but Nick felt happy. He felt he had left everything behind, the need for thinking, the need to write, other needs. It was all back of him.

From the time he had gotten down off the train and the baggage man had thrown his pack out of the open car door things had been different. Seney was burned, the country was burned over and changed, but it did not matter. It could not all be burned. He knew that. He hiked along the road, sweating in the sun, climbing to cross the range of hills that separated the railway from the pine plains.

The road ran on, dipping occasionally, but always climbing. Nick went on up. Finally the road after going parallel to the burnt hillside reached the top. Nick leaned back against a stump and slipped out of the pack harness. Ahead of him, as far as he could see, was the pine plain. The burned country stopped off at the left with the range of hills. On ahead islands of dark pine trees rose out of the plain. Far off to the left was the line of the river. Nick followed it with his eye and caught glints of the water in the sun.

There was nothing but the pine plain ahead of him, until the far blue hills that marked the Lake Superior height of land. He could hardly see them, faint and far away in the head-light over the plain. If he looked too steadily they were gone. But if he only half-looked they were there, the far-off hills of the height of land.

Nick sat down against the charred stump and smoked a cigarette. His pack balanced on top of the stump, harness holding ready, a hollow moulded in it from his back. Nick sat smoking, looking out over the country. He did not need to get his map out. He knew where he was from the position of the river.

As he smoked, his legs stretched out in front of him, he noticed a grasshopper walk along the ground and up on to his woollen sock. The grasshopper was black. As he had walked along the road, climbing, he had started many grasshoppers from the dust. They were all black. They were not the big grasshoppers with yellow and black or red and black wings whirring out from their black wing sheathing as they fly up. These were just ordinary hoppers, but all a sooty black in colour. Nick had wondered about them as he walked, without really thinking about them. Now, as he watched the black hopper that was nibbling at the wool of his sock with its fourway lip, he realized that they had all turned black from living in the burned–over land. He realized that the fire must have come the year before, but the grasshoppers were all black now. He wondered how long they would stay that way.

Carefully he reached his hand down and took hold of the hopper by the wings. He turned him up, all his legs walking in the air, and looked at his jointed belly. Yes, it was black too, iridescent where the back and head were dusty.

'Go on, hopper,' Nick said, speaking out loud for the first time. 'Fly away somewhere.'

He tossed the grasshopper into the air and watched him sail away to a charcoal stump across the road.

Nick stood up. He leaned his back against the weight of his pack where it rested upright on the stump and got his arms through the shoulder straps. He stood with the pack on his back on the brow of the hill looking out across the country toward the distant river and then stuck down the hillside away from the road. Underfoot the ground was good walking. Two hundred yards down the hillside the fire line stopped. Then it was sweet fern, growing ankle high, to walk through, and clumps of jack pines; a long undulating country with frequent rises and descents, sandy underfoot and the country alive again.

Nick kept his direction by the sun. He knew where he wanted to strike the river and he kept on through the pine plain, mounting small rises to see other rises ahead of him and sometimes from the top of a rise a great solid island of pines off to his right or his left. He broke off some sprigs of the heathery sweet fern, and put them under his pack straps. The chafing crushed it and he smelled it as he walked.

He was tired and very hot, walking across the uneven, shadeless pine plain. At any time he knew he would strike the river by turning off to his left. It could not be more than a mile away. But he kept on toward the north to hit the river as far upstream as he could go in one day's walking.

For some time as he walked Nick had been in sight of one of the big islands of pine standing out above the rolling high ground he was crossing. He dipped down and then as he came slowly up to the crest of the ridge he turned and made toward the pine trees.

There was no underbrush in the island pine trees. The trunks of the trees went straight up or slanted toward each other. The trunks were straight and brown without branches. The branches were high above. Some interlocked to make a solid shadow on the brown forest floor. Around the grove of trees was a bare space. It was brown and soft underfoot as Nick walked on it. This was the over-lapping of the pine needle floor, extending out beyond the width of the high branches. The trees had grown tall and the branches moved high, leaving in the sun this bare space they had once covered with shadow. Sharp at the edge of this extension of the forest floor commenced the sweet fern.

Nick slipped off his pack and lay down in the shade. He lay on his back and looked up into the pine trees. His neck and back and the small of his back rested as he stretched. The earth felt good against his back. He looked up at the sky, through the branches, and then shut his eyes. He opened them and looked up again. There was a wind high up in the branches. He shut his eyes again and went to sleep.

Nick woke stiff and cramped. The sun was nearly down. His pack was heavy and the straps painful as he lifted it on. He leaned over with the pack on and picked up the leather rod-case and started out from the pine trees across the sweet fern swale, toward the river. He knew it could not be more than a mile.

He came down a hillside covered with stumps into a meadow. At the edge of the meadow flowed the river. Nick was glad to get to the river. He walked upstream through the meadow. His trousers were soaked with the dew as he walked. After the hot day, the dew had come quickly and heavily. The river made no sound. It was too fast and smooth. At the edge of the meadow, before he mounted to a piece of high ground to make camp, Nick looked down the river at the trout rising. They were rising to insects come from the swamp on the other side of the stream when the sun went down. The trout jumped out of water to take them. While Nick walked through the little stretch of meadow alongside the stream, trout had jumped high out of water. Now as he looked down the river, the insects must be settling on the surface, for the trout were feeding steadily all down the stream. As far down the long stretch as he could see, the trout were rising, making circles all down the surface of the water, as though it were starting to rain.

The ground rose, wooded and sandy, to overlook the meadow, the stretch of river and the swamp. Nick dropped his pack and rod-case and looked for a level piece of ground. He was very hungry and he wanted to make his camp before he cooked. Between two jack-pines, the ground was quite level. He took the axe out of the pack and chopped out two projecting roots. That levelled a piece of ground large enough to sleep on. He smoothed out the sandy soil with his hand and pulled all the sweet fern bushes by their roots. His hands smelled good from the sweet fern. He smoothed the up-rooted earth. He did not want anything making lumps under the blankets. When he had the ground smooth, he spread his three blankets. One he folded double, next to the ground, The other two he spread on top.

With the axe he slit off a bright slab of pine from one of the stumps and split it into pegs for the tent. He wanted them long and solid to hold in the ground. With the tent unpacked and spread on the ground, the pack, leaning against a jack-pine, looked much smaller. Nick tied the rope that served the tent for a ridge-pole to the trunk of one of the pine trees and pulled the tent up off the ground with the other end of the rope and tied it to the other pine. The tent hung on the rope like a canvas blanket on a clothes line. Nick poked a pole he had cut up under the back peak of the canvas and then made it a tent by pegging out the sides. He pegged the sides out taut and drove the pegs deep, hitting them down into the ground with the flat of the axe until the rope loops were buried and the canvas was drum tight.

Across the mouth of the tent Nick fixed cheesecloth to keep out mosquitoes. He crawled inside under the mosquito bar with various things from the pack to put at the head of the bed under the slant of the canvas. It smelled pleasantly of canvas. Already there was something mysterious and home-like. Nick was happy as he crawled inside the tent. He had not been unhappy all day. This was different though. Now things were done. There had been this to do. Now it was done. It had been a hard trip. He was very tired. That was done. He had made his camp. He was settled. Nothing could touch him. It was a good place to camp. He was there, in the good place. He was in his home where he had made it. Now he was hungry.

He came out, crawling under the cheesecloth. It was quite dark outside. It was lighter in the tent.

Nick went over to the pack and found, with his fingers, a long nail in a paper sack of nails, in the bottom of the pack. He drove it

into the pine tree, holding it close and hitting it gently with the flat
of the axe. He hung the pack up on the nail. All his supplies were
in the pack. They were off the ground and sheltered now.

Nick was hungry. He did not believe he had ever been hungrier.
He opened and emptied a can of pork and beans and a can of
spaghetti into the frying pan.

'I've got a right to eat this kind of stuff, if I'm willing to carry it,'
Nick said. His voice sounded strange in the darkening woods. He
did not speak again.

He started a fire with some chunks of pine he got with the axe
from a stump. Over the fire he stuck a wire grill, pushing the four
legs down into the ground with his boot. Nick put the frying-pan
on the grill over the flames. He was hungrier. The beans and
spaghetti warmed. Nick stirred them and mixed them together.
They began to bubble, making little bubbles that rose with difficulty
to the surface. There was a good smell. Nick got out a bottle of
tomato catchup and cut four slices of bread. The little bubbles
were coming faster now. Nick sat down beside the fire and lifted the
frying-pan off. He poured about half the contents out into a tin
plate. It spread slowly on the plate. Nick knew it was too hot. He
poured on some tomato catchup. He knew the beans and spaghetti
were still too hot. He looked at the fire, then at the tent, he was not
going to spoil it all by burning his tongue. For years he had never
enjoyed fried bananas because he had never been able to wait for
them to cool. His tongue was very sensitive. He was very hungry.
Across the river in the swamp, in the almost dark, he saw a mist
rising. He looked at the tent once more. All right. He took a full
spoonful from the plate.

'Chrise,' Nick said. 'Geezus Chrise,' he said happily.

He ate the whole plateful before he remembered the bread. Nick
finished the second plateful with the bread, mopping the plate shiny.
He had not eaten since a cup of coffee and a ham sandwich in the
station restaurant at St. Ignace. It had been a very fine experience.
He had been that hungry before, but had not been able to satisfy it.
He could have made camp hours before if he had wanted to. There
were plenty of good places to camp on the river. But this was good.

Nick tucked two big chips of pine under the grill. The fire flared
up. He had forgotten to get water for the coffee. Out of the pack
he got a folding canvas bucket and walked down the hill, across the

edge of the meadow to the stream. The other bank was in the white mist. The grass was wet and cold as he knelt on the bank and dipped the canvas bucket into the stream. It bellied and pulled hard in the current. The water was ice cold. Nick rinsed the bucket and carried it full up to the camp. Up away from the stream it was not so cold.

Nick drove another big nail and hung up the bucket full of water. He dipped the coffee pot half full, put some more chips under the grill on to the fire and put the pot on. He could not remember which way he made coffee. He could remember an argument about it with Hopkins, but not which side he had taken. He decided to bring it to a boil. He remembered now that was Hopkins's way. He had once argued about everything with Hopkins. While he waited for the coffee to boil, he opened a small can of apricots. He liked to open cans. He emptied the can of apricots out into a tin cup. While he watched the coffee on the fire, he drank the juice syrup of the apricots, carefully at first to keep from spilling, then meditatively, sucking the apricots down. They were better than fresh apricots.

The coffee boiled as he watched. The lid came up and coffee and grounds ran down the side of the pot. Nick took it off the grill. It was a triumph for Hopkins. He put sugar in the empty apricot cup and poured some of the coffee out to cool. It was too hot to pour and he used his hat to hold the handle of the coffee pot. He would not let it steep in the pot at all. Not for the first cup. It should be straight Hopkins all the way. Hop deserved that. He was a very serious coffee drinker. He was the most serious man Nick had ever known. Not heavy, serious. That was a long time ago. Hopkins spoke without moving his lips. He had played polo. He made millions of dollars in Texas. He had borrowed car fare to go to Chicago, when the wire came that his first big well had come in. He could have wired for money. That would have been too slow. They called Hop's girl the Blonde Venus. Hop did not mind because she was not his real girl. Hopkins said very confidently that none of them would make fun of his real girl. He was right. Hopkins went away when the telegram came. That was on the Black River. It took eight days for the telegram to reach him. Hopkins gave away his ·22 calibre Colt automatic pistol to Nick. He gave his camera to Bill. It was to remember him always by. They were all going fishing again next summer. The Hop Head was rich. He would get a yacht and they would all cruise along the north shore of Lake Superior. He was excited but serious. They said good-bye and all felt bad. It broke up the trip. They never saw Hopkins again. That was a long time ago on the Black River.

Nick drank the coffee, the coffee according to Hopkins. The coffee was bitter. Nick laughed. It made a good ending to the story. His mind was starting to work. He knew he could choke it because he was tired enough. He spilled the coffee out of the pot and shook the grounds loose into the fire. He lit a cigarette and went inside the tent. He took of his shoes and trousers, sitting on the blankets, rolled the shoes up inside the trousers for a pillow and got in between the blankets.

Out through the front of the tent he watched the glow of the fire, when the night wind blew on it. It was a quiet night. The swamp was perfectly quiet. Nick stretched under the blanket comfortably. A mosquito hummed close to his ear. Nick sat up and lit a match. The mosquito was on the canvas, over his head, Nick moved the match quickly up to it. The mosquito made a satisfactory hiss in the flame. The match went out. Nick lay down again under the blanket. He turned on his side and shut his eyes. He was sleepy. He felt sleep coming. He curled up under the blanket and went to sleep.

Part II

IN THE morning the sun was up and the tent was starting to get hot. Nick crawled out under the mosquito netting stretched across the mouth of the tent, to look at the morning. The grass was wet on his hands as he came out. He held his trousers and his shoes in his hands. The sun was just up over the hill. There was the meadow, the river and the swamp. There were birch trees in the green of the swamp on the other side of the river.

The river was clear and smoothly fast in the early morning. Down about two hundred yards were three logs all the way across the stream. They made the water smooth and deep above them. As Nick watched, a mink crossed the river on the logs and went into the swamp. Nick was excited. He was excited by the early morning and the river. He was really too hurried to eat breakfast, but he knew he must. He built a little fire and put on the coffee pot.

While the water was heating in the pot he took an empty bottle and went down over the edge of the high ground to the meadow.

The meadow was wet with dew and Nick wanted to catch grass-hoppers for bait before the sun dried the grass. He found plenty of good grasshoppers. They were at the base of the grass stems. Sometimes they clung to a grass stem. They were cold and wet with the dew, and could not jump until the sun warmed them. Nick picked them up taking only the medium-sized brown ones, and put them into the bottle. He turned over a log and just under the shelter of the edge were several hundred hoppers. It was a grass-hopper lodging house. Nick put about fifty of the medium browns into the bottle. While he was picking up the hoppers the others warmed in the sun and commenced to hop away. They flew when they hopped. At first they made one flight and stayed stiff when they landed, as though they were dead.

Nick knew that by the time he was through with breakfast they would be as lively as ever. Without dew on the grass it would take him all day to catch a bottle full of good grasshoppers and he would have to crush many of them, slamming at them with his hat. He washed his hands at the stream. He was excited to be near it. Then he walked up to the tent. The hoppers were already jumping stiffly in the grass. In the bottle, warmed by the sun, they were jumping in a mass. Nick put in a pine stick as a cork. It plugged the mouth of the bottle enough, so the hoppers could not get out and left plenty of air passage.

He had rolled the log back and knew he could get grasshoppers there every morning.

Nick laid the bottle full of jumping grasshoppers against a pine trunk. Rapidly he mixed some buckwheat flour with water and stirred it smooth, one cup of flour, one cup of water. He put a hand-ful of coffee in the pot and dipped a lump of grease out of a can and slid it sputtering across the hot skillet. On the smoking skillet he poured smoothly the buckwheat batter. It spread like lava, the grease spitting sharply. Around the edges the buckwheat cake began to firm, then brown, then crisp. The surface was bubbling slowly to porousness. Nick pushed under the browned under surface with a fresh pine chip. He shook the skillet sideways and the cake was loose on the surface. I won't try and flop it, he thought. He slid the chip of clean wood all the way under the cake, and flopped it over on to its face. It sputtered in the pan.

When it was cooked Nick regreased the skillet. He used all the batter. It made another big flapjack and one smaller one.

Nick ate a big flapjack and a smaller one, covered with apple butter. He put apple butter on the third cake, folded it over twice, wrapped it in oiled paper and put it in his shirt pocket. He put the apple butter jar back in the pack and cut bread for two sandwiches.

In the pack he found a big onion. He sliced it in two and peeled the silky outer skin. Then he cut one half into slices and made onion sandwiches. He wrapped them in oiled paper and buttoned them in the other pocket of his khaki shirt. He turned the skillet upside down on the grill, drank the coffee, sweetened and yellow brown with the condensed milk in it, and tidied up the camp. It was a good camp.

Nick took his fly rod out of the leather rod-case, jointed it, and shoved the rod-case back into the tent. He put on the reel and threaded the line through the guides. He had to hold it from hand to hand, as he threaded it, or it would slip back through its own weight. It was a heavy, double tapered fly line. Nick had paid eight dollars for it a long time ago. It was made heavy to lift back in the air and come forward flat and heavy and straight to make it possible to cast a fly which has no weight. Nick opened the aluminium leader box. The leaders were coiled between the damp flannel pads. Nick had wet the pads at the water cooler on the train up to St. Ignace. In the damp pads the gut leaders had softened and Nick unrolled one and tied it by a loop at the end of the heavy fly line. He fastened a hook on the end of the leader. It was a small hook; very thin and springy.

Nick took it from his hook book, sitting with the rod across his lap. He tested the knot and the spring of the rod by pulling the line taut. It was a good feeling. He was careful not to let the hook bite into his finger.

He started down to the stream, holding his rod, the bottle of grasshoppers hung from his neck by a thong tied in half hitches around the neck of the bottle. His landing net hung by a hook from his belt. Over his shoulder was a long flour sack tied at each corner into an ear. The cord went over his shoulder. The sack flapped against his legs.

Nick felt awkward and professionally happy with all his equipment hanging from him. The grasshopper bottle swung against his chest. In his shirt the breast pockets bulged against him with the lunch and his fly book.

He stepped into the stream. It was a shock. His trousers clung tight to his legs. His shoes felt the gravel. The water was a rising cold shock.

Rushing, the current sucked against his legs. Where he stepped in, the water was over his knees. He waded with the current. The gravel slid under his shoes. He looked down at the swirl of water below each leg and tipped up the bottle to get a grasshopper.

The first grasshopper gave a jump in the neck of the bottle and went out into the water. He was sucked under in the whirl by Nick's right leg and came to the surface a little way downstream. He floated rapidly, kicking. In a quick circle, breaking the smooth surface of the water, he disappeared. A trout had taken him.

Another hopper poked his face out of the bottle. His antennæ wavered. He was getting his front legs out of the bottle to jump. Nick took him by the head and held him while he threaded the slim hook under his chin, down through his thorax and into the last segments of his abdomen. The grasshopper took hold of the hook with his front feet, spitting tobacco juice on it. Nick dropped him into the water.

Holding the rod in his right hand he let out line against the pull of the grasshopper in the current. He stripped off line from the reel with his left hand and let it run free. He could see the hopper in the little waves of the current. It went out of sight.

There was a tug on the line. Nick pulled against the taut line. It was his first strike. Holding the now living rod across the current, he brought in the line with his left hand. The rod bent in jerks, the trout pumping against the current. Nick knew it was a small one. He lifted the rod straight up in the air. It bowed with the pull.

He saw the trout in the water jerking with his head and body against the shifting tangent of the line in the stream.

Nick took the line in his left hand and pulled the trout, thumping tiredly against the current, to the surface. His back was mottled the clear, water-over-gravel colour, his side flashing in the sun. The rod under his right arm, Nick stooped, dipping his right hand into the current. He held the trout, never still, with his moist right hand, while he unhooked the barb from his mouth, then dropped him back into the stream.

He hung unsteadily in the current, then settled to the bottom beside a stone. Nick reached down his hand to touch him, his arm to the elbow under the water. The trout was steady in the moving stream resting on the gravel, beside a stone. As Nick's fingers

touched him, touched his smooth, cool, underwater feeling he was gone, gone in a shadow across the bottom of the stream.

He's all right, Nick thought. He was only tired.

He had wet his hand before he touched the trout, so he would not disturb the delicate mucus that covered him. If a trout was touched with a dry hand, a white fungus attacked the unprotected spot. Years before when he had fished crowded streams, with fly fishermen ahead of him and behind him, Nick had again and again come on dead trout, furry with white fungus, drifted against a rock, or floating belly up in some pool. Nick did not like to fish with other men on the river. Unless they were of your party, they spoiled it.

He wallowed down the stream, above his knees in the current, through the fifty yards of shallow water above the pile of logs that crossed the stream. He did not rebait his hook and held it in his hand as he waded. He was certain he could catch small trout in the shallows, but he did not want them. There would be no big trout in the shallows this time of day.

Now the water deepened up his thighs sharply and coldly. Ahead was the smooth dammed-back flood of water above the logs. The water was smooth and dark; on the left, the lower edge of the meadow; on the right the swamp.

Nick leaned back against the current and took a hopper from the bottle. He threaded the hopper on the hook and spat on him for good luck. Then he pulled several yards of line from the reel and tossed the hopper out ahead on to the fast, dark water. It floated down toward the logs, then the weight of the line pulled the bait under the surface. Nick held the rod in his right hand, letting the line run out through his fingers.

There was a long tug. Nick struck and the rod came alive and dangerous, bent double, the line tightening, coming out of water, tightening, all in a heavy, dangerous, steady pull. Nick felt the moment when the leader would break if the strain increased and let the line go.

The reel racheted into a mechanical shriek as the line went out in a rush. Too fast. Nick could not check it, the line rushing out, the reel note rising as the line ran out.

With the core of the reel showing, his heart feeling stopped with the excitement, leaning back against the current that mounted icily his thighs. Nick thumbed the reel hard with his left hand. It was awkward getting his thumb inside the fly reel frame.

As he put on pressure the line tightened into sudden hardness and beyond the logs a huge trout went high out of water. As he jumped, Nick lowered the tip of the rod. But he felt, as he dropped the tip to ease the strain, the moment when the strain was too great; the hardness too tight. Of course, the leader had broken. There was no mistaking the feeling when all spring left the line and it became dry and hard. Then it went slack.

His mouth dry, his heart down, Nick reeled in. He had never seen so big a trout. There was a heaviness, a power not to be held, and then the bulk of him, as he jumped. He looked as broad as a salmon.

Nick's hand was shaky. He reeled in slowly. the thrill had been too much. He felt, vaguely, a little sick, as though it would be better to sit down.

The leader had broken where the hook was tied to it. Nick took it in his hand. He thought of the trout somewhere on the bottom, holding himself steady over the gravel, far down below the light, under the logs, with the hook in his jaw. Nick knew the trout's teeth would cut through the snell of the hook. The hook would imbed itself in his jaw. He'd bet the trout was angry. Anything that size would be angry. That was a trout. He had been solidly hooked. Solid as a rock. He felt like a rock, too, before he started off. By God, he was a big one. By God, he was the biggest one I ever heard of.

Nick climbed out on the meadow and stood, water running down his trousers and out of his shoes, his shoes squelchy. He went over and sat on the logs. He did not want to rush his sensations any.

He wriggled his toes in the water, in his shoes, and got out a cigarette from his breast pocket. He lit it and tossed the match into
the fast water below the logs. A tiny trout rose at the match, as it
swung around in the fast current. Nick laughed. He would finish the
cigarette.

He sat on the logs, smoking, drying in the sun, the sun warm on
his back, the river shallow ahead entering the woods, curving into
the woods, shallows, light glittering, big water-smooth rocks, cedars
along the bank and white birches, the logs warm in the sun, smooth
to sit on, without bark, grey to the touch; slowly the feeling of disappointment left him. It went away slowly, the feeling of disappointment that came sharply after the thrill that made his shoulders
ache. It was all right now. His rod lying out on the logs, Nick tied
a new hook on the leader, pulling the gut tight until it grimped into
itself in a hard knot.

He baited it, then picked up the rod and walked to the far end of
the logs to get into the water, where it was not too deep. Under and
beyond the logs was a deep pool. Nick walked around the shallow
shelf near the swamp shore until he came out on the shallow bed of
the stream.

On the left, where the meadow ended and the woods began, a
great elm tree was uprooted. Gone over in a storm, it lay back into
the woods, its roots clotted with dirt, grass growing in them, rising
a solid bank beside the stream. The river cut to the edge of the uprooted tree. From where Nick stood he could see deep channels, like
ruts, cut in the shallow bed of the stream by the flow of the current.
Pebbly where he stood and pebbly and full of boulders beyond;
where it curved near the tree roots, the bed of the stream was marly
and between the ruts of deep water green weed fronds swung in the
current.

Nick swung the rod back over his shoulder and forward, and the
line, curving forward, laid the grasshopper down on one of the deep
channels in the weeds. A trout struck and Nick hooked him.

Holding the rod far out toward the uprooted tree and sloshing
backward in the current, Nick worked the trout, plunging, the rod
bending alive, out of the danger of the weeds into the open river.
Holding the rod, pumping alive against the current, Nick brought
the trout in. He rushed, but always came, the spring of the rod
yielding to the rushes, sometimes jerking under water, but always

bringing him in. Nick eased downstream with the rushes. The rod above his head he led the trout over the net, then lifted.

The trout hung heavy in the net, mottled trout back and silver sides in the meshes. Nick unhooked him; heavy sides, good to hold, big undershot jaw, and slipped him, heaving and big sliding, into the long sack that hung from his shoulders in the water.

Nick spread the mouth of the sack against the current and it filled heavy with water. He held it up, the bottom in the stream, and the water poured out through the sides. Inside at the bottom was the big trout, alive in the water.

Nick moved downstream. The sack out ahead of him sunk heavy in the water, pulling from his shoulders.

It was getting hot, the sun hot on the back of his neck.

Nick had one good trout. He did not care about getting many trout. Now the stream was shallow and wide. There were trees along both banks. The trees of the left bank made short shadows on the current in the forenoon sun. Nick knew there were trout in each shadow. In the afternoon, after the sun had crossed toward the hills, the trout would be in the cool shadows on the other side of the stream.

The very biggest ones would lie up close to the bank. You could always pick them up there on the Black. When the sun was down they all moved out into the current. Just when the sun made the water blinding in the glare before it went down, you were liable to strike a big trout anywhere in the current. It was almost impossible to fish then, the surface of the water was blinding as a mirror in the sun. Of course, you could fish upstream, but in a stream like the Black, or this, you had to wallow against the current and in a deep place, the water piled up on you. It was no fun to fish upstream with this much current.

Nick moved along through the shallow stretch watching the banks for deep holes. A beech tree grew close beside the river, so that the branches hung down into the water. The stream went back in under the leaves. There were always trout in a place like that.

Nick did not care about fishing that hole. He was sure he would get hooked in the branches.

It looked deep though. He dropped the grasshopper so the current took it under water, back in under the overhanging branch. The line pulled hard and Nick struck. The trout threshed heavily, half out of water in the leaves and branches. The line was caught. Nick pulled hard and the trout was off. He reeled in and holding the hook in his hand, walked down the stream.

Ahead, close to the left bank, was a big log. Nick saw it was hollow; pointing up river the current entered it smoothly, only a little ripple spread each side of the log. The water was deepening. The top of the hollow log was grey and dry. It was partly in the shadow.

Nick took the cork out of the grasshopper bottle and a hopper clung to it. He picked him off, hooked him and tossed him out. He held the rod far out so that the hopper on the water moved into the current flowing into the hollow log. Nick lowered the rod and the hopper floated in. There was a heavy strike. Nick swung the rod against the pull. It felt as though he were hooked into the log itself, except for the live feeling.

He tried to force the fish out into the current. It came, heavily.

The line went slack, and Nick thought the trout was gone. Then he saw him very near, in the current, shaking his head, trying to get the hook out. His mouth was clamped shut. He was fighting the hook in the clear flowing current.

Looping the line with his left hand, Nick swung the rod to make the line taut and tried to lead the trout toward the net, but he was gone, out of sight, the line pumping. Nick fought him against the current, letting him thump in the water against the spring of the rod. He shifted the rod to his left hand, worked the trout upstream, holding his weight, fighting on the rod, and then let him down into the net. He lifted him clear of the water, a heavy half circle in the net, the net dripping, unhooked him and slid him into the sack.

He spread the mouth of the sack and looked down in at the two big trout alive in the water.

Through the deepening water, Nick waded over to the hollow log. He took the sack off, over his head, the trout flopping as it came out of water, and hung it so the trout were deep in the water. Then he pulled himself up on the log and sat, the water from his trousers and boots running down in the stream. He laid his rod down, moved along to the shady end of the log and took the sandwiches out of his pocket. He dipped the sandwiches in the cold water. The current carried away the crumbs. He ate the sandwiches and dipped his hat full of water to drink, the water running out through his hat just ahead of his drinking.

It was cool in the shade, sitting on the log. He took a cigarette out and struck a match to light it. The match sunk into the grey wood, making a tiny furrow. Nick leaned over the side of the log, found a hard place and lit the match. He sat smoking and watching the river.

Ahead the river narrowed and went into a swamp. The river became smooth and deep and the swamp looked solid with cedar trees, their trunks close together, their branches solid. It would not be possible to walk through a swamp like that. The branches grew so low. You would have to keep almost level with the ground to move at all. You could not crash through the branches. That must be why the animals that lived in swamps were built the way they were, Nick thought.

He wished he had brought something to read. He felt like reading. He did not feel like going on into the swamp. He looked down the river. A big cedar slanted all the way across the stream. Beyond that the river went into the swamp.

Nick did not want to go in there now. He felt a reaction against deep wading with the water deepening up under his armpits, to hook big trout in places impossible to land them. In the swamp the banks were bare, the big cedars came together overhead, the sun did not come through, except in patches; in the fast deep water, in the half light, the fishing would be tragic. In the swamp fishing was a tragic adventure. Nick did not want it. He did not want to go down the stream any farther to-day.

He took out his knife, opened it and stuck it in the log. Then he pulled up the sack, reached into it and brought out one of the trout. Holding him near the tail, hard to hold, alive, in his hand, he whacked him against the log. The trout quivered, rigid. Nick laid him on the log in the shade and broke the neck of the other fish the same way. He laid them side by side on the log. They were fine trout.

Nick cleaned them, slitting them from the vent to the tip of the jaw. All the insides and the gills and tongue came out in one piece. They were both males; long grey-white strips of milt, smooth and clean. All the insides clean and compact, coming out all together. Nick tossed the offal ashore for the minks to find.

He washed the trout in the stream. When he held them back up in the water they looked like live fish. Their colour was not gone yet. He washed his hands and dried them on the log. Then he laid the trout on the sack spread out on the log, rolled them up in it, tied the bundle and put it in the landing net. His knife was still standing, blade stuck in the log. He cleaned it on the wood and put it in his pocket.

Nick stood up on the log holding his rod, the landing net handing heavy, then stepped into the water and splashed ashore. He climbed the bank and cut up into the woods, toward the high ground. He was going back to camp. He looked back. The river just showed through the trees. There were plenty of days coming when he could fish the swamp.

HIGHLAND RIVER
Neil M. Gunn

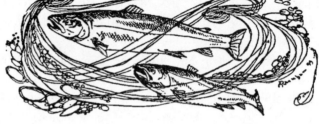

Neil Gunn was the son of a fishing-boat skipper and owner. Apart from a spell working in the Excise Service he devoted his life to writing about the Scottish Highlands. He wrote several fine novels, from one of which, Highland River *the following extract is taken.*

THE near side of the pool was solid rock which the water hit as it entered before swirling out into a round basin with a stony beach on the off side. It was not a large pool, but it was deep and, as the boys saw, impenetrably dark.

'Black as peat,' said Angus, with his friendly smile, when presently they stood on the low rock scanning the water. Then he glanced quickly over each shoulder and stepped down to a narrow ledge. Though only some eighteen inches broad and not really his own length, he yet managed to curl up on it and peer down into the dark current. As he lay there, his nose in the water and his cap held in his right hand close to his head, with its snout lipping the water, Kenn wondered how on earth he expected to see anything, for the ledge in the pool's throat lay at a slant to the incoming dark current which flowed past at some speed carrying continuous legions of round white foam petals.

But he wondered with the excitement that knew Angus was not going through this performance for the fun of it. This was an example of that secret knowledge of the river which he himself hoped yet to attain; the knowledge that finally got into the bone and remained there for ever. Without this knowledge, all talk of loving a river was so much sailing froth; pretty, and to be smiled at in that pleasant, derisive way Angus had at times.

Angus was now lying still as the rock itself. Kenn glanced about him, holding his breath to listen. Angus lifted his head and slowly turned up his face. The water trickled unheeded from the hair on his forehead and from his nose. He was smiling, 'A beauty!' he said, in quiet tones, and levered himself on to his feet. As he squeezed his hair and his nose, he looked about him. 'A fine fish – about ten pounds. And clean.' He vaulted up beside Kenn.

Presently he got Kenn down on the ledge. 'Wait a bit.' He glanced at the sky. 'You won't see a thing unless you get a beam of sun. When you lie down bring your eyes close to the water. Make a shadow with your bonnet and look down the shadows. Keep staring down. He's about six inches out from the rock and his body moves from side to side a little with the current, a very slow waggle like a clout in a stream. . . . Now! I'll hold your jacket.'

Kenn got down and Angus directed him into position. But though Kenn stared earnestly, he could see nothing but the dark-brown water, foam-pattered, flowing immediately under his eyes.

'Keep the foam off if you can with the edge of your hand or the snout of your bonnet. Make a sort of calm water and keep on staring straight down. I'll hold you.'

The brown of the water beneath him became all at once irradiated with sunlight and Kenn realised that he was staring into depth, a brown depth full of myriads of specks of matter. Far down the specks ran into a treacly thickness. Stare as he liked he could not see the bottom, could not see any shape, could distinguish nothing at all beyond a tiny pale fleck that disappeared even as he looked at it.

He hated having to admit defeat. 'I cannot see him,' he said at last, wiping his nose slowly.

'Did you see nothing at all?'

'No. There was a wee little white thing –'

'That's about his back fin,' said Angus, 'Down you go, you've got to learn to see him.'

Angus's tone was eager. Kenn was his partner, had to be initiated. With a quickening in his breast, Kenn got down again. And this time all unconsciously he guarded the foam away with his whole forearm. He flicked the flowing water with his lashes. He stared until the depth ran a golden brown. He saw the tiny fleck again. It wavered towards the rock and disappeared. It came again. It disappeared. The whole depth vanished and came again – and suddenly for an instant a dark shadow the length of a sea-trout wavered beneath it. Then it was gone.

Kenn reared up, the water running from him unheeded, and looked doubtfully at Angus. 'I thought – something like a trout.'

Angus nodded. 'That's him. Ten pounds. Maybe twelve. And clean run.'

'Was that him?'

'Yes. Great, isn't it?'

'Yes,' said Kenn on a solemn breath, and was aware of a lovely lightheartedness in life; saw it sparkle in Angus's eyes: and climbed up and sat down, tremulous a little and weak.

'You go down round the corner of the trees there and see if there's any life on the flat. Then go up through the wood to the top. By the time you're back, I'll be ready.'

The tremulous feeling merely made him noiseless and extraordinarily nimble. He felt light as air; swung under the branches, round rocks, paused, slipped away, listened, stood for a long half-minute screened by a birch, gazing down the flat, saw a rabbit hop from its burrow and cock its ears, began to climb, holding his breath till it came out of him in little gasps, wondered what signal he would give if Gordon stepped out beside him – from round that rock; went round the rock, waited till his heart eased and his mouth grew moist again, and finally stood among the last of the trees on the crest and followed the moor road till it vanished beyond the burying ground. He descended as noiselessly as he had gone up and while still some distance above the pool saw Angus tying a large cod-hook to the end of a hazel stick. The funnel in the trees down which he looked isolated Angus with startling clearness. His slightest movement, his absorbed expression, the stick, the hook, the shake of the white line – everything was so vivid that Kenn had a momentary sensation of prying. With a hawk-like movement, Angus glanced over each shoulder, then put a loop over the hook and pulled it tight, satisfied no human eye was seeing him.

For a moment Kenn could not move. How easy it would be for

a keeper to lie low and then rush out and capture at the critical moment! But what held Kenn was something deeper than that; something not of thought but of vision. Down this arrested moment of time, he himself was the Invisible Watcher, and held all the security of the position, like God or Death. Not, of course, that any such image touched him then. But he remembers now the distinct expression of security and of prying, of the moment as one of extreme clarity like time held spellbound. A faint warmth of shame came out of the prying. Were he God or Death, to have advanced on that bright living figure would surely have broken his heart.

Actually he advanced so quietly that Angus looked up with a start, lowered his eyes, and swiftly, as if he'd caught or missed something, looked at Kenn again.

Kenn shook his head. 'No-one.'

'Come on then. You stand here above me. When I hook him and lift the stick up, you grab it and heave. If I wait till I get up off my belly, he'll have got a grip of the water and tear off.'

Carefully Angus explained the situation and pointed to the ledge on to which Kenn was to heave the fish. 'Jump on him then and hold like grim death.'

Angus was now nervously alive and keen, with the joy of battle in him. He took off his jacket and turned up his right sleeve. 'Here goes!' and he flashed a smile.

Flat on the ledge, he shadowed the water with the cap held in his left hand, while slowly he sank the stick. Kenn watched it go down, down, at arm's length from the rock but coming in gradually. He could see the wobble on it set up by the current. The hand touched the water and remained there. He had got bottom. Slowly the hand brought the stick nearer, still nearer, inch by inch, until it rested again.

Kenn took a swift glance at the ledge of rock. He would have to stoop swiftly, catch the stick, and heave.

Angus now seemed to have got frozen to the rock. He was taking a terrible time. Suddenly he wriggled as if forcing his body down through the rock to see better; then lay motionless again. The blood was congesting his features. At last Kenn saw the right hand grip, felt the pause, and crouched.

The strike was swift enough, but no stick handle was thrust at Kenn.

Angus pulled the stick clear of the water, and with intense dismay

said, 'I missed him!' He stamped about the rock. What a fool! What
an idiot! 'We'll never get him now though we wait till the crack of
doom!' He spoke out loud. He did not care who heard him. What
did it matter? The one and only chance on the river to-day!

He rapped out short sentences. Had lost sight of the hook.
Difficult to feel the touch of the fish. Strong current. Rumble on
the stick. Had felt something once – twice – then timed for the third
touch and struck. While speaking he had got down on the ledge
again, and rose with wet face. Nothing! What did one expect? Kenn
asked him where the fish was lying now.

'Out there, and he might as well be in the Atlantic. Come on!
We'll put the fear of death in him.'

They heaved great stones into the pool. The noise was terrific.
When the water had settled, Angus got down on the ledge again,
but the fish had not come back. They searched the throat, poking
under flags, slashing the running water. But they saw nothing. 'He
may be swimming about.' Angus stoned the pool once more; then
they both withdrew on to the rocks above.

As they lay together, Kenn listened to Angus describe at greater
length exactly what had happened. They could not tell each other
enough about it.

It was a great pity!

A wren, no bigger than a curled brown leaf, landed on a stunted
willow, and let out a song of astonishing fullness and power. *Spink!*
Spink! came from the branches higher up, and from the trees round-
ing towards the flat descended a song of clear single notes, a slow-
tumbling sunny cataract, with memories floating in it.

'It's fine up here,' said Kenn.

'Great getting away, isn't it?'

'Yes.'

'You can see the smoke yonder against the sky. They're hard at it!'
Kenn smiled too. 'When will they be coming back?'

'Not till four or five o'clock. And it can hardly be one yet. Not
much more.' They both looked at the sun in the cloud-moving sky.

'Quiet up here.'

'Yes,' said Kenn. 'I have two wrens' nests.'

'Where? . . . Have you a robin's?'

'Yes.'

'In the serpent grass behind the mill?'

'Yes. But I think I have another one making.'

'If it's in the grass ditch in the park it's a yellow yarling's.'

'I have that one already and two more – all with eggs in them.'

'I'll tell you one you haven't got?'

'What?'

'A blackbird's.'

Kenn rolled over with mirth. Even little boys had a blackbird's nest. 'You'll be saying a sparrow's next!'

They recalled the walk last Sunday morning and the return with eleven peewits' eggs for breakfast. Kenn had eaten two hens' eggs and two peewits' for it had been Peace Sunday. Joe had been at home and there had been much secret fun. It had been exciting, spread out and breasting the fields in the windy morning. And their parents had not said much because there was a long tradition behind the gathering of the peewits' eggs for this festival. Their mother was always at her best when there was plenty to give away. She had the overflowing hand.

Happiness was crawling in their flesh again. 'Let's have a look,' said Angus. 'You never know.' From nibbling odds and ends, the taste of the earth was in their mouths, in their blood. They felt secure from fear, snake-quick under it.

Angus stepped down the rock deliberate as a dancer, and subsided on the narrow ledge, and laid his forehead on the water.

Kenn glanced about him, along the crests, the flats, at Angus, and then swept the pool. It would be fun if he saw. . . . His heart gave a quick turn over as if the dark edge of a stone in eighteen inches of water near the other side of the pool was the salmon. It was just the shadow of a stone-edge. It was the length that deceived. The length was just about right. . . . It really was awfully like it.

Angus uprose, his face dripping. 'Nothing. Rotten, isn't it? What are you looking at?'

'Nothing. It was just that out there – look.'

Angus came beside him. 'Shut up!' he said in a hushed voice and hit Kenn in the ribs with his elbow. 'Shut up your mouth!' He looked about him; picked up the stick; began tying on the hook. 'A blind man couldn't help getting him there.' He was charged with a tremendous excited gaiety. 'Can't you see his head? He's facing *down* the pool.'

The dark outline of the fish came into focus against its blurred background and Kenn said, 'I thought all the time it was him, but I was frightened to say.'

'You're getting the eye.'

Kenn was quivering with pleasure. 'I felt sure it was him; will I run up to see if –'

'Naah!' said Angus, with a large gesture. 'Keep your eyes skinned, that's all. I'll give him the dirty heave – if he'll lie.'

'Do you think he'll lie?'

'He'll see me – see the hook and everything. You watch!'

'He's awfully difficult to see, isn't he?' said Kenn, wanting more praise.

'You'll see him better in a minute!' Angus stepped up under the willow bush, and then leapt from boulder to boulder until he had crossed the stream.

His approach to the side of the pool was noiseless. His left foot levered against a stone on the water's edge, his crouching body slowly arched over the water as the stick went out at arm's length and the hook down in a movement so slow that it fascinated Kenn. Like a drooping summer branch with a white leaf at its tip. The leaf drifted to the salmon's side. The salmon never moved, but lay as if waiting to be stroked. The white hook drifted under the ventral fin until it vanished from Kenn's sight. A final movement of delicate poise and Angus struck.

There was a swift boil – and then nothing but a drifting dance of a dozen silver spangles where the salmon had been.

For the second time Angus had missed.

A darkness in his face, he stared at the scales, then at his hook, muttering fiercely, incoherently, out of his hot blood. Arching out over the water, he examined the bottom on which the salmon had lain and found his explanation. Protruding just above the gravel was the leaning edge of a stone (like the first leg of a V), some four inches in length and an inch or so in depth. It had been invisible to Angus. When he had thought his point was under the ventral fin it actually was under the sloping stone and when he had struck, the stone had thrown the point off the belly of the fish on to its back which it had merely scored. It was the sort of odd chance that might happen once or twice in a lifetime.

When Angus came back, he explained exactly what had happened, but with less than his usual exuberance. The darkness was still in his face and his eyes were stormy.

From place to place he went, peering along the shallow edges, getting down on hands and knees, watching for bubbles, staring a long time from the ledge and turning away from it without speaking to Kenn. At last he started stoning the pool. Kenn could see he was forgotten and without a word went and helped in the stone-throwing. When Angus stopped he stopped. When Angus had once more examined all visible resting places, he said shortly, 'Come on!' and Kenn followed him under the willow and away from that place of ill fortune.

They emerged on a narrow flat of grey grass and old bracken. As they went on, Angus began to speak.

'Sometimes a fellow gets luck like that. Once Lachie-the-Fish took three days to get a salmon out of the Serpent Pool – in the height of summer with clear water. He stripped; swam with the gaff in his mouth; tried the three hooks; tried everything; but the fish wouldn't lie. It happens like that. As if the fish put a hoodoo on you. Nothing you ever do is right. You are too quick or too slow; too wild or too careful; and in the end the fish always moves just when you are about to strike. Becomes uncanny. I heard Joe telling about it. The pale mouth opening and shutting, opening and shutting. Wait till you see one swimming like that, up and down, up and down, its mouth opening and shutting.'

'Did you ever see one like that?'

'Yes. The summer before last in the Broch Pool. He was lying by the sloping flag. I got him in the side, but the stone I had my foot on moved, and he got off. Alie, who was up on the Broch point watching, could see the white gash quite distinctly going up and down the pool. Took me two days to get him – and the whole world could see you yonder.'

8 GONE FISHING

'You got him in the end, though?'

'I did. Lachie got him too. You have to get him.'

'Yes,' said Kenn.

They went on in silence.

'I saw in a book about the Celtic people,' said Kenn, 'they were people somewhere in the olden times. I forget what it was all about, except two lines, and they were something about 'the hazel nuts of knowledge and the salmon of wisdom.' It made me think of the strath. Funny, wasn't it?'

'Not much sense in it.'

'No,' said Kenn at once. 'Only I thought it was queer at the time.'

'They believed in anything in the olden times.'

'Yes,' said Kenn.

They went on in silence until they came to the Smugglers' Pool. There was a shallow cave in the solid rock still blackened from ancient smoke. Angus explained to Kenn about the whisky smugglers, how the men used to meet here and make the white spirits.

Kenn gaped at the cave; climbed up a few paces to its floor level, and saw part of the fleece of a sheep, with white skull and jaw bones lying apart. 'What's that?' he asked, pointing to myriads of brown things like roasted coffee beans in the belly of the fleece. Angus stirred them with his toe. 'Maggot shells.'

A feather of sickness touched Kenn's throat and he backed away. In a small dried water-course behind him grew a bunch of primroses, with four flowers full open. When he saw them, he picked two of the flowers and smelt them, and kept them against his mouth as he followed Angus to the pool and looked up wonderingly at the rock. He nibbled the stalk of one of the primroses. He was not thinking of what he was doing. The stalk was very tender. The yellow petals were softer than any human skin. He crushed them against his mouth, and dropped them, and went forward in a little run of escape, the scent in his nostrils.

Angus was climbing down a crevice to river level. From a precarious hold, he peered into the dark water, but not for very long. He climbed back shaking his head. It was a long, narrow, deep pool. Angus gazed at it for some time. He loved looking at pools.

'You can only work that one with a net,' he said. 'I could tell you ever so many stories about it. In the neck – just there – is a big flat flag. When the water goes down a bit you can see it and stand on it, just over the ankles. They lie under that flag.'

'Is that the flag where last year you progged – and the fish came out with a wild boil and then you –'

'Yes. That chap Harry from Edinburgh was fairly astonished! He though it was magic! Queer . . .'

In the middle of his story Angus stopped and said abruptly, 'Come on back.'

He went swiftly and did not speak again until they were at Achglas Pool.

He examined the pool with a concentrated patience. His last move was to reverse himself on the ledge and peer along the base of the rock where no fish normally lay. He even stretched out his cap a foot or two in front of his head for a last glance. And in that last glance he saw the salmon.

'He's here.' There was excitement, but it was almost bitterly controlled. He made Kenn get down, and after a time in a piercing beam of underwater sunlight, Kenn saw the salmon's head, the round eyes, and the pale line of the mouth so distinctly that he started back with instinctive care.

'It's going to be difficult,' muttered Angus. 'You'll keep hold of the line and play him.'

When he had fixed on the hook he brought the line along to the end of the stick and after a double hitch passed the remainder of it to Kenn.

He was lying with his right shoulder against the rock. To strike with his right hand, he would have to lie over on his left side, when the least little jerk outward would land him in the current. It was a delicate position, but the only one. In getting at the fish he also had to crane forward off the narrow ledge, and to make matters still worse the fish was again facing downstream, was in fact staring right into the window of light in which Angus operated. He was lying at a slant against a broken piece of under-rock, which no doubt sent an invisible eddy of water back over the gills. There was no way of getting at him from upstream because of the wall of rock.

But Angus already knew that salmon lying in deep water are not the wary, frightened creatures many make them out to be. That he was directly in the window of the fish's vision he could see for himself. Both eyes of the fish indeed stared up at him through the clear shadow he made with cap and arm. Yet as his stick kept going down, the fish made no slightest move, exhibited no least trace of uneasiness. Angus took care that the stick grounded beyond the head of course, and then with infinite caution he brought the white visible hook – the water here was two feet shallower than at the other end of the ledge – towards the gill-covers. And the fish lay as if enchanted.

The hook passed out of sight under its head which, although appearing to lie on the bottom, must at least have been two inches clear. The point, thought Angus to himself quite deliberately, must now be directly under the white triangle of the lower jaw. He knew the spot, knew exactly what it felt like to the exploring touch of fingers. A fish gaffed there is at its least powerful.

But still he was not satisfied, and with the utmost care he brought the stick against the salmon's head until he actually felt its weight, felt it as distinctly as if he had brought his own cupped palm under its chin. And still the salmon did not move.

Then Angus struck straight up.

Because of his position on the rock he was powerless, yet in the first few seconds his instinct made him hang on to the stick. The fish got a grip of the water and his pull was tremendous. Realising that the hook would get torn out, he let the stick go and scrambled to his knees. But Kenn was now so excited that instead of paying out line, he held on as he had seen Angus do. 'Let him go!' shouted Angus, grabbing outward at the line. He caught it and so increased the strain. 'Let go, you fool!' Kenn let go. From the whirlpool in the water, the line came away slack and Angus hauled in an empty gaff.

It was maddening; beyond human power to endure: 'Why on earth didn't you let go?'

Kenn felt the attack bitterly. It was a dark, horrible moment, a pit in which the brightness of the day vanished, in which their lovely friendship was smothered.

Angus's fists were tight-clenched. He looked away. 'God damn it!' he said.

Very rarely did the boys of that river swear. 'A dirty mouth' was a reproach amongst them, and a grown man at sound of even an ambiguous oath would quickly enough warm a cheek. Angus's expression was thus like the going out of the sun.

Kenn did not speak. They stood on the rock and stared at the pool. While they stared the quiet tail-reach began to undulate. The salmon became dimly visible, his body moving with a slow waggle like an eel. He nosed the edge of the green flagstone, left it, came into the outgoing current – and went with it over the tail-race into a short comparatively quiet run of water less than two feet deep, with stones here and there. Beyond were boulders and broken shallows. No sooner had he entered this place, however, than he turned towards the pool. He was going back.. . . . His head fell off and with the same slow sinuous movement of the whole body, he began to explore this shallow of refreshing, running water.

Angus had Kenn's arm in a strong grip. 'Don't move,' he muttered, keeping his very lips stiff, as if the salmon might see them.

But the salmon could find no place to rest. Twice it tried to wriggle into a comfortable lie, lay for a moment, and then came away again towards the near side. As its head got the current it balanced and went slowly forward towards the pool.

Angus's fingers dug into Kenn's bone. But Kenn kept the quiver of pain to himself.

The head fell away, and the fingers relaxed.

The salmon began to rub into the bottom and turned half over; the silver under-body flashed rose-gleams through the brown water. In this fashion was scooped the bridal bed.

'Sick!' muttered Angus.

At last it lay still, wholly visible in the shallow water. Slowly the boys backed into the brae, went round some trees and came at the fish from below.

Angus well knew that this was a very different affair from approaching a fish in deep water. Besides, the salmon must be restless, terrified of its enemy. Angus crouched and approached upstream, approached until he could have touched it with the stick at full stretch.

And the salmon did not move.

It lay at a slant to the current, curved like an unstrung bow, sheltering as it were behind its own back, exactly as Angus or Kenn on bare land would shelter from the wind.

Angus's body slid forward again. The stick went out until it over-shot the fish, then the hook drifted back with the current and in behind the shoulder. But he could not get the hook under the body, and yet he was fearful of an instant rush back into the pool, when all would be lost, for if the fish went to earth in the deeps now it would never more move.

He must take his chance, he nervously decided. He struck. The hook glanced off the hard shoulder, and now a strange thing happened. Instead of flashing into the pool like a torpedo the fish circled slowly where it was. Quicker than thought Angus gaffed it on the move and walked ashore with it. It hung limp as if played out by a fisherman, and not until Angus was about to deliver the *coup de grâce* did it give a last show of its strength. while they had been watching it, the wound under the jaw had been draining its life away.

Its size was astonishing to Kenn, for even in the shallows it had not looked very big. It was fully twelve pounds, fresh run, blue-green and silver bright, and of all shapes surely the most perfect in creation.

My memories of fishing in Scotland are not quite so fruitful as Neil Gunn's. I first fished there when I was in my late teens.

'Inverness August 31st - September 7th 1935

Monday 1st September

Rain, Rain, Rain. Some very nice people, Mr and Mrs Pitt of Boxmoor who came last night for a week, took me down to the Oely and we salmon fished the river rising and rising and not a fish to be seen. We've been sitting in the hotel ever since. The rain stopped at about 7.30 after being at it for about 24 hours and by now the loch stretches about 500 yards further west up the glen than it should. The trees peeping out of the face of the waters make me feel like Noah though the inn makes a comfortable ark with not too many animals . . . some good "mots" though. Scots fisherman off for a weekend in his swack tells his boy to go and get his provisions. Boy returns with 24 bottles of whisky and a loaf of bread. "Och" says the fisherman "and what's all the bread for?"'

from

SALAR THE SALMON
Henry Williamson

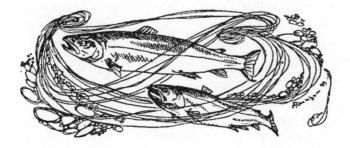

Perhaps best known for Tarka the Otter, *Henry Williamson moved to North Devon in the early twenties. Its countryside and wildlife inspired both this novel and* Salar the Salmon, *a study of river lore which draws on his intimate knowledge and scientific observation of the wildlife around him. I think his real gift however was the power he had of actually seeing life from the point of view of the animals he describes.*

As I arrived at 'Jordan' on Dartmoor in 1925 we may have been fishing not far from one another.

THE elvers were running. They darkened the green shallows of the river. The eddies were thick tangles of them. They had come into the estuary on the flood-tide, and in a gelatinous mass had moved into the still water of the tide-head. All fish in the river sped from them, for elvers were gill-twisting torture and death.

For nearly three years as thin glassy threads the young eels had been crossing the Atlantic, drifting in warm currents of the Gulf Stream from the Sargasso Sea. Here in deep water far under floating beds of clotted marine wreckage all the mature eels of the northern hemisphere, patient travellers from inland ponds and ditches, brooks and rivers, came together to shed themselves of life for immortal reasons. From blue dusk of ocean's depth they passed into death: and from darkness the elvers arose again, to girdle the waters of half the earth.

Salar lay in fast water between Sloping Weir and the road bridge. He lay in front of a large stone, in the swift flume rising to pass over it. The flume streamed by his head and gills and shoulders without local eddy. No elver could reach his gill without violent wriggling, which he would feel. He was swift with the swiftness of the water. There was the least friction between fish and river, for his skin exuded a mucus or lubricant by which the water slipped. The sweep of strong water guarded his life. Other salmon were lying in like lodges in the stony surges. Salar lodged there until dusk, when he moved forward again. Gralaks moved beside him. They recognised and knew each other without greeting.

Many fish were at Sloping Weir before them, waiting beside the lessening weight of white water, in the swarming bubbles of the eddy. They lay close to one another. As soon as one fish waggled tail and dipped and rose to get a grip of the water, to test its own pulse of power, another fish took its place, ready for the take-off. Salar idled, alert, apprehensive, seventeenth in line. Sometimes two or three fish left the phalanx at the same time and after nervous ranging set themselves to swim up through the heavy water.

At the edge of the turning pool, where Shiner the poacher had waited and watched during the day, stood Old Nog the heron. The bird was picking up elvers as fast as he could snick them. His throat and neck ached. A continuous loose rope of elvers wove itself on the very edge of the water, where frillets sliding down the concrete apron-edge scarcely washed into the grass. Old Nog had eaten his first thousand elvers too quickly, gulping with head downheld until his tongue refused work.

After a return to the tree-top heronry where three hernlets had craked and fought to thrust their beaks down his throat to take what he had, Old Nog flew back to the weir and picked and swallowed slowly, his excitement gone. All afternoon he flew back and forth. At dusk he rested, sleeping for three hours. By the light of the full moon rising he returned with his mate to the weir. They crammed their crops and necks and flew back to their filthy nest, where by midnight the three hernlets were crouching, huddled and dour with overmuch feeding. Old Nog then flew back to the weir, to feed himself. Most of the elvers were now gone, but he managed to satisfy his hunger.

On the way home, however, an elver wriggled down his wind-
pipe, causing him to choke and sputter and disgorge; the mass fell
beside a badger below rubbing against its scratching-thorn, causing
it to start and grunt with alarm. Having cautiously sniffed for some
minutes, from various angles, the badger dared to taste; after which
it ate all up and searched for more. For the next few nights it
returned specially to rub itself against the thorn, in the hope of finding such food there again. As for Old Nog, not an elver that year
reached his long pot, as countrymen do call the guts.

During the time of the moon's high tides, more than two hundred
salmon passed over the weir. Salar swam up on his second attempt;
at first he had been unsure of himself, and dropped back almost as
soon as he had got a grip on the central cord or spine of water.
Swimming again with all his power, he moved slowly into the
glissade of water above the white surge, stayed a third of the way up,
as though motionless, vibrating; then had gained over the water and
swum stronger in jubilation, and suddenly found the sill moving
away under him, release of weight from his sides, and calm deep
water before him. He flung himself out for joy, and a young dog-
otter, who was rolling on its back on grass at the pool's edge, where
a bitch–otter had touched earlier in the night, instantly lifted its head,
slipped to the edge, put its head under, and slid tail last into the
water.

Salar saw the otter swimming above him, shining in a broken
envelope of air on head and fur and legs. The pool took the dull
blows of his acceleration and in three seconds, when the otter had
swum nine yards against the current, Salar had gone twenty yards
upstream into the mill-pool, swerved from a sunken tree trunk
lodged in the silt, zigzagged forward to the further bank, startling
other salmon resting there, and hidden himself under a ledge of rock.
The otter, which was not hunting salmon, since in deep water it
could never catch any, unless a fish were injured, crawled out on the
bank again to enjoy through its nose what it imagined visually.

An elver wriggled against Salar, and he swam on. The pool was long
and deep and dark. He swam on easily, restfully, slower than the otter
had pretended to chase him. The wound in his side began to ache
dully, and he rested near the surface, near water noisy over a branch
of alder. At dawn he was three miles above Sloping Weir, lying under
a ledge of rock hollow curving above him, and therefore protecting

him from behind, with an immediate way of escape from danger
into deep water. The salmon slept, only the white-grey tip of the
kype – hooked end of lower jaw – showing as the mouth slightly
opened. Fifteen times a minute water passed the gills, which opened
imperceptibly.

Salar slept. The water lightened with sunrise. He lay in shadow.
His eyes were fixed, passively susceptible to all movement. The sun
rose up. Leaves and stalks of loose weed and water-moss passing were
seen but unnoticed by the automatic stimulus of each eye's retina.
The eyes worked together with the unconscious brain, while the
nerves, centres of direct feeling, rested themselves. One eye noticed
a trout hovering in the water above, but Salar did not see it.

The sun rose higher, and shone down on the river, and slowly
the shadow of the ledge shrank into its base. Light revealed Salar, a
grey-green uncertain dimness behind a small pale spot appearing and
disappearing regularly.

Down there Salar's right eye was filled with the sun's blazing fog.
His left eye saw the wall of rock and the water above. The trout right
forward of him swam up, inspected that which had attracted it, and
swam down again; but Salar's eye perceived no movement. The
shadow of the trout in movement did not fall on the salmon's right
eye.

A few moments later there was a slight splash left forward of
Salar. Something swung over, casting the thinnest shadow; but it
was seen by the eye, which awakened the conscious brain. Salar was
immediately alert.

The thing vanished. A few moments later, it appeared nearer to him.

With his left eye Salar watched the thing moving overhead. It swam in small jerks, across the current and just under the surface, opening and shutting, gleaming, glinting, something trying to get away. Salar, curious and alert, watched it until it was disappearing and then he swam up and around to take it ahead of its arc of movement. The surface water, however, was flowing faster than the river at mid-stream, and he misjudged the opening of his mouth, and the thing, which recalled sea feeding, escaped.

On the bank upriver fifteen yards away a fisherman with fourteen-foot split-cane rod said to himself, excitedly, 'Rising short'; and pulling loops of line between reel and lowest ring of rod, he took a small pair of scissors from a pocket and snipped off the thing which had attracted Salar.

No wonder Salar had felt curious about it, for human thought had ranged the entire world to imagine that lure. It was called a fly: but no fly like it ever swam in air or flew through water. Its tag, which had glinted, was of silver from Nevada and silk of a moth from Formosa; its tail, from the feather of an Indian crow; its butt, black herl of African ostrich; its body, yellow floss-silk veiled with orange breast-feather of the South American toucan, and black Macclesfield silk ribbed with silver tinsel. This fly was given the additional attraction of wings for water-flight, made of strips of feathers from many birds: turkey from Canada, peahen and peacock from Japan, swan from Ireland, bustard from Arabia, golden-pheasant from China, teal and wild duck and mallard from the Hebrides. Its throat was made of the feather of an English speckled hen, its side of Bengal jungle-cock's neck feathers, its cheeks came from a French kingfisher, its horns from the tail of an Amazonian macaw. Wax, varnish, and enamel secured the 'marriage' of the feathers. It was one of hundreds of charms, or materialised river-side incantations, made by men to persuade sleepy or depressed salmon to rise and take. Invented after a bout of seasickness by a Celt as he sailed the German ocean between England and Norway, for nearly a hundred years this fly had borne his name, Jock Scott.

While the fisherman was tying a smaller pattern of the same fly to the end of the gut cast, dark stained by nitrate of silver against under-water glint, Salar rose to mid-water and hovered there.

Behind him lay the trout, which, scared by the sudden flash of the big fish turning, had dropped back a yard. So Salar had hovered three years before in his native river, when, as parr spotted like a trout, and later as silvery smolt descending to the sea, he had fed eagerly on nymphs of the olive dun and other ephemeridae coming down with the current.

He opened his mouth and sucked in a nymph as it was swimming to the surface. The fisherman saw a swirl on the water, and threw his fly, with swish of double-handed rod, above and to the right of the swirl. Then, lowering the rod point until it was almost parallel to the water, he let the current take the fly slowly across the stream, lifting the rod tip and lowering it slightly and regularly to make it appear to be swimming.

Salar saw the fly and slowly swam up to look at it. He saw it clear in the bright water and sank away again, uninterested in the lifelessness of its bright colours. Again it reappeared, well within his skylight window. He ignored it, and it moved out of sight. Then it fell directly over him, jigging about in the water, and with it a dark thin thing which he regarded cautiously. This was the gut cast. Once more it passed over, and then again, but he saw only the dark thinness moving there. It was harmless. He ignored it. Two other salmon below Salar, one in a cleft of rock and the other beside a sodden oak log wedged under the bank, also saw the too-bright thing, and found no vital interest in it.

The fisherman pulled in the line through the rod-rings. It was of plaited silk, tapered and enamelled for ease of casting. The line fell over his boot. Standing still, he cut off the fly, and began a search for another in a metal box, wherein scores of mixed feathers were ranged on rows of metal clasps. First he moved one with his forefinger, then another, staring at this one and frowning at that one, recalling in its connection past occasions of comparative temperatures of air and river, of height and clearness of water, of sun and shade, while the angler's familiar feeling, of obscurity mingled with hope and frustration, came over him. While from the air he tried to conjure certainty for choice of fly, Salar, who had taken several nymphs of the olive dun during the time the angler had been cogitating, leapt and fell back with a splash that made the old fellow take a small Black Doctor and tie the gut to the loop of the steel hook with a single Cairntonjam knot.

Salar saw this lure and fixed one eye on it as it approached and then ignored it, a thing without life. As it was being withdrawn from the water a smolt which had seen it only then leapt open-mouthed at a sudden glint and fell back, having missed it.

Many times a similar sort of thing moved over Salar, who no longer heeded their passing. He enjoyed crushing the tiny nymphs on his tongue, and tasting their flavour. Salar was not feeding, he was not hungry; but he was enjoying remembrance of his river-life with awareness of an unknown great excitement before him. He was living by the spirit of running water. Indeed Salar's life was now the river: as he explored it higher, so would he discover his life.

On the bank the fisherman sat down and perplexedly re-examined his rows and rows of flies. He had tried all recommended for the water, and several others as well; and after one short rise, no fish had come to the fly. Mar Lodge and Silver Grey, Dunkeld and Black Fairy, Beauly Snow Fly, Fiery Brown, Silver Wilkinson, Thunder and Lightning, Butcher, Green Highlander, Blue Charm, Candlestick Maker, Bumbee, Little Inky Boy, all were no good. Then in one corner of the case he saw an old fly of which most of the mixed plumage was gone: a Black Dog which had belonged to his grandfather. Grubs of moths had fretted away hackle, wing, and topping. It was thin and bedraggled. Feeling that it did not matter much what fly was used, he sharpened the point with a slip of stone, tied it on and carelessly flipped it into the water. He was no longer fishing; he was no longer intent, he was about to go home; the cast did not fall straight, but crooked; the line also was crooked. Without splash the fly moved down a little less fast than the current, coming thus into Salar's skylight. It was like the nymphs he had been taking, only larger; and with a leisurely sweep he rose and turned across the current, and took it, holding it between tongue and vomer as he went down to his lie again, where he would crush and taste it. The sudden resistance of the line to his movement caused the point of the hook to prick the corner of his mouth. He shook his head to rid himself of it, and this action drove the point into the gristle, as far as the barb.

A moment later, the fisherman, feeling a weight on the line, lifted the rod-point, and tightened the line, and had hardly thought to himself, *salmon*, when the blue-grey tail of a fish broke half out of water and its descending weight bended the rod.

Salar knew of neither fisherman nor rod nor line. He swam down to the ledge of rock and tried to rub the painful thing in the corner of his mouth against it. But his head was pulled away from the rock. He saw the line, and was fearful of it. He bored down to his lodge at the base of the rock, to get away from the line, while the small brown trout swam behind his tail, curious to know what was happening.

Salar could not reach his lodge. He shook his head violently, and, failing to get free, turned down-stream and swam away strongly, pursued by the line and a curious buzzing vibration just outside his jaw.

Below the pool the shallow water jabbled before surging in broken white crests over a succession of rocky ledges. Salar had gone about sixty yards from his lodge, swimming hard against the backward pull of line, when the pull slackened, and he turned head to current, and lay close to a stone, to hide from his enemy.

When the salmon had almost reached the jabble, the fisherman, fearing it would break away in the rough water, had started to run down the bank, pulling line from the reel as he did so. By thus releasing direct pull on the fish, he had turned it. Then, by letting the current drag line in a loop below it, he made Salar believe that the enemy was behind him. Feeling the small pull of the line from behind, Salar swam up into deeper water, to get away from it. The fisherman was now behind the salmon, in a position to make it tire itself by swimming upstream against the current.

Salar, returning to his lodge, saw it occupied by another fish, which his rush, and the humming line cutting the water, had disturbed from the lie by the sodden log. This was Gralaks the grilse. Again Salar tried to rub the thing against the rock, again the pull, sideways and upwards, was too strong for him. He swam downwards, but could make no progress towards the rock. This terrified him and he turned upwards and swam with all his strength, to shake it from his mouth. He leapt clear of the water and fell back on his side, still shaking his head.

On the top of the leap the fisherman had lowered his rod, lest the fly be torn away as the salmon struck the water.

Unable to get free by leaping, Salar sank down again and settled himself to swim away from the enemy. Drawing the line after him, and beset again by the buzzing vibration, he travelled a hundred yards to the throat of the pool, where water quickened over gravel.

He lay in the riffle spreading away from a large stone, making himself heavy, his swim-bladder shrunken, trying the press himself into the gravel which was his first hiding place in life. The backward pull on his head nearly lifted him into the fast water, but he held himself down, for nearly five minutes, until his body ached and he weakened and he found himself being taken down sideways by the force of shallow water. He recalled the sunken tree and it became a refuge, and he swam down fast, and the pull ceased with the buzz against his jaw. Feeling relief, he swam less fast over his lodge, from which Gralaks sped away, alarmed by the line following Salar.

But before he could reach the tree the weight was pulling him back, and he turned and bored down to bottom, scattering a drove of little grey shadows which were startled trout. Again the pull was too much for him, and he felt the ache of his body spreading back to his tail. He tried to turn on his side to rub the corner of his mouth on something lying on the bed of the pool – an old cartwheel – again and again, but he could not reach it.

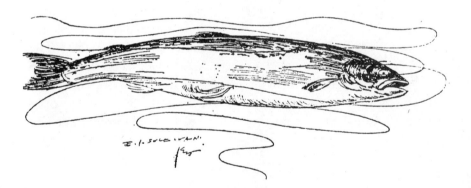

A jackdaw flying silent over the river, paper in beak for nest-lining, saw the dull yellow flashes and flew faster in alarm of them and the man with the long curving danger.

Fatigued and aching, Salar turned downstream once more, to swim away with the river, to escape the enemy which seemed so much bigger because he could not close his mouth. As he grew heavier, slower, uncertain, he desired above all to be in the deeps of the sea, to lie on ribbed sand and rest and rest and rest. He came to rough water, and let it take him down, too tired to swim. He bumped into a rock, and was carried by the current around it, on his side, while the gut cast, tautened by the dragging weight, twanged and jerked his head up-stream, and he breathed again, gulping water quickly and irregularly. Still the pull was trying to take him forward, so with a renewal by fear he turned and re-entered fast water and went down and down, until he was in another deep pool at a bend of the river. Here he remembered a hole under the roots of a tree, and tried to hide there, but had not strength enough to reach the refuge of darkness.

Again he felt release, and swam forward slowly, seeking the deepest part of the pool, to lie on the bottom with his mouth open. Then he was on his side, dazed and weary, and the broken-quicksilvery surface of the pool was becoming whiter. He tried to swim away, but the water was too thick-heavy; and after a dozen sinuations it became solid. His head was out of water. A shock passed through him as he tried to breathe. He lay there, held by line taut over fisherman's shoulder. He felt himself being drawn along just under the surface, and only then did he see his enemy – flattened, tremulant-spreading image of the fisherman. A new power of fear broke in the darkness of his lost self. When it saw the tailer coming down to it, the surface of the water was lashed by the desperately scattered self. The weight of the body falling over backwards struck the taut line; the tail-fin was split. The gut broke just above the hook, where it had been frayed on the rock. Salar saw himself sinking down into the pool, and he lay there, scattered about himself and unable to move away, his tail curved round a stone, feeling only a distorted head joined to the immovable river-bed.

from

COMING UP FOR AIR
George Orwell

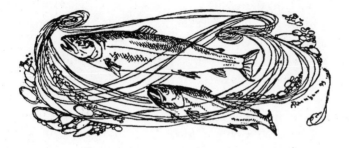

In Coming up for Air *the narrator goes back to the stamping ground of his youth, Lower Binfield, where he fishes for carp in a pool he remembers from thirty years before. I returned to the Dart, the river of my childhood, in 1948. The war over, I fished once more with Peggy Howard, a long-time fishing companion. My diary of that day is filled with similar nostalgia:*

'Peggy on her bank and I on mine. . .The view from the Head looking down the Double Dart valley with the Combestone sunk into the hill opposite seen from my bedroom window in the early morning brought the lost world back dreadfully. With some reservations I would have given anything to be back in 1925.'

FOR the next seven years, from when I was eight to when I was fifteen, what I chiefly remember is fishing. We went many a time to old Brewer's pool, and took tiny carp and tench out of it, and once a whopping eel, and there were other cow-ponds that had fish in them and were within walking distance on Saturday afternoons. But after we got bicycles we started fishing in the Thames below Burford Weir. It seemed more grown-up than fishing in cow-ponds. There were no farmers chasing you away, and there are some thumping fish in the Thames – though so far as I know, nobody's ever been known to catch one.

It's queer, the feeling I had for fishing – and still have, really. I can't call myself a fisherman. I've never in my life caught a fish two feet long, and it's thirty years now since I've had a rod in my hands. And yet when I look back the whole of my boyhood from eight to fifteen seems to have revolved round the days when we went fishing. Every detail has stuck clear in my memory. I can remember individual days and individual fish, there isn't a cow-pond or a backwater that I can't see a picture of if I shut my eyes and think. I could write a book on the technique of fishing. When we were kids we didn't have much in the way of tackle, it cost too much and most of our three-pence a week (which was the usual pocket-money in those days) went on sweets and Lardy Busters. Very small kids generally fish with a bent pin, which is too blunt to be much use, but you can make a pretty good hook (though of course it's got no barb) by bending a needle in a candle flame with a pair of pliers. The farm lads knew how to plait horsehair so that it was almost as good as gut, and you can take a small fish on a single horsehair. Later we got to having two-shilling fishing-rods and even reels of sorts. God, what hours I've spent gazing into Wallace's window.! Even the ·410 guns and saloon pistols didn't thrill me so much as the fishing tackle. And the copy of Gamage's catalogue that I picked up somewhere, on a rub-bish dump I think, and studied as though it had been the Bible! Even now I could give you all the details about gut-substitute and gimp and Limerick hooks and priests and disgorgers and Nottingham reels and God knows how many other technicalities.

Then there were the kinds of bait we used to use. In our shop there were always plenty of mealworms, which were good but not very good. Gentles were better. You had to beg them of old Gravitt, the butcher, and the gang used to draw lots or do ena-mena-mina-mo to decide who should go and ask, because Gravitt wasn't usually too pleasant about it. He was a big, rough-faced old devil with a voice like a mastiff, and when he barked, as he generally did when speak-ing to boys, all the knives and steels on his blue apron would give a jangle. You'd go in with an empty treacle-tin in your hand, hang round till any customers had disappeared and then say very humbly:

'Please, Mr. Gravitt, y'got any gentles today?'

Generally he'd roar out: 'What! Gentles! Gentles in my shop! Ain't seen such a thing in years. Think I got blow-flies in my shop?'

He had, of course. They were everywhere. He used to deal with them with a strip of leather on the end of a stick, with which he could reach out to enormous distances and smack a fly into paste. Sometimes you had to go away without any gentles, but as a rule he'd shout after you just as you were going:

''Ere! Go round the backyard an' 'ave a look. P'raps you might find one or two if you looked careful.'

You used to find them in little clusters everywhere. Gravitt's backyard smelt like a battlefield. Butchers didn't have refrigerators in those days. Gentles live longer if you keep them in sawdust.

Wasp grubs are good, though it's hard to make them stick on the hook, unless you bake them first. When someone found a wasps' nest we'd go out at night and pour turpentine down it and plug up the hole with mud. Next day the wasps would all be dead and you could dig out the nest and take the grubs. Once something went wrong, the turps missed the hole or something, and when we took the plug out the wasps, which had been shut up all night, came out all together with a zoom. We weren't very badly stung, but it was a pity there was no one standing by with a stop-watch. Grasshoppers are about the best bait there is, especially for chub. You stick them on the hook without any shot and just flick them to and fro on the surface – 'dapping,' they call it. But you can never get more than two or three

grasshoppers at a time. Greenbottle flies, which are also damned difficult to catch, are the best bait for dace, especially on clear days. You
want to put them on the hook alive, so that they wriggle. A chub will
even take a wasp, but it's a ticklish job to put a live wasp on the hook.

God knows how many other baits there were. Bread paste you
make by squeezing water through white bread in a rag. Then there
are cheese paste and honey paste and paste with aniseed in it. Boiled
wheat isn't bad for roach. Redworms are good for gudgeon. You
find them in very old manure heaps. And you also find another kind
of worm called a brandling, which is striped and smells like an
earwig, and which is very good bait for perch. Ordinary earthworms
are good for perch. You have to put them in moss to keep them
fresh and lively. If you try to keep them in earth they die. Those
brown flies you find on cow-dung are pretty good for roach. You
can take a chub on a cherry, so they say, and I've seen roach taken
with a currant out of a bun.

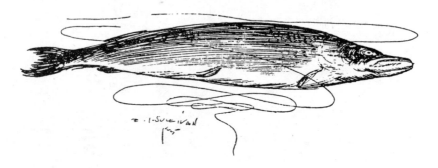

In those days, from the sixteenth of June (when the coarse-fishing
season starts) till mid-winter I wasn't often without a tin of worms or
gentles in my pocket. I had some fights with Mother about it, but in
the end she gave in, fishing came off the list of forbidden things and
Father even gave me a two-shilling fishing-rod for Christmas in 1903.
Joe was barely fifteen when he started going after girls, and from then
on he seldom came out fishing, which he said was a kid's game. But
there were about half a dozen others who were as mad on fishing as
I was. Christ, those fishing days! The hot sticky afternoons in the big
schoolroom when I've sprawled across my desk, with old Blowers's
voice grating away about predicates and subjunctives and relative
clauses, and all that's in my mind is the backwater near Burford Weir
and the green pool under the willows with the dace gliding to and

fro. And then the terrific rush on bicycles after tea, up Chamford Hill and down to the river to get in an hour's fishing before dark. The still summer evening, the faint splash of the weir, the rings on the water where the fish are rising, the midges eating you alive, the shoals of dace swarming round your hook and never biting. And the kind of passion with which you'd watch the black backs of the fish swarming round, hoping and praying (yes, literally praying) that one of them would change his mind and grab your bait before it got too dark. And then it was always 'Let's have five minutes more,' and then 'Just five minutes more,' until in the end you had to walk your bike into the town because Towler, the copper, was prowling round and you could be 'had up' for riding without a light. And the times in the summer holidays when we went out to make a day of it with boiled eggs and bread and butter and a bottle of lemonade, and fished and bathed and then fished again and did occasionally catch something. At night you'd come home with filthy hands and so hungry that you'd eaten what was left of your bread paste, with three or four smelly dace wrapped up in your handkerchief. Mother always refused to cook the fish I brought home. She would never allow that river fish were edible, except trout and salmon. 'Nasty muddy things,' she called them. The fish I remembered best of all are the ones I didn't catch. Especially the monstrous fish you always used to see when you went for a walk along the towpath on Sunday afternoons and hadn't a rod with you. There was no fishing on Sundays, even the Thames Conservancy Board didn't allow it. On Sundays you had to go for what was called a 'nice walk' in your thick black suit and the Eton collar that sawed your head off. It was on a Sunday that I saw a pike a yard long asleep in shallow water by the bank and nearly got him with a stone. And sometimes in the green pools on the edge of the reeds you'd see a huge Thames trout go sailing past. The trout grow to vast sizes in the Thames, but they're practically never caught. They say that one of the real Thames fishermen, the old bottle-nosed blokes that you see muffled up in overcoats on camp-stools with twenty-foot roach-poles at all seasons of the year, will willingly give up a year of his life to catching a Thames trout. I don't blame them, I see their point entirely, and still better I saw it then.

Of course other things were happening. I grew three inches in a year, got my long trousers, won some prizes at school, went to confirmation classes, told dirty stories, took to reading and had crazes for white mice, fretwork and postage stamps. But it's always fishing that I remember. Summer days, and the flat water-meadows and the blue hills in the distance, and the willows up the backwater and the pools underneath like a kind of deep green glass. Summer evenings, the fish breaking the water, the nightjars hawking round your head, the smell of nightstocks and Latakia. Don't mistake what I'm talking about. It's not that I'm trying to put across any of that poetry of childhood stuff. I know that's all baloney. Old Porteous (a friend of mine, a retired schoolmaster, I'll tell you about him later) is great on the poetry of childhood. Sometimes he reads me stuff about it out of books. Wordsworth. Lucy Gray. *There was a time when meadow, grove* – and all that. Needless to say he's got no kids of his own. The truth is that kids aren't in any way poetic, they're merely savage little animals, except that no animal is a quarter as selfish. A boy isn't interested in meadows, groves and so forth. He never looks at a landscape, doesn't give a damn for flowers, and unless they affect him in some way, such as being good to eat, he doesn't know one plant from another. Killing things – that's about as near to poetry as a boy gets. And yet all the while there's that peculiar intensity, the power of longing for things as you can't long when you're grown up, and the feeling that time stretches out and out in front of you and that whatever you're doing you could go on for ever.

I was rather an ugly little boy, with butter-coloured hair which was always cropped short except for a quiff in front. I don't idealise my childhood, and unlike many people I've no wish to be young again. Most of the things I used to care for would leave me something more than cold. I don't care if I never see a cricket ball again, and I wouldn't give you threepence for a hundredweight of sweets. But I've still got, I've always had, that peculiar feeling for fishing. You'll think it damned silly, no doubt, but I've actually half a wish to go fishing even now, when I'm fat and forty-five and got two kids and a house in the suburbs? Why? Because in a manner of speaking I *am* sentimental about my childhood – not my own particular childhood, but the civilisation which I grew up in and which is now, I suppose, just about at its last kick. And fishing is somehow typical of that civilisation. As soon as you think of fishing you think of things that don't belong to the modern world. The very idea of sitting all day under a willow tree beside a quiet pool – and being able to find a quiet pool to sit beside – belongs to the time before the war, before the radio, before aeroplanes, before Hitler. There's a kind of peace-fulness even in the names of English coarse fish. Roach, rudd, dace, bleak, barbel, bream, gudgeon, pike, chub, carp, tench. They're solid kind of names. The people who made them up hadn't heard of machine-guns, they didn't live in terror of the sack or spend their time eating aspirins, going to the pictures and wondering how to keep out of the concentration camp.

Does anyone go fishing nowadays, I wonder? Anywhere within a hundred miles of London there are no fish left to catch. A few dismal fishing-clubs plant themselves in rows along the banks of canals, and millionaires go trout-fishing in private waters round Scotch hotels, a sort of snobbish game of catching hand-reared fish with artificial flies. But who fishes in mill-streams or moats or cow-ponds any longer? Where are the English coarse fish now? When I was a kid every pond and stream had fish in it. Now all the ponds are drained, and when the streams aren't poisoned with chemicals from factories they're full of rusty tins and motor-bike tyres.

My best fishing-memory is about some fish that I never caught. That's usual enough, I suppose.

When I was about fourteen Father did a good turn of some kind to old Hodges, the caretaker at Binfield House. I forget what it was – gave him some medicine that cured his fowls of the worms, or something, Hodges was a crabby old devil, but he didn't forget a good turn. On day a little while afterwards when he'd been down to the shop to buy chicken-corn he met me outside the door and stopped me in his surly way. He had a face like something carved out of a bit of root, and only two teeth, which were dark brown and very long.

'Hey, young 'un! Fisherman, ain't you?'

'Yes.'

'Thought you was. You listen, then. If so be you wanted to, you could bring your line and have a try in that they pool up ahind the Hall. There's plenty bream and jack in there. But don't you tell no one as I told you. And don't you go for to bring any of them other young whelps, or I'll beat the skin off their backs.'

Having said this he hobbled off with his sack of corn over his shoulder, as though feeling that he'd said too much already. the next Saturday afternoon I biked up to Binfield House with my pockets full of worms and gentles, and looked for old Hodges at the lodge. At that time Binfield House had already been empty for ten or twenty years. Mr. Farrel, the owner, couldn't afford to live in it and either couldn't or wouldn't let it. He lived in London on the rent of his farms and let the house and grounds go to the devil. All the fences were green and rotting, the park was a mass of nettles, the plantations were like a jungle and even the gardens had gone back to meadow, with only a few old gnarled rose-bushes to show you where the beds had been. But it was a very beautiful house, especially from a distance. It was a great white place with colonnades and long-shaped windows, which had been built, I suppose, about Queen Anne's time by someone who'd travelled in Italy. If I went there now I'd probably get a certain kick out of wandering around the general desolation thinking about the life that used to go on there, and the people who built such places because they imagined that the good days would last for ever. As a boy I didn't give either the house or the grounds a second look. I dug out old Hodges, who'd just finished his dinner and was a bit surly, and got him to show me the way down to the pool. It was several hundred yards behind the house and completely hidden in the beech woods, but it was a good-sized pool, almost a lake, about a hundred and fifty yards across. It was astonishing, and even at that age it astonished me, that there, a dozen miles from Reading and not fifty from London, you could have such solitude. You felt as much alone as if you'd been on the banks of the Amazon. The pool was ringed completely round by the enormous beech trees, which in one place came down to the edge and were reflected in the water. On the other side there was a patch of grass where there was a hollow with beds of wild pepper-mint, and up at one end of the pool an old wooden boathouse was rotting among the bulrushes.

The pool was swarming with bream, small ones, about four to six inches long. Every now and again you'd see one of them turn half over and gleam reddy-brown under the water. There were pike there too, and they must have been big ones. You never saw them, but sometimes one that was basking among the weeds would turn over and plunge with a splash that was like a brick being bunged into the water. It was no use trying to catch them, though of course I always tried every time I went there. I tried them with dace and minnows I'd caught in the Thames and kept alive in a jam-jar, and even with a spinner made out of a bit of tin. But they were gorged with fish and wouldn't bite, and in any case they'd have broken any tackle I possessed. I never came back from the pool without at least a dozen small bream. Sometimes in the summer holidays I went there for a whole day, with my fishing-rod and a copy of *Chums* or the *Union Jack* or something, and a hunk of bread and cheese which Mother had wrapped up for me. And I've fished for hours and then lain in the grass hollow and read the *Union Jack*, and then the smell of my bread paste and the plop of a fish jumping somewhere would send me wild again, and I'd go back to the water and have another go, and so on all through a summer's day. And the best of all was to be alone, utterly alone, though the road wasn't a quarter of a mile away. I was just old enough to know that it's good to be alone occasionally. With the trees all round you it was as though the pool belonged to you, and nothing ever stirred except the fish ringing the water and the pigeons passing overhead. And yet, in the two years or so that I went fishing there, how many times did I really go, I wonder? Not more than a dozen. It was a three-mile bike ride from home and took up a whole afternoon at least. And sometimes other things turned up, and sometimes when I'd meant to go it rained. You know the way things happen.

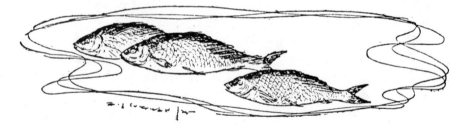

One afternoon the fish weren't biting and I began to explore at the end of the pool farthest from Binfield House. There was a bit of an overflow of water and the ground was boggy, and you had to fight your way through a sort of jungle of blackberry bushes and rotten boughs that had fallen off the trees. I struggled through it for about fifty yards, and then suddenly there was a clearing and I came to another pool which I had never known existed. It was a small pool not more than twenty yards wide, and rather dark because of the boughs that overhung it. But is was very clear water and immensely deep. I could see ten or fifteen feet down into it. I hung about for a bit, enjoying the dampness and the rotten boggy smell, the way a boy does. And then I saw something that almost made me jump out of my skin.

It was an enormous fish. I don't exaggerate when I say it was enormous. It was almost the length of my arm. It glided across the pool, deep under water, and then became a shadow and disappeared into the dark water on the other side. I felt as if a sword had gone through me. It was far the biggest fish I'd ever seen, dead or alive. I stood there without breathing, and in a moment another huge thick shape glided through the water, and then another and then two more close together. The pool was full of them. They were carp, I suppose. Just possibly they were bream or tench, but more probably carp. Bream or tench wouldn't grow so huge. I knew what had happened. At some time this pool had been connected with the other, and then the stream had dried up and the woods had closed round the small pool and it had just been forgotten. It's a thing that happens occasionally. A pool gets forgotten somehow, nobody fishes in it for years and decades and the fish grow to monstrous sizes. The brutes that I was watching might be a hundred years old. And not a soul in the world knew about them except me. Very likely it was twenty years since anyone had so much as looked at the pool, and probably even old Hodges and Mr. Farrel's bailiff had forgotten its existence.

Well, you can imagine what I felt. After a bit I couldn't even bear the tantalisation of watching. I hurried back to the other pool and got my fishing things together. It was no use trying for those colossal brutes with the tackle I had. They'd snap it as if it had been a hair. And I couldn't go on fishing any longer for the tiny bream. The sight of the big carp had given me a feeling in my stomach almost as if I was going to be sick. I got on to my bike and whizzed down the hill and home. It was a wonderful secret for a boy to have. There was the dark pool hidden away in the woods and the monstrous fish sailing round it – fish that had never been fished for and would grab the first bait you offered them. It was only a question of getting hold of a line strong enough to hold them. Already I'd made all the arrangements. I'd buy the tackle that would hold them if I had to steal the money out of the till. Somehow, God knew how, I'd get hold of half a crown and buy a length of silk salmon line and some thick gut or gimp and Number 5 hooks, and còme back with cheese and gentles and paste and mealworms and brandlings and grasshoppers and every mortal bait a carp might look at. The very next Saturday afternoon I'd come back and try for them.

But as it happened I never went back. One never does go back. I never stole the money out of the till or bought the bit of salmon line or had a try for those carp. Almost immediately afterwards something turned up to prevent me, but if it hadn't been that it would have been something else. It's the way things happen.

I know, of course, that you think I'm exaggerating about the size of those fish. You think, probably, that they were just medium-sized fish (a foot long, say) and that they've swollen gradually in my memory. But it isn't so. People tell lies about the fish they've caught and still more about the fish that are hooked and get away, but I never caught any of these or even tried to catch them, and I've no motive for lying. I tell you they were enormous.

Fishing! Here I'll make a confession, or rather two. The first is that when I look back through my life I can't honestly say that anything I've ever done has given me quite such a kick as fishing. Everything else has been a bit of a flop in comparison, even women.

from

THE LITTLE FISHES
H. E. Bates

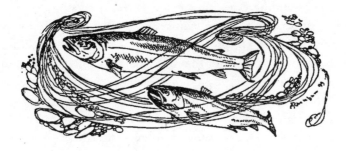

H. E. Bates is one of the greatest exponents of the short story. In
The Little Fishes *he captures perfectly a little boy's admiration for*
his Uncle Silas who tells him great fishing stories of days gone by
when the fish were 'as big as hippoptomassiz'.

MY UNCLE Silas was very fond of fishing. It was an occupation that
helped to keep him from thinking too much about work and also
about how terribly hard it was.

If you went through the bottom of my Uncle Silas's garden, past
the gooseberry bushes, the rhubarb and the pigsties, you came to a
path that went alongside a wood where primroses grew so richly
in spring that they blotted out the floor of oak and hazel leaves. In
summer wild strawberries followed the primroses and by July the
meadows beyond the wood were frothy with meadow-sweet, red
clover and the seed of tall soft grasses.

At the end of the second meadow a little river, narrow in parts and
bellying out into black deep pools in others, ran along between
willows and alders, occasional clumps of dark high reeds and a few
wild crab trees. Some of the pools, in July, would be white with water
lilies, and snakes would swim across the light flat leaves in the sun.
Moorhens talked to each other behind the reeds and water rats would
plop suddenly out of sight under clumps of yellow monkey flower.

Here in this little river, my Uncle Silas used to tell me when I was a boy, 'the damn pike used to be as big as hippopotomassiz'.

'Course they ain't so big now,' he would say. 'Nor yit the tench. Nor yit the perch. Nor yit the —'

'Why aren't they so big?'

'Well, I'm a-talkin' about fifty years agoo. Sixty year agoo. Very near seventy years agoo.'

'If they were so big then,' I said, 'all that time ago, they ought to be even bigger now.'

'Not the ones we catched,' he said. 'They ain't there.'

You couldn't, as you see from this, fox my Uncle Silas very easily, but I was at all times a very inquisitive, persistent little boy.

'How big were the tench?' I said.

'Well, I shall allus recollect one as me and Sammy Twizzle caught,' he said. 'Had to lay it in a pig trough to carry it home.'

'And how big were the perch?'

'Well,' he said, rolling his eye in recollection, in that way he had of bringing the wrinkled lid slowly down over it, very like a fish ancient in craftiness himself, 'I don' know as I can jistly recollect the size o' that one me and Arth Sugars nipped out of a September morning one time. But I do know as I cleaned up the back fin and used it for a horse comb for about twenty year.'

'Oh! Uncle Silas,' I would say, 'let's go fishing! Let's go and see if they're still as big as hippopotomassiz!'

But it was not always easy, once my Uncle Silas had settled under the trees at the end of the garden on a hot July afternoon, to persuade him that it was worth walking across two meadows just to see if the fish were as big as they used to be. Nevertheless I was, as I say, a very inquisitive, persistent little boy and finally my Uncle Silas would roll over, take the red handkerchief off his face and grunt:

'If you ain't the biggest whittle-breeches I ever knowed I'll goo t'Hanover. Goo an' git the rod and bring a bit o' dough. They'll be no peace until you do, will they?'

'Shall I bring the rod for you too?'

'Rod?' he said 'For me. Rod?' He let fall over his eye a tremulous bleary ash-like lid of scorn. 'When me and Sammy Twizzle went a-fishin', all we had to catch 'em with wur we bare hands and a drop o' neck-oil.'

'What's neck-oil?'

'Never you mind,' he said. 'You git the rod and I'll git the neck-oil.'

And presently we would be walking out of the garden, past the wood and across the meadows; I carrying the rod, the dough and perhaps a piece of carraway cake in a paper bag, my Uncle Silas waddling along in his stony-coloured corduroy trousers, carrying the neck-oil.

Sometimes I would be very inquisitive about the neck-oil, which was often pale greenish-yellow, rather the colour of cowslip, or perhaps of parsnips, and sometimes purplish-red, rather the colour of elderberries, or perhaps of blackberries or plums.

On one occasion I noticed that the neck-oil was very light in colour, almost white, or perhaps more accurately like straw-coloured water.

'Is it a new sort of neck-oil you've got?' I said.

'New flavour.'

'What is it made of?'

'Taters.'

'And you've got two bottles today,' I said.

'Must try to git used to the new flavour.'

'And do you think,' I said, 'we shall catch a bigger fish now that you've got a new kind of neck-oil?'

'Shouldn't be a bit surprised, boy,' he said, 'if we don't git one as big as a donkey.'

That afternoon it was very hot and still as we sat under the shade of a big willow, by the side of a pool that seemed to have across it an oiled black skin broken only by minutest winks of sunlight when the leaves of the willow parted softly in gentle turns of air.

'This is the place where me and Sammy tickled that big 'un out,' my Uncle Silas said.

'The one you carried home in a pig trough?'

'That's the one.'

I said how much I too should like to catch one I could take home in a pig trough and my Uncle Silas said:

'Well, you never will if you keep whittlin' and talkin' and ompolodgin' about.' My Uncle Silas was the only man in the world who ever used the word ompolodgin'. It was a very expressive word and when my Uncle Silas accused you of ompolodgin' it was a very serious matter. It meant that you had buttons on your bottom and if you didn't drop it he would damn well ding your ear.

'You gotta sit still and wait and not keep fidgetin' and very like in another half-hour you'll see a big 'un layin' aside o' that log. But not if you keep ompolodgin'! See?'

'Yes, Uncle.'

'That's why I bring the neck-oil,' he said. 'It quiets you down so's you ain't a-whittlin' and a-ompolodgin' all the time.'

'Can I have a drop of neck-oil?'

'When you git thirsty,' my Uncle Silas said, 'there's that there spring in the next medder.'

After this my Uncle Silas took a good steady drink of neck-oil and settled down with his back against the tree. I put a big lump of paste on my hook and dropped it into the pool. The only fish I could see in the pool were shoals of little silver tiddlers that flickered about a huge fallen willow log a yard or two upstream or came to play inquisitively about my little white and scarlet float, making it quiver up and down like the trembling scraps of sunlight across the water.

Sometimes the bread paste got too wet and slipped from the hook and I quietly lifted the rod from the water and put another lump on the hook. I tried almost not to breathe as I did all this and every time I took the rod out of the water I glanced furtively at my Uncle Silas to see if he thought I was ompolodgin'.

Every time I looked at him I could see that he evidently didn't think so. He was always far too busy with the neck-oil.

I suppose we must have sat there for nearly two hours on that hot windless afternoon of July, I not speaking a word and trying not to breathe as I threw my little float across the water, my Uncle Silas never uttering a sound either except for a drowsy grunt or two as he uncorked one bottle of neck-oil or felt to see if the other was safe in his jacket pocket.

All that time there was no sign of a fish as big as a hippopotamus or even of one you could take home in a pig trough and all the time my Uncle Silas kept tasting the flavour of the neck-oil, until at last his head began to fall forward on his chest. Soon all my bread paste was gone and I got so afraid of disturbing my Uncle Silas that I scotched my rod to the fallen log and walked into the next meadow to get myself a drink of water from the spring.

The water was icy cold from the spring and very sweet and good and I wished I had brought myself a bottle too, so that I could fill

it and sit back against a tree, as my Uncle Silas did, and pretend that
it was neck-oil.

Ten minutes later, when I got back to the pool, my Uncle Silas
was fast asleep by the tree trunk, one bottle empty by his side and
the other still in his jacket pocket. There was, I thought, a remarkable expression on his face, a wonderful rosy fogginess about his
mouth and nose and eyes.

But what I saw in the pool, as I went to pick my rod from the
water, was a still more wonderful thing.

During the afternoon the sun had moved some way round
and under the branches of the willow, so that now, at the first touch
of evening, there were clear bands of pure yellow light across the
pool.

In one of these bands of light, by the fallen log, lay a long lean
fish, motionless as a bar of steel, just under the water, basking in the
evening sun.

When I woke my Uncle Silas he came to himself with a fumbling
start, red eyes only half open, and I thought for a moment that perhaps he would ding my ear for ompolodgin'.

'But it's as big as a hippopotamus,' I said. 'It's as big as the one in
the pig trough.'

'Wheer, boy? Wheer?'

When I pointed out the fish my Uncle Silas could not, at first, see
it lying there by the log. But after another nip of neck-oil he started
to focus it correctly.

'By Jingo, that's a big 'un,' he said. 'By Jingo, that's a walloper.'

'What sort is it?'

'Pike,' he said. 'Git me a big lump o' paste and I'll dangle it a-top
of his nose.'

'The paste has all gone.'

'Then give us a bit o' carraway and we'll tiddle him up wi' that.'

'I've eaten all the carraway,' I said. 'Besides, you said you and
Sammy Twizzle used to catch them with your hands. You said you
used to tickle their bellies –'

'Well, that wur –'

'Get him! Get him! Get him!' I said. 'He's as big as a donkey!'

Slowly, and with what I thought was some reluctance, my Uncle
Silas heaved himself to his feet. He lifted the bottle from his pocket
and took a sip of neck-oil. Then he slapped the cork back with the

palm of his hand, wiped his lips with the back of his hand and put the bottle back in his pocket.

'Now you stan' back,' he said, 'and dammit, don't git ompolodgin'!'

I stood back. My Uncle Silas started to creep along the fallen willow-log on his hands and knees. Below him, in the band of sunlight, I could see the long dark lean pike, basking.

For nearly two minutes my Uncle Silas hovered on the end of the log. Then slowly he balanced himself on one hand and dipped his other into the water. Over the pool it was marvellously, breathlessly still and I knew suddenly that this was how it had been in the good great old days, when my Uncle Silas and Sammy Twizzle had caught the mythical mammoth ones, fifty years before.

'God A'mighty!' my Uncle Silas suddenly yelled. 'I'm a-gooin' over!'

My Uncle Silas was indeed gooin' over. Slowly, like a turning spit, the log started heeling, leaving my Uncle Silas half-slipping, half-dancing at its edge, like a man on a greasy pole.

In terror I shut my eyes. When I opened them and looked again my Uncle Silas was just coming up for air, yelling 'God A'mighty, boy, I believe you ompolodged!'

I thought for a moment he was going to be very angry with me. Instead he started to cackle with crafty, devilish, stentorian laughter, his wet lips dribbling, his eyes more fiery than ever under the dripping water, his right hand triumphant as he snatched it up from the stream.

'Jist managed to catch it, boy,' he yelled and in triumph he held up the bottle of neck-oil.

And somewhere downstream, startled by his shout, a whole host of little tiddlers jumped from the water, dancing in the evening sun.

from

THE SONG OF HIAWATHA
Henry Wadsworth Longfellow

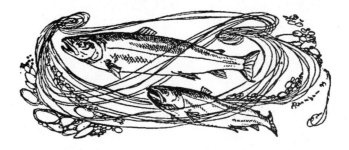

Henry Wadsworth Longfellow's narrative poem The Song of
Hiawatha *was published in 1855 and achieved instant popularity.
In this extract Hiawatha sets out to catch the King of Fishes, Nahma
the sturgeon and ends up being swallowed by the mighty fish.*

> Forth upon the Gitche Gumee,
> On the shining Big-Sea-Water,
> With his fishing-line of cedar,
> Of the twisted bark of cedar,
> Forth to catch the sturgeon, Nahma,
> Mishe-Nahma, King of Fishes,
> In his birch canoe exulting
> All alone went Hiawatha.
>   Through the clear, transparent water
> He could see the fishes swimming
> Far down in the depths below him:
> See the yellow perch, the Sahwa,
> Like a sunbeam in the water,
> See the Shawgashee, the crawfish,
> Like a spider on the bottom,
> On the white and sandy bottom.
>   At the stern sat Hiawatha,
> With his fishing-line of cedar;

In his plumes the breeze of morning
Played as in the hemlock branches;
On the bows, with tail erected,
Sat the squirrel, Adjidaumo;
In his fur the breeze of morning
Played as in the prairie grasses.

On the white sand of the bottom
Lay the monster Mishe-Nahma,
Lay the sturgeon, King of Fishes;
Through his gills he breathed the water,
With his fins he fanned and winnowed,
With his tail he swept the sand-floor.

There he lay in all his armour;
On each side a shield to guard him,
Plates of bone upon his forehead,
Down his sides and back and shoulders
Plates of bone with spines projecting!
Painted was he with his war-paints,
Stripes of yellow, red, and azure,
Spots of brown and spots of sable;
And he lay there on the bottom,
Fanning with his fins of purple,
As above him Hiawatha
In his birch canoe came sailing,
With his fishing-line of cedar.

'Take my bait!' cried Hiawatha
Down into the depths beneath him,
'Take my bait, O Sturgeon, Nahma!
Come up from below the water,
Let us see which is the stronger!'
And he dropped his line of cedar
Through the clear, transparent water,
Waited vainly for an answer,
Long sat waiting for an answer,
And repeating loud and louder:
'Take my bait, O King of Fishes!'

Quiet lay the sturgeon, Nahma,
Fanning slowly in the water,
Looking up at Hiawatha,

Listening to his call and clamour,
His unnecessary tumult,
Till he wearied of the shouting;
And he said to the Kenozha,
To the pike, the Maskenozha:
'Take the bait of this rude fellow,
Break the line of Hiawatha!'
    In his fingers Hiawatha
Felt the loose line jerk and tighten;
As he drew it in, it tugged so
That the birch canoe stood endwise,
Like a birch log in the water,
With the squirrel, Adjidaumo,
Perched and frisking on the summit.
    Full of scorn was Hiawatha
When he saw the fish rise upward,
Saw the pike, the Maskenozha,
Coming nearer, nearer to him,
And he shouted through the water:
'Esa! esa! shame upon you!
You are but the pike, Kenozha,
You are not the fish I wanted,
You are not the King of Fishes!'

★ ★ ★

And again the sturgeon, Nahma,
Heard the shout of Hiawatha,
Heard his challenge of defiance,
The unnecessary tumult,
Ringing far across the water,
    From the white sand of the bottom
Up he rose with angry gesture,
Quivering in each nerve and fibre,
Clashing all his plates of armour,
Gleaming bright with all his war-paint;
In his wrath he darted upward,
Flashing leaped into the sunshine,
Opened his great jaws, and swallowed
Both canoe and Hiawatha.

from

A RIVER RUNS THROUGH IT
Norman Maclean

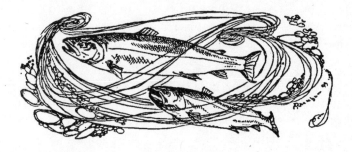

'I am haunted by waters,' says Norman Maclean in the last line of his powerful novella, A River Runs Through It. *I discovered this book one Christmas but have never seen the film by Robert Redford which I understand to be very good. The story vividly evokes the relationship between man and landscape and describes how in this particular family, fly fishing is practically the only means to communication.*

IN OUR family, there was no clear line between religion and fly fishing. We lived at the junction of great trout rivers in western Montana, and our father was a Presbyterian minister and a fly fisherman who tied his own flies and taught others. He told us about Christ's disciples being fishermen, and we were left to assume, as my brother and I did, that all first-class fishermen on the Sea of Galilee were fly fishermen and that John, the favorite, was a dry-fly fisherman.

Paul and I fished a good many big rivers, but when one of us referred to the 'the big river' the other knew it was the Big Blackfoot. It isn't the biggest river we fished, but it is the most powerful, and per pound, so are its fish. It runs straight and hard – on a map or from an airplane it is almost a straight line running due west from its headwaters at Rogers Pass on the Continental Divide to Bonner, Montana, where it empties into the South Fork of the Clark Fork of the Columbia. It runs hard all the way.

Near its headwaters on the Continental Divide there is a mine with a thermometer that stopped at 69.7 degrees below zero, the lowest temperature ever officially recorded in the United States (Alaska omitted). From its headwaters to its mouth it was manufactured by glaciers. The first sixty-five miles of it are smashed against the southern wall of its valley by glaciers that moved in from the north, scarifying the earth; its lower twenty-five miles were made overnight when the great glacial lake covering northwestern Montana and northern Idaho broke its ice dam and spread the remains of Montana and Idaho mountains over hundreds of miles of the plains of eastern Washington. It was the biggest flood in the world for which there is geological evidence; it was so vast a geological event that the mind of man could only conceive of it but could not prove it until photographs could be taken from earth satellites.

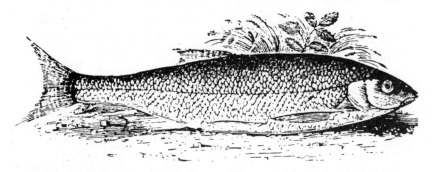

The straight line on the map also suggests its glacial origins; it has no meandering valley, and its few farms are mostly on its southern tributaries which were not ripped up by glaciers; instead of opening into a wide flood plain near its mouth, the valley, which was cut overnight by a disappearing lake when the great ice dam melted, gets narrower and narrower until the only way a river, an old logging railroad, and an automobile road can fit into it is for two of them to take to the mountainsides.

It is a tough place for a trout to live – the river roars and the water is too fast to let algae grow on the rocks for feed, so there is no fat on the fish, which must hold most trout records for high jumping.

Besides, it is the river we knew best. My brother and I had fished the Big Blackfoot since nearly the beginning of the century – my father before then. We regarded it as a family river, as a part of us, and I surrender it now only with great reluctance to dude ranches, the unselected inhabitants of Great Falls, and the Moorish invaders from California.

Early next morning Paul picked me up in Wolf Creek, and we drove across Rogers Pass where the thermometer is that stuck at three-tenths of a degree short of seventy below. As usual, especially if it were early in the morning, we sat silently respectful until we passed the big Divide, but started talking the moment we thought we were draining into another ocean. Paul nearly always had a story to tell in which he was the leading character but not the hero.

He told his Continental Divide stories in a seemingly light-hearted, slightly poetical mood such as reporters often use in writing 'human-interest' stories, but, if the mood were removed, his stories would appear as something about him that would not meet the approval of his family and that I would probably find out about in time anyway. He also must have felt honor-bound to tell me that he lived other lives, even if he presented them to me as puzzles in the form of funny stories. Often I did not know what I had been told about him as we crossed the divide between our two worlds.

'You know,' he began, 'it's been a couple of weeks since I fished the Blackfoot.' At the beginning, his stories sounded like factual reporting. He had fished alone and the fishing had not been much good, so he had to fish until evening to get his limit. Since he was returning directly to Helena he was driving up Nevada Creek along an old dirt road that followed section lines and turned at right angles at section corners. It was moonlight, he was tired and feeling in need of a friend to keep him awake, when suddenly a jackrabbit jumped on to the road and started running with the headlights. 'I didn't push him too hard,' he said, 'because I didn't want to lose a friend.' He drove, he said, with his head outside the window so he could feel close to the rabbit. With his head in the moonlight, his account took on poetic touches. The vague world of moonlight was pierced by the intense white triangle from the headlights. In the center of the penetrating isosceles was the jackrabbit, which, except for the length of his jumps, had become a snowshoe rabbit. The phosphorescent jackrabbit was doing his best to keep in the center of the isosceles but was afraid he was losing ground and, when he looked back to check, his eyes shone with whites and blues gathered up from the universe. My brother said, 'I don't know how to explain what happened next, but there was a right-angle turn in this section-line road, and the rabbit saw it, and I didn't.'

Later, he happened to mention that it cost him $175.00 to have his car fixed, and in 1937 you could almost get a car rebuilt for $175.00. Of course, he never mentioned that, although he did not drink when he fished, he always started drinking when he finished.

I rode part of the way down the Blackfoot wondering whether I had been told a little human-interest story with hard luck turned into humor or whether I had been told he had taken too many drinks and smashed hell out of the front end of his car.

Since it was no great thing either way, I finally decided to forget it, and, as you see, I didn't. I did, though, start thinking about the canyon where we were going to fish.

The canyon above the old Clearwater bridge is where the Blackfoot roars loudest. The backbone of a mountain would not break, so the mountain compresses the already powerful river into sound and spray before letting it pass. Here, of course, the road leaves the river; there was no place in the canyon for an Indian trail; even in 1806 when Lewis left Clark to come up the Blackfoot, he skirted the canyon by a safe margin. It is no place for small fish or small fisher-men. Even the roar adds power to the fish or at least intimidates the fisherman.

When we fished the canyon we fished on the same side of it for the simple reason that there is no place in the canyon to wade across. I could hear Paul start to pass me to get to the hole above, and, when I realized I didn't hear him anymore, I knew he had stopped to watch me. Although I have never pretended to be a great fisherman, it was always important to me that I was a fisherman and looked like one, especially when fishing with my brother. Even before the silence continued, I knew that I wasn't looking like much of anything.

Although I have a warm personal feeling for the canyon, it is not an ideal place for me to fish. It puts a premium upon being able to cast for distance, and yet most of the time there are cliffs or trees right behind the fisherman so he has to keep all his line in front of him. It's like a baseball pitcher being deprived of his windup, and it forces the fly fisherman into what is called a 'roll cast,' a hard cast that I have never mastered. The fisherman has to work enough line into his cast to get distance without throwing any line behind him, and then he has to develop enough power from a short arc to shoot it out across the water.

He starts accumulating the extra amount of line for the long cast by retrieving his last cast so slowly that an unusual amount of line stays in the water and what is out of it forms a slack semiloop. The loop is enlarged by raising the casting arm straight up and cocking the wrist until it points to 1:30. There, then, is a lot of line in front of the fisherman, but it takes about everything he has to get it high in the air and out over the water so that the fly and leader settle ahead of the line – the arm is a piston, the wrist is a revolver that uncocks, and even the body gets behind the punch. Important, too is the fact that the extra amount of line remaining in the water until the last moment gives a semisolid bottom to the cast. It is a little like a rattlesnake striking, with a good piece of his tail on the ground as something to strike from. All this is easy for a rattlesnake, but has always been hard for me.

Paul knew how I felt about my fishing and was careful not to seem superior by offering advice, but he had watched to long that he couldn't leave now without saying something. Finally he said, 'The fish are out farther.' Probably fearing he had put a strain on family relations, he quickly added, 'Just a little farther.'

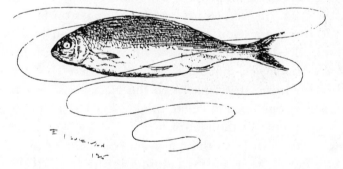

I reeled in my line slowly, not looking behind so as not to see him. Maybe he was sorry he had spoken, but, having said what he said, he had to say something more. 'Instead of retrieving the line straight toward you, bring it in on a diagonal from the downstream side. The diagonal will give you a more resistant base to your loop so you can put more power into your forward cast and get a little more distance.'

Then he acted as if he hadn't said anything and I acted as if I hadn't heard it, but as soon as he left, which was immediately,

I started retrieving my line on a diagonal, and it helped. The moment I felt I was getting a little more distance I ran for a fresh hole to make a fresh start in life.

It was a beautiful stretch of water, either to a fisherman or a photographer, although each would have focused his equipment on a different point. It was a barely submerged waterfall. The reef of rock was about two feet under the water, so the whole river rose into one wave, shook itself into spray, then fell back on itself and turned blue. After it recovered from the shock, it came back to see how it had fallen.

No fish could live out there where the river exploded into the colors and curves that would attract photographers. The fish were in that slow backwash, right in the dirty foam, with the dirt being one of the chief attractions. Part of the speckles would be pollen from pine trees, but most of the dirt was edible insect life that had not survived the waterfall.

I studied the situation. Although maybe I had just added three feet to my roll cast, I still had to do a lot of thinking before casting to compensate for some of my other shortcomings. But I felt I had already made the right beginning – I had already figured out where the big fish would be and why.

Then an odd thing happened. I saw him. A black back rose and sank in the foam. In fact, I imagined I saw spines on his dorsal fin until I said to myself, 'God, he couldn't be so big you could see his fins.' I even added, 'You wouldn't even have seen the fish in all that foam if you hadn't first thought he would be there.' But I couldn't shake the conviction that I had seen the black back of a big fish, because, as someone often forced to think, I know that often I would not see a thing unless I thought of it first.

Seeing the fish that I first thought would be there led me to wondering which way he would be pointing in the river. 'Remember, when you make the first cast,' I thought, 'that you saw him in the backwash where the water is circling upstream, so he will be looking downstream, not upstream, as he would be if he were in the main current.'

I was led by association to the question of what fly I would cast, and to the conclusion that it had better be a large fly, a number four or six, if I was going after the big hump in the foam.

From the fly, I went to the other end of the cast, and asked myself where the hell I was going to cast from. There were only gigantic rocks at this waterfall, so I picked one of the biggest, saw how I could crawl up it, and knew from that added height I would get added distance, but then I had to ask myself, 'How the hell am I going to land the fish if I hook him while I'm standing up there?' So I had to pick a smaller rock, which would shorten my distance but would let me slide down it with a rod in my hand and a big fish on.

I was gradually approaching the question all river fishermen should ask before they make the first cast, 'If I hook a big one, where the hell can I land him?'

One great thing about fly fishing is that after a while nothing exists of the world but thoughts about fly fishing. It is also interesting that thoughts about fishing are often carried on in dialogue form where Hope and Fear – or, many times, two Fears – try to outweigh each other.

One Fear looked down the shoreline and said to me (a third person distinct from the two fears), 'There is nothing but rocks for thirty yards, but don't get scared and try to land him before you get all the way down to the first sandbar.'

The Second Fear said, 'It's forty, not thirty, yards to the first sandbar and the weather has been warm and the fish's mouth will be soft and he will work off the hook if you try to fight him forty yards downriver. It's not good but it will be best to try to land him on a rock that is closer.'

The First Fear said, 'There is a big rock in the river that you will have to take him past before you land him, but, if you hold the line tight enough on him to keep him this side of the rock, you will probably lose him.'

The Second Fear said, 'But if you let him get on the far side of the rock, the line will get caught under it, and you will be sure to lose him.'

That's how you know when you have thought too much – when you become a dialogue between *You'll probably lose* and *You're sure to lose*. But I didn't entirely quit thinking, although I did switch subjects. It is not in the book, yet it is human enough to spend a moment before casting in trying to imagine what the fish is thinking, even if one of its eggs is as big as its brain and even if, when you swim underwater, it is hard to imagine that a fish has anything

to think about. Still, I could never be talked into believing that all a
fish knows is hunger and fear. I have tried to feel nothing but hunger
and fear and don't see how a fish could ever grow to six inches
if that were all he ever felt. In fact, I go so far sometimes as to
imagine that a fish thinks pretty thoughts. Before I made the cast,
I imagined the fish with the black back lying cool in the carbonated
water full of bubbles from the waterfalls. He was looking downriver
and watching the foam with food in it backing upstream like a floating cafeteria coming to wait on its customers. And he probably
was imagining that the speckled foam was eggnog with nutmeg
sprinkled on it, and, when the whites of eggs separated and he saw
what was on shore, he probably said to himself, 'What a lucky son
of a bitch I am that this guy and not his brother is about to fish this
hole.'

I thought all these thoughts and some besides that proved of no
value, and then I cast and I caught him.

I kept cool until I tried to take the hook out of his mouth. He
was lying covered with sand on the little bar where I had landed him.
His gills opened with his penultimate sighs. Then suddenly he stood
up on his head in the sand and hit me with his tail and the sand flew.
Slowly at first my hands began to shake, and, although I thought
they made a miserable sight, I couldn't stop them. Finally, I managed
to open the large blade to my knife which several times slid off his
skull before it went through his brain.

Even when I bent him he was way too long for my basket, so his
tail stuck out.

There were black spots on him that looked like crustaceans. He
seemed oceanic, including barnacles. When I passed my brother at
the next hole, I saw him study the tail and slowly remove his hat,
and not out of respect to my prowess as a fisherman.

I had a fish, so I sat down to watch a fisherman.

He took his cigarettes and matches from his shirt pocket and put
them in his hat and pulled his hat down tight so it wouldn't leak.
Then he unstrapped his fish basket and hung it on the edge of his
shoulder where he could get rid of it quick should the water get too
big for him. If he studied the situation he didn't take any separate
time to do it. He jumped off a rock into the swirl and swam for a
chunk of cliff that had dropped into the river and parted it. He swam
in his clothes with only his left arm – in his right hand, he held his

rod high and sometimes all I could see was the basket and rod, and when the basket filled with water sometimes all I could see was the rod.

The current smashed him into the chunk of cliff and it must have hurt, but he had enough strength remaining in his left fingers to hang to a crevice or he would have been swept into the blue below. Then he still had to climb to the top of the rock with his left fingers and his right elbow which he used like a prospector's pick. When he finally stood on top, his clothes looked hydraulic, as if they were running off him.

Once he quit wobbling, he shook himself duck-dog fashion, with his feet spread apart, his body lowered and his head flopping then he steadied himself and began to cast and the whole world turned to water.

Below him was the multitudinous river, and, where the rock had parted it around him, big-grained vapor rose. The mini-molecules of water left in the wake of his line made momentary loops of gossamer, disappearing so rapidly in the rising big-grained vapor that they had to be retained in memory to be visualized as loops. The spray emanating from him was finer-grained still and enclosed him in a halo of himself. The halo of himself was always there and always disappearing, as if he were candlelight flickering about three inches from himself. The images of himself and his line kept disappearing into the rising vapors of the river, which continually circled to the tops of the cliffs where, after becoming a wreath in the wind, they became rays of the sun.

The river above and below his rock was all big Rainbow water, and he would cast hard and low upstream, skimming the water with his fly but never letting it touch. Then he would pivot, reverse his line in a great oval above his head, and drive his line low and hard downstream, again skimming the water with his fly. He would complete this grand circle four or five times, creating an immensity of motion which culminated in nothing if you did not know, even if you could not see, that now somewhere out there a small fly was washing itself on a wave. Shockingly, immensity would return as the Big Blackfoot and the air above it became iridescent with the arched sides of a great Rainbow.

He called this 'shadow casting,' and frankly I don't know whether to believe the theory behind it – that the fish are alerted by the shadows of flies passing over the water by the first casts, so hit the fly the moment it touches the water. It is more or less the 'working up an appetite' theory, almost too fancy to be true, but then every fine fisherman has a few fancy stunts that work for him and for almost no one else. Shadow casting never worked for me, but maybe I never had the strength of arm and wrist to keep line circling over the water until fish imagined a hatch of flies was out.

My brother's wet clothes made it easy to see his strength. Most great casters I have known were big men over six feet, the added height certainly making it easier to get more line in the air in a bigger arc. My brother was only five feet ten, but he had fished so many years his body had become partly shaped by his casting. He was thirty-two now, at the height of his power, and he could put all his body and soul into a four-and-a-half-ounce magic totem pole. Long ago, he had gone far beyond my father's wrist casting, although his right wrist was always so important that it had become larger than his left. His right arm, which our father had kept tied to the side to emphasize the wrist, shot out of his shirt as if it were engineered, and it, too, was larger than his left arm. His wet shirt bulged and came unbuttoned with his pivoting shoulders and hips. It was also not hard to see why he was a street fighter, especially since he was committed to getting in the first punch with his right hand.

Rhythm was just as important as color and just as complicated. It was one rhythm superimposed upon another, our father's four-count rhythm of the line and wrist being still the base rhythm. But superimposed upon it was the piston two count of his arm and the long overriding four count of the completed figure eight of his reversed loop.

The canyon was glorified by rhythms and colors.

from

NOBODY SAID ANYTHING
Raymond Carver

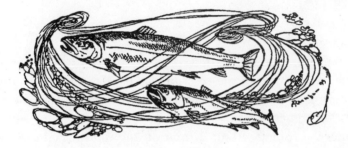

At the time of his death in 1988, Raymond Carver was acknowl-edged one of the great practitioners of the American short story. The story chosen here is a fine example. Not only does it capture the need within every boy to show off his catch but also, on a deeper and more tragic level, it reveals the breakdown in communication within a family.

IT WAS nice out. It was fall. But it wasn't cold yet except at night. At night they would light the smudgepots in the orchards and you would wake up in the morning with a black ring of stuff in your nose. But nobody said anything. They said the smudging kept the young pears from freezing, so it was all right.

To get to Birch Creek, you go to the end of our street where you hit Sixteenth Avenue. You turn left on Sixteenth and go up the hill past the cemetery and down to Lennox, where there is a Chinese restaurant. From the crossroads there, you can see the airport, and Birch Creek is below the airport. Sixteenth changes to View Road at the crossroads. You follow View for a little way until you come to the bridge. There are orchards on both sides of the road. Sometimes when you go by the orchards you see pheasants running down the rows, but you can't hunt there because you might get shot by a Greek named Matsos. I guess it is about a forty-minute walk all in all.

I was halfway down Sixteenth when a woman in a red car pulled onto the shoulder ahead of me. She rolled down the window on the passenger's side and asked if I wanted a lift. She was thin and had little pimples around her mouth. Her hair was up in curlers. But she was sharp enough. She had a brown sweater with nice boobs inside.

'Playing hooky?'

'Guess so.'

'Want a ride?'

I nodded.

'Get in. I'm kind of in a hurry.'

I put the fly rod and the creel on the back seat. There were a lot of grocery sacks from Mel's on the floorboards and back seat. I tried to think of something to say.

'I'm going fishing.' I said. I took off my cap hitched the canteen around so I could sit, and parked myself next to the window.

'Well, I never would have guessed.' She laughed. She pulled back onto the road. 'Where are you going? Birch Creek?'

I nodded again. I looked at my cap. My uncle had bought it for me in Seattle when he had gone to watch a hockey game. I couldn't think of anything more to say. I looked out the window and sucked my cheeks. You always see yourself getting picked up by this woman. You know you'll fall for each other and that she'll take you home with her and let you screw her all over the house. I began to get a boner thinking about it. I moved the cap over my lap and closed my eyes and tried to think about baseball.

'I keep saying that one of these days I'll take up fishing.' she said. 'They say it's very relaxing. I'm a nervous person.'

I opened my eyes. We were stopped at the crossroads. I wanted to say, *Are you real busy? Would you like to start this morning?* But I was afraid to look at her.

'Will this help you? I have to turn here. I'm sorry I'm in a hurry this morning,' she said.

'That's okay. this is fine.' I took my stuff out. Then I put my cap on and took it off again while I talked. 'Good–bye. Thanks. Maybe next summer,' but I couldn't finish.

'You mean fishing? Sure thing.' She waved with a couple of fingers the way women do.

I started walking, going over what I should have said. I could think of a lot of things. What was wrong with me? I cut the air with the fly rod and hollered two or three times. What I should have done to start things off was ask if we could have lunch together. No one was home at my house. Suddenly we are in my bedroom under the covers. She asks me if she can keep her sweater on and I say it's okay with me. She keeps her pants on too. That's all right, I say. I don't mind.

A Piper Cub dipped low over my head as it came in for a landing. I was a few feet from the bridge. I could hear the water running. I hurried down the embankment, unzipped, and shot off five feet over the creek. It must have been a record. I took a while eating the other sandwich and the peanut-butter crackers. I drank up half the water in the canteen. Then I was ready to fish.

★ ★ ★

I tried to think where to start. I had fished here for three years, ever since we had moved. Dad used to bring George and me in the car and wait for us, smoking, baiting our hooks, tying up new rigs for us if we snagged. We always started at the bridge and moved down, and we always caught a few. Once in a while, at the first of the season, we caught the limit. I rigged up and tried a few casts under the bridge first.

Now and then I cast under a bank or else in behind a big rock. But nothing happened. One place where the water was still and the bottom full of yellow leaves, I looked over and saw a few crawdads crawling there with their big ugly pinchers raised. Some quail flushed out of a brush pile. When I threw a stick, a rooster pheasant jumped up cackling about ten feet away and I almost dropped the rod.

The creek was slow and not very wide. I could walk across almost anywhere without it going over my boots. I crossed a pasture full of cow pads and came to where the water flowed out of a big pipe. I knew there was a little hole below the pipe, so I was careful. I got down on my knees when I was close enough to drop the line. It had just touched the water when I got a strike, but I missed him. I felt him roll with it. Then he was gone and the line flew back. I put another salmon egg on and tried a few more casts. But I knew I had jinxed it.

I went up the embankment and climbed under a fence that had a KEEP OUT sign on the post. One of the airport runways started here. I stopped to look at some flowers growing in the cracks in the pavement. You could see where the tires had smacked down on the pavement and left oily skid marks all around the flowers. I hit the creek again on the other side and fished along for a little way until I came to the hole. I thought this was as far as I would go. When I had first been up here three years ago, the water was roaring right up to the top of the banks. It was so swift then that I couldn't fish. Now the creek was about six feet below the bank. It bubbled and hopped through this little run at the head of the pool where you could hardly see bottom. A little farther down, the bottom sloped up and got shallow again as if nothing had happened. The last time I was up here I caught two fish about ten inches long and turned one that looked twice as big – a summer steelhead, Dad said when I told him about it. He said they come up during the high water in early spring but that most of them return to the river before the water gets low.

I put two more shot on the line and closed them with my teeth. Then I put a fresh salmon egg on and cast out where the water dropped over a shelf into the pool. I let the current take it down. I could feel the sinkers tap-tapping on rocks, a different kind of tapping than when you are getting a bite. Then the line tightened and the current carried the egg into sight at the end of the pool.

I felt lousy to have come this far up for nothing. I pulled out all kinds of line this time and made another cast. I laid the fly rod over a limb and lit the next to last weed. I looked up the valley and began to think about the woman. We were going to her house because she wanted help carrying in the groceries. Her husband was overseas. I touched her and she started shaking. We were French-kissing on the couch when she excused herself to go to the bathroom. I followed her. I watched as she pulled down her pants and sat on the toilet. I had a big boner and she waved me over with her hand. Just as I was going to unzip, I heard a plop in the creek. I looked and saw the tip of my fly rod jiggling.

★ ★ ★

He wasn't very big and didn't fight much. But I played him as long as I could. He turned on his side and lay in the current down below. I didn't know what he was. He looked strange. I tightened the line and lifted him over the bank into the grass, where he started wiggling. He was a trout. But he was green. I never saw one like him before. He had green sides with black trout spots, a greenish head, and like a green stomach. He was the color of moss, that color green. It was as if he had been wrapped up in moss a long time, and the color had come off all over him. He was fat, and I wondered why he hadn't put up more of a fight. I wondered if he was all right. I looked at him for a time longer, then I put him out of his pain.

I pulled some grass and put it in the creel and laid him in there on the grass.

I made some more casts, and then I guessed it must be two or three o'clock. I thought I had better move down to the bridge. I thought I would fish below the bridge awhile before I started home. And I decided I would wait until night before I thought about the woman again. But right away I got a boner thinking about the boner I would get that night. Then I thought I had better stop doing it so much. About a month back, a Saturday when they were all gone, I had picked up the Bible right after and promised and swore I wouldn't do it again. But I got jism on the Bible, and the promising and swearing lasted only a day or two, until I was by myself again.

★ ★ ★

I didn't fish on the way down. When I got to the bridge, I saw a bicycle in the grass. I looked and saw a kid about George's size running down the bank. I started in his direction. Then he turned and started toward me, looking in the water.

'Hey, what is it!' I hollered. 'What's wrong?' I guessed he didn't hear me. I saw his pole and fishing bag on the bank, and I dropped my stuff. I ran over to where he was. He looked like a rat or something. I mean, he had buckteeth and skinny arms and this ragged long-sleeved shirt that was too small for him.

'God, I swear there's the biggest fish here I ever saw!' he called. 'Hurry! Look! Look here! Here he is!'

I looked where he pointed and my heart jumped.

It was as long as my arm.

'God, oh God, will you look at him!' the boy said.

I kept looking. It was resting in a shadow under a limb that hung over the water. 'God almighty,' I said to the fish, 'where did you come from?'

'What'll we do?' the boy said. 'I wish I had my gun.'

'We're going to get him,' I said. 'God, look at him! Let's get him into the riffle.'

'You want to help me, then? We'll work it together!' the kid said.

The big fish had drifted a few feet downstream and lay there finning slowly in the clear water.

'Okay, what do we do?' the kid said.

'I can go up and walk down the creek and start him moving,' I said. 'You stand in the riffle, and when he tries to come through, you kick the living shit out of him. Get him onto the bank some-way, I don't care how. Then get a good hold of him and hang on.'

'Okay. Oh shit, look at him! Look, he's going! Where's he going?' the boy screamed.

I watched the fish move up the creek again and stop close to the bank. 'He's not going anyplace. There's no place for him to go. See him? He's scared shitless. He knows we're here. He's just cruising around now looking for someplace to go. See, he stopped again. He can't go anyplace. He knows that. He knows we're going to nail him. He knows it's tough shit. I'll go up and scare him down. You get him when he comes through.'

'I wish I had my gun,' the boy said. 'That would take care of him,' the boy said.

I went up a little way, then started wading down the creek. I watched ahead of me as I went. Suddenly the fish darted away from the bank, turned right in front of me in a big cloudy swirl, and bar-rel-assed downstream.

'Here he comes!' I hollered. 'Hey, hey, here he comes!' But the fish spun around before it reached the riffle and headed back. I splashed and hollered, and it turned again. 'He's coming! Get him, get him! Here he comes!'

But the dumb idiot had himself a club, the asshole, and when the fish hit the riffle, the boy drove at him with the club instead of trying to kick the son of a bitch out like he should have. The fish veered off, going crazy, shooting on his side through the shallow water. He made it. The asshole idiot kit lunged for him and fell flat.

He dragged up onto the bank sopping wet. 'I hit him!' the boy hollered. 'I think he's hurt, too. I had my hands on him, but I couldn't hold him.'

'You didn't have anything!' I was out of breath. I was glad the kid fell in. 'You didn't even come close, asshole. What were you doing

with that club? You should have kicked him. He's probably a mile
away by now.' I tried to spit. I shook my head. 'I don't know. We
haven't got him yet. We just may not get him,' I said.

'Goddamn it, I hit him!' the boy screamed. 'Didn't you see? I hit
him, and I had my hands on him too. How close did you get?
Besides, whose fish it it?' He looked at me. Water ran down his
trousers over his shoes.

I didn't say anything else, but I wondered about that myself. I
shrugged. 'Well, okay. I thought it was both ours. Let's get him
this time. No goof-ups, either one of us,' I said.

We waded downstream. I had water in my boots, but the kid was
wet up to his collar. He closed his buckteeth over his lip to keep his
teeth from chattering.

★ ★ ★

The fish wasn't in the run below the riffle, and we couldn't see him
in the next stretch, either. We looked at each other and began to
worry that the fish really had gone far enough downstream to reach
one of the deep holes. But then the goddamn thing rolled near the
bank, actually knocking dirt into the water with his tail, and took
off again. He went through another riffle, his big tail sticking out of
the water. I saw him cruise over near the bank and stop, his tail half
out of the water, finning just enough to hold against the current.

'Do you see him?' I said. the boy looked. I took his arm and
pointed his finger. 'Right *there*. Okay now, listen. I'll go down to
that little run between those banks. See where I mean? You wait
here until I give you a signal. Then you start down. Okay? And this
time don't let him get by you if he heads back.'

'Yeah,' the boy said and worked his lip with those teeth. 'Let's get
him this time,' the boy said, a terrible look of cold in his face.

I got up on the bank and walked down, making sure I moved
quiet. I slid off the bank and waded in again. But I couldn't see the
great big son of a bitch and my heart turned. I thought It might have
taken off already. A little farther downstream and it would get to
one of the holes. We would never get him then.

'He still there?' I hollered. I held my breath.

The kid waved.

'Ready!' I hollered again.

'Here goes!' the kid hollered back.

My hands shook. The creed was about three feet wide and ran between dirt banks. The water was low but fast. The kid was moving down the creek now, water up to his knees, throwing rocks ahead of him, splashing and shouting.

'Here he comes!' The kid waved his arms. I saw the fish now; it was coming right at me. He tried to turn when he saw me, but it was too late. I went down on my knees, grasping in the cold water. I scooped him with my hands and arms, up, up, raising him, throwing him out of the water, both of us falling onto the bank. I held him against my shirt, him flopping and twisting, until I could get my hands up his slippery sides to his gills. I ran one hand in and clawed through to his mouth and locked around his jaw. I knew I had him. He was still flopping and hard to hold, but I had him and I wasn't going to let go.

'We got him!' the boy hollered as he splashed up. 'We got him, by God! Ain't he something! Look at him! Oh God, let me hold him,' the boy hollered.

' We got to kill him first,' I said. I ran my other hand down the throat. I pulled back on the head as hard as I could, trying to watch out for the teeth, and felt the heavy crunching. He gave a long slow tremble and was still. I laid him on the bank and we looked at him. He was at least two feet long, queerly skinny, but bigger than anything I had ever caught. I took hold of his jaw again.

'Hey,' the kid said but didn't say any more when he saw what I was going to do. I washed off the blood and laid the fish back on the bank.

'I want to show him to my dad so bad,' the kid said.

We were wet and shivering. We looked at him, kept touching him. We pried open his big mouth and felt his rows of teeth. His sides were scarred, whitish welts as big as quarters and kind of puffy. There were nicks out of his head around his eyes and on his snout where I guess he had banged into the rocks and been in fights. But he was so skinny, too skinny for how long he was, and you could hardly see the pink stripe down his sides, and his belly was gray and slack instead of white and solid like it should have been. But I thought he was something.

★ ★ ★

'I guess I'd better go pretty soon,' I said. I looked at the clouds over the hills where the sun was going down. 'I better get home.'

'I guess so. Me too. I'm freezing,' the kid said. 'Hey, I want to carry him,' the kid said.

'Let's get a stick. We'll put it through his mouth and both carry him,' I said.

The kid found a stick. We put it through the gills and pushed until the fish was in the middle of the stick. Then we each took an end and started back, watching the fish as he swung on the stick.

'What are we going to do with him?' the kid said.

'I don't know,' I said. 'I guess I caught him,' I said.

'We both did. Besides, I saw him first.'

'That's true,' I said. 'Well, you want to flip for him or what?' I felt with my free hand, but I didn't have any money. And what would I have done if I had lost?

Anyway, the kid said, 'No, let's not flip.'

I said, 'All right. It's okay with me.' I looked at that boy, his hair standing up, his lips gray. I could have taken him if it came to that. But I didn't want to fight.

We got to where we left our things and picked up our stuff with one hand, neither of us letting go of his end of the stick. Then we walked up to where his bicycle was. I got a good hold on the stick in case the kid tried something.

Then I had an idea. 'We could half him,' I said.

'What do you mean?' the boy said, his teeth chattering again. I could feel him tighten his hold on the stick.

'Half him. I got a knife. We cut him in two and each take half. I don't know, but I guess we could do that.'

He pulled at a piece of his hair and looked at the fish. 'You going to use that knife?'

'You got one?' I said.

The boy shook his head.

'Okay,' I said.

I pulled the stick out and laid the fish in the grass beside the kid's bicycle. I took out the knife. A plane taxied down the runway as I measured a line. 'Right here?' I said. the kid nodded. The plane roared down the runway and lifted up right over our heads. I started cutting down into him. I came to his guts and turned him over and stripped everything out. I kept cutting until there was only a flap of skin on his belly holding him together. I took the halves and worked them in my hands and I tore him in two.

I handed the kid the tail part.

'No,' he said, shaking his head. 'I want that half.'

I said, 'They're both the same! Now goddamn, watch it, I'm going to get mad in a minute.'

'I don't care,' the boy said. 'If they're both the same, I'll take that one. They're both the same, right?'

'They're both the same,' I said. 'But I think I'm keeping this half here. I did the cutting.'

'I want it,' the kid said, 'I saw him first.'

'Whose knife did we use?' I said.

'I don't want the tail,' the kid said.

I looked around. There were no cars on the road and nobody else fishing. There was an airplane droning, and the sun was going down. I was cold all the way through. The kid was shivering hard, waiting.

'I got an idea,' I said. I opened the creel and showed him the trout. 'See? It's a green one. It's the only green one I ever saw. So who-ever takes the head, the other guy gets the green trout and the tail part. Is that fair?'

The kid looked at the green trout and took it out of the creel and held it. He studied the halves of the fish.

'I guess so,' he said. 'Okay, I guess so. You take that half. I got more meat on mine.'

'I don't care,' I said. 'I'm going to wash him off. Which way do you live?' I said.

'Down on Arthur Avenue.' He put the green trout and his half of the fish into a dirty canvas bag. 'Why?'

'Where's that? Is that down by the ball park?' I said.

'Yeah, but why, I said.' That kid looked scared.

'I live close to there,' I said. 'So I guess I could ride on the handle-bars. We could take turns pumping. I got a weed we could smoke, if it didn't get wet on me.'

But the kid only said, 'I'm freezing.'

I washed my half in the creek. I held his big head under water and opened his mouth. The stream poured into his mouth and out the other end of what was left of him.

'I'm freezing,' the kid said.

★ ★ ★

I saw George riding his bicycle at the other end of the street. He didn't see me. I went around to the back to take off my boots. I unslung the creel so I could raise the lid and get set to march into the house, grinning.

I heard their voices and looked through the window. They were sitting at the table. Smoke was all over the kitchen. I saw it was coming from a pan on the burner. But neither of them paid any attention.

'What I'm telling you is the gospel truth,' he said. 'What do kids know? You'll see.'

She said, 'I'll see nothing. If I thought that, I'd rather see them dead first.'

He said, 'What's the matter with you? You better be careful what you say!'

She started to cry. He smashed out a cigarette in the ashtray and stood up.

'Edna, do you know this pan is burning up?' he said.

She looked at the pan. She pushed her chair back and grabbed the pan by its handle and threw it against the wall over the sink.

He said, 'Have you lost your mind? Look what you've done!' He took a dish cloth and began to wipe up stuff from the pan.

I opened the back door. I started grinning. I said, 'You won't believe what I caught at Birch Creek. Just look. Look here. Look at this. Look what I caught.'

My legs shook. I could hardly stand. I held the creel out to her, and she finally looked in. 'Oh, oh, my God! What is it? A snake! What is it? Please, please take it out before I throw up.'

'Take it out!' he screamed. 'Didn't you hear what she said? Take it out of here!' he screamed.

I said, 'But look, Dad. Look what it is.'

He said, 'I don't want to look.'

I said, 'It's a gigantic summer steelhead from Birch Creek. Look! Isn't he something? It's a monster! I chased him up and down the creek like a madman!' My voice was crazy. But I could not stop. 'There was another one, too,' I hurried on. 'A green one. I swear! It was green! Have you ever seen a green one?'

He looked into the creel and his mouth fell open.

He screamed, 'Take that goddamn thing out of here! What in the hell is the matter with you? Take it the hell out of the kitchen and throw it in the goddamn garbage!'

I went back outside. I looked into the creel. What was there looked silver under the porch light. What was there filled the creel.

I lifted him out. I held him. I held that half of him.

from

WALDEN; OR LIFE IN THE WOODS
Henry Thoreau

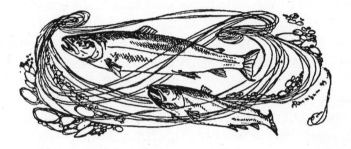

Henry Thoreau left his home in Concord, Massachusetts in 1845 to live in a hut in the woods beside Walden Pond. There he communed with and observed nature and wrote a journal. The journal became his most famous book Walden; or Life in the Woods *published in 1854. As this extract shows, he created a masterpiece of natural history. Thoreau is my idea of a true philosopher.*

THE PONDS

SOMETIMES, having had a surfeit of human society and gossip, and worn out all my village friends, I rambled still farther westward than I habitually dwell, into yet more unfrequented parts of the town, "to fresh woods and pastures new," or, while the sun was setting, made my supper of huckleberries and blueberries on Fair Haven Hill, and laid up a store for several days. The fruits do not yield their true flavor to the purchaser of them, nor to him who raises them for the market. There is but one way to obtain it, yet few take that way. If you would know the flavor of huckleberries, ask the cowboy or the partridge. It is a vulgar error to suppose that you have tasted huckle-berries who never plucked them. A huckleberry never reaches Boston; they have not been known there since they grew on her three hills. The ambrosial and essential part of the fruit is lost with the bloom which is rubbed off in the market cart, and they become mere provender. As long as Eternal Justice reigns, not one innocent huckleberry can be transported thither from the country's hills.

Occasionally, after my hoeing was done for the day, I joined some impatient companion who had been fishing on the pond since morning, as silent and motionless as a duck or a floating leaf, and, after practicing various kinds of philosophy, had concluded commonly, by the time I arrived, that he belonged to the ancient sect of Cenobites. There was one older man, an excellent fisher and skilled in all kinds of woodcraft, who was pleased to look upon my house as a building erected for the convenience of fishermen; and I was equally pleased when he sat in my doorway to arrange his lines. Once in a while we sat together on the pond, he at one end of the boat, and I at the other; but not many words passed between us, for he had grown deaf in his later years, but he occasionally hummed a psalm, which harmonized well enough with my philosophy. Our intercourse was thus altogether one of unbroken harmony, far more pleasing to remember than if it had been carried on by speech. When, as was commonly the case, I had none to commune with, I used to raise the echoes by striking with a paddle on the side of my boat, filling the surrounding woods with circling and dilating sound, stirring them up as the keeper of a menagerie his wild beasts, until I elicited a growl from every wooded vale and hillside.

In warm evenings I frequently sat in the boat playing the flute, and saw the perch, which I seem to have charmed, hovering around me, and the moon traveling over the ribbed bottom, which was strewed with the wrecks of the forest. Formerly I had come to this pond adventurously, from time to time, in dark summer nights, with a companion, and making a fire close to the water's edge, which we thought attracted the fishes, we caught pouts with a bunch of worms strung on a thread, and when we had done, far in the night, threw the burnings brands high into the air like skyrockets, which, coming down into the pond, were quenched with a loud hissing, and we were suddenly groping in total darkness. Through this, whistling a tune, we took our way to the haunts of men again. But now I had made my home by the shore.

Sometimes, after staying in a village parlor till the family had all retired, I have returned to the woods, and, partly with a view to the next day's dinner, spent the hours of midnight fishing from a boat by moonlight, serenaded by owls and foxes, and hearing, from time to time, the creaking note of some unknown bird close at hand. These experiences were very memorable and valuable to me, anchored in forty feet of water, and twenty or thirty rods from the shore, surrounded sometimes by thousands of small perch and shiners, dimpling the surface with their tails in the moonlight, and communicating by a long flaxen line with mysterious nocturnal fishes which had their dwelling forty feet below, or sometimes dragging sixty feet of line about the pond as I drifted in the gentle night breeze, now and then feeling a slight vibration along it, indicative of some life prowling about its extremity, of dull uncertain blundering purpose there, and slow to make up its mind. At length you slowly raise, pulling hand over hand, some horned pout squeaking and squirming to the upper air. It was very queer, especially in dark nights, when your thoughts had wandered to vast and cosmogonal themes in other spheres, to feel this faint jerk, which came to interrupt your dreams and link you to Nature again. It seemed as if I might next cast my line upward into the air, as well as downward into this element, which was scarcely more dense. Thus I caught two fishes as it were with one hook.

★ ★ ★

The scenery of Walden is on a humble scale and, though very beautiful, does not approach to grandeur, nor can it much concern one who has not long frequented it or lived by its shore; yet this pond is so remarkable for its depth and purity as to merit a particular description. It is a clear and deep green well, half a mile long and a mile and three quarters in circumference, and contains about sixty-one and a half acres; a perennial spring in the midst of pine and oak woods, without any visible inlet or outlet except by the clouds and evaporation. The surrounding hills rise abruptly from the water to the height of forty to eighty feet, though on the southeast and east they attain to about one hundred and one hundred and fifty feet respectively, within a quarter and a third of a mile. They are exclusively woodland. All our Concord waters have two colors at least; one when viewed at a distance, and another, more proper, close at hand. The first depends more on the light, and follows the sky. In clear weather, in summer, they appear blue at a little distance, especially if agitated, and at a great distance all appear alike. In stormy weather they are sometimes of a dark slate color. The sea, however, is said to be blue one day and green another without any perceptible change in the atmosphere. I have seen our river, when, the landscape being covered with snow, both water and ice were almost as green as grass. Some consider blue "to be the color of pure water, whether liquid or solid." But, looking directly down into our waters from a boat, they are seen to be of very different colors. Walden is blue at one time and green at another, even from the same point of view. Lying between the earth and the heavens, it partakes of the color of both. Viewed from a hilltop it reflects the color of the sky; but near at hand it is of a yellowish tint next the shore where you can see the sand, then a light green, which gradually deepens to a uniform dark green in the body of the pond. In some lights, viewed even from a hilltop, it is of a vivid green next the shore. Some have referred this to the reflection of the verdure; but it is equally green there against the railroad sand-bank, and in the spring, before the leaves are expanded, and it may be simply the result of the prevailing blue mixed with the yellow of the sand. Such is the color of its iris. This is that portion, also, where in the spring, the ice being warmed by the heat of the sun reflected from the bottom, and also transmitted through the earth, melts first and forms a narrow canal about the still frozen middle. Like the rest of our waters, when much agitated, in clear weather, so that the surface of the waves may reflect the sky at the right angle, or because there is more light mixed with it, it appears at a little distance of a darker blue than the sky itself; and at such a time, being on its surface, and looking with divided vision, so as to see the reflection, I have discerned a matchless and indescribable light blue, such as watered or changeable silks and sword blades suggest, more cerulean than the sky itself, alternating with the original dark green on the opposite sides of the waves, which last appeared but muddy in comparison. It is a vitreous greenish blue, as I remember it, like those patches of the winter sky seen through cloud vistas in the west before sundown. Yet a single glass of its water held up to the light is as colorless as an equal quantity of air. It is well known that a large plate of glass will have a green tint, owing, as the makers say, to its "body," but a small piece of the same will be colorless. How large a body of Walden water would be required to reflect a green tint, I have never proved. The water of our river is black or a very dark brown to one looking directly down on it, and, like that of most ponds, imparts to the body of one bathing in it a yellowish tinge; but this water is of such crystalline purity that the body of the bather appears of an alabaster whiteness, still more unnatural, which, as the limbs are magnified and distorted withal, produces a monstrous effect, making fit studies for a Michaelangelo.

The water is so transparent that the bottom can easily be discerned at the depth of twenty-five or thirty feet. Paddling over it, you may see many feet beneath the surface the schools of perch and shiners, perhaps only an inch long, yet the former easily distinguished by their transverse bars, and you think that they must be ascetic fish that find a subsistence there. Once, in the winter, many years ago, when I had been cutting holes through the ice in order to catch pickerel, as I stepped ashore I tossed my axe back onto the ice, but, as if some evil genius had directed it, it slid four or five rods directly into one of the holes, where the water was twenty-five feet deep. Out of curiosity, I lay down on the ice and looked through the hole, until I saw the axe a little on one side, standing on its head, with its helve erect and gently swaying to and fro with the pulse of the pond; and there it might have stood erect and swaying till in the course of time the handle rotted off, if I had not disturbed it. Making another hole directly over it with an ice chisel which I had, and cutting down the longest birch which I could find in the neighbourhood with my knife, I made a slip noose, which I attached to its end, and, letting it down carefully, passed it over the knob of the handle, and drew it by a line along the birch, and so pulled the axe out again.

The shore is composed of a belt of smooth rounded white stones like paving-stones, excepting one or two short sand beaches, and is so steep that in many places a single leap will carry you into water over your head; and were it not for its remarkable transparency, that would be the last to be seen of its bottom till it rose on the opposite side. Some think it is bottomless. It is nowhere muddy, and a casual observer would say that there were no weeds at all in it; and of noticeable plants, except in the little meadows recently over-flowed, which do not properly belong to it, a closer scrutiny does not detect a flag nor a bulrush, nor even a lily, yellow or white, but only a few small heartleaves and potamogetons, and perhaps a water target or two; all of which however a bather might not perceive; and these plants are clean and bright like the element they grow in. The stones extend a rod or two into the water, and then the bottom is pure sand, except in the deepest parts, where there is usually a little sediment, probably from the decay of the leaves which have been wafted onto it so many successive falls, and a bright green weed is brought up on anchors even in midwinter.

We have one other pond just like this, White Pond, in Nine Acre Corner, about two and a half miles westerly; but, though I am acquainted with most of the ponds within a dozen miles of this center, I do not know a third of this pure and well-like character. Successive nations perchance have drank at, admired, and fathomed it, and passed away, and still its water is green and pellucid as ever. Not an intermitting spring! Perhaps on that spring morning when Adam and Eve were driven out of Eden, Walden Pond was already in existence, and even then breaking up in a gentle spring rain accompanied with mist and a southerly wind, and covered with myriads of ducks and geese, which had not heard of the fall, when still such pure lakes sufficed them. Even then it had commenced to rise and fall, and had clarified its waters and colored them of the hue they now wear, and obtained a patent of Heaven to be the only Walden Pond in the world and distiller of celestial dews. Who knows in how many unremembered nations' literatures this has been the Castalian Fountain? or what nymphs presided over it in the Golden Age? It is a gem of the first water which Concord wears in her coronet.

Yet perchance the first who came to this well have left some trace of their footsteps. I have been surprised to detect encircling the pond, even where a thick wood has just been cut down on the shore, a narrow shelflike path in the steep hillside, alternately rising and falling, approaching and receding from the water's edge, as old probably as the race of man here, worn by the feet of aboriginal hunters, and still from time to time unwittingly trodden by the present occupants of the land. This is particularly distinct to one standing on the middle of the pond in winter, just after a light snow has fallen, appearing as a clear undulating white line, unobscured by weeds and twigs, and very obvious a quarter of a mile off in many places where in summer it is hardly distinguishable close at hand. The snow reprints it, as it were, in clear white type alto-relievo. The ornamented grounds of villas which will one day be built here may still preserve some trace of this.

The pond rises and falls, but whether regularly or not, and within what period, nobody knows, though, as usual, many pretend to know. It is commonly higher in the winter and lower in the summer, though not corresponding to the general wet and dryness. I can remember when it was a foot or two lower, and also when it was at least five feet higher, than when I lived by it. There is a narrow sandbar running into it, with very deep water on one side, on which I helped boil a kettle of chowder, some six rods from the main shore, about the year 1824, which it has not been possible to do for twenty-five years; and, on the other hand, my friends used to listen with incredulity when I told them, that a few years later I was accustomed to fish from a boat in a secluded cove in the woods, fifteen rods from the only shore they knew, which place was long since converted into a meadow. But the pond has risen steadily for two years, and now, in the summer of '52, is just five feet higher than when I lived there, or as high as it was thirty years ago, and fishing goes on again in the meadow. This makes a difference of level, at the outside, of six or seven feet; and yet the water shed by the surrounding hills is insignificant in amount, and this overflow must be referred to causes which affect the deep springs. This same summer the pond has begun to fall again. It is remarkable that this fluctuation, whether periodical or not, appears thus to require many years for its accomplishment. I have observed one rise and a part of two falls, and I expect that a dozen or fifteen years hence the water will again be as low as I have ever known it. Flints' Pond, a mile eastward, allowing for the disturbance occasioned by its inlets and outlets, and the smaller intermediate ponds also, sympathize with Walden, and recently attained their greatest height at the same time with the latter. The same is true, as far as my observation goes, of White Pond.

The rise and fall of Walden at long intervals serves this use at least: the water standing at this great height for a year or more, though it makes it difficult to walk round it, kills the shrubs and trees which have sprung up about its edge since the last rise – pitch pines, birches, alders, aspens, and others – and, falling again, leaves an unobstructed shore; for, unlike many ponds and all waters which are subject to a daily tide, its shore is cleanest when the water is lowest. On the side of the pond next my house a row of pitch pines, fifteen feet high, has been killed and tipped over as if by a lever, and thus a stop put to their encroachments; and their size indicates how many years have elapsed since the last rise to this height. By this fluctuation the pond asserts its title to a shore, and thus the *shore* is *shorn*, and the trees cannot hold it by right of possession. These are the lips of the lake on which no beard grows. It licks its chaps from time to time. When the water is at its height, the alders, willows, and maples send forth a mass of fibrous red roots several feet long from all sides of their stems in the water, and to the height of three or four feet from the ground, in the effort to maintain themselves; and I have known the high-blueberry bushes about the shore, which commonly produce no fruit, bear an abundant crop under these circumstances.

Some have been puzzled to tell how the shore became so regularly paved. My townsmen have all heard the tradition, the oldest people tell me that they heard it in their youth, that anciently the Indians were holding a powwow upon a hill here, which rose as high into the heavens as the pond now sinks deep into the earth, and they used much profanity, as the story goes, though this vice is one of which the Indians were never guilty, and while they were thus engaged the hill shook and suddenly sank, and only one old squaw, named Walden, escaped, and from her the pond was named. It has been conjectured that when the hill shook these stones rolled down its side and became the present shore. It is very certain, at any rate, that once there was no pond here, and now there is one; and this Indian fable does not in any respect conflict with the account of that ancient settler whom I have mentioned, who remembers so well when he first came here with his divining rod, saw a thin vapor rising from the sward, and the hazel pointed steadily downward, and he concluded to dig a well here. As for the stones, many still think that they are hardly to be accounted for by the action of the waves on these hills; but I observe that the surrounding hills are remarkably full of the same kind of stones, so that they have been obliged to pile them up in walls on both sides of the railroad cut nearest the pond; and, moreover, there are most stones where the shore is most abrupt; so that, unfortunately, it is no longer a mystery to me. I detect the paver. If the name was not derived from that of some English locality – Saffron Walden, for instance – once might suppose that it was called originally *Walled-in* Pond.

The pond was my well ready dug. For four months in the year its water is as cold as it is pure at all times; and I think that it is then as good as any, if not the best, in the town. In the winter, all water which is exposed to the air is colder than springs and wells which are protected from it. The temperature of the pond water which had stood in the room where I sat from five o'clock in the afternoon till noon the next day, the sixth of March, 1846, the thermometer having been up to 65° or 70° some of the time, owing partly to the sun on the roof, was 42°, or one degree colder than the water of one of the coldest wells in the village just drawn. The temperature of the Boiling Spring the same day was 45°, or the warmest of any water tried, though it is the coldest that I know of in summer, when, besides, shallow and stagnant surface water is not mingled with it. Moreover, in summer, Walden never becomes so warm as most water which is exposed to the sun, on account of its depth. In the warmest weather I usually placed a pailful in my cellar, where it became cool in the night, and remained so during the day; though I also resorted to a spring in the neighborhood. It was as good when a week old as the day it was dipped, and had no taste of the pump. Whoever camps for a week in summer by the shore of a pond, needs only bury a pail of water a few feet deep in the shade of his camp to be independent of the luxury of ice.

There have been caught in Walden pickerel, one weighing seven pounds – to say nothing of another which carried off a reel with great velocity, which the fisherman safely set down at eight pounds because he did not see him – perch and pouts, some of each weighing over two pounds, shiners, chivins or roach (*Leuciscus pulchellus*), a very few breams, and a couple of eels, one weighing four pounds – I am thus particular because the weight of a fish is commonly its only title to fame, and these are the only eels I have heard of here – also, I have a faint recollection of a little fish some five inches long, with silvery sides and a greenish back, somewhat dace-like in its character, which I mention here chiefly to link my facts to fable. Nevertheless, this pond is not very fertile in fish. Its pickerel, though not abundant, are its chief boast. I have seen at one time lying on the ice pickerel of at least three different kinds: a long and shallow one, steel-colored, most like those caught in the river; a bright golden kind, with greenish reflections and remarkably deep, which is the most common here; and another, golden-colored, and shaped like the last, but peppered on the sides with small dark brown or black spots, intermixed with a few faint blood-red ones, very much like a trout. The specific name *reticulatus* would not apply to this; it should be *guttatus* rather. These are all very firm fish, and weigh more than their size promises. The shiners, pouts, and perch also, and indeed all the fishes which inhabit this pond, are much cleaner, handsomer, and firmer fleshed than those in the river and most other ponds, as the water is purer, and they can easily be distinguished from them. Probably many ichthyologists would make new varieties of some of them. There are also a clean race of frogs and tortoises, and a few muscles in it; muskrats and minks leave their traces about it, and occasionally a traveling mud-turtle visits it. Sometimes, when I pushed off my boat in the morning, I disturbed a great mud-turtle which had secreted himself under the boat in the night. Ducks and geese frequent it in the spring and fall, the while-bellied swallows (*Hirundo bi-color*) skim over it, and the peetweets (*Totanus Macularius*) 'teter' along its stony shores all summer. I have sometimes disturbed a fish hawk sitting on a white pine over the water; but I doubt if it is ever profaned by the wing of a gull, like Fair Haven. At most, it tolerates one annual loon. These are all the animals of consequence which frequent it now.

You may see from a boat, in calm weather, near the sandy eastern shore, where the water is eight or ten feet deep, and also in some other parts of the pond, some circular heaps half a dozen feet in diameter by a foot in height, consisting of small stones less than a hen's egg in size, where all around is bare sand. At first you wonder if the Indians could have formed them on the ice for any purpose, and so, when the ice melted, they sank to the bottom; but they are too regular and some of them plainly too fresh for that. They are similar to those found in rivers; but as there are no suckers nor lampreys here, I know not by what fish they could be made. Perhaps they are the nests of the chivin. These lend a pleasing mystery to the bottom.

The shore is irregular enough not to be monotonous. I have in my mind's eye the western indented with deep bays, the bolder northern, and the beautifully scolloped southern shore, where successive capes overlap each other and suggest unexplored coves between. The forest has never so good a setting, nor is so distinctly beautiful, as when seen from the middle of a small lake amid hills which rise from the water's edge; for the water in which it is reflected not only makes the best foreground in such a case, but, with its winding shore, the most natural and agreeable boundary to it. There is no rawness nor imperfection in its edge there, as where the axe has cleared a part, or a cultivated field abuts on it. The trees have ample room to expand on the water side, and each sends forth its most vigorous branch in that direction. There Nature has woven a natural selvage, and the eye rises by just gradations from the low shrubs of the shore to the highest trees. There are few traces of man's hand to be seen. The water laves the shore as it did a thousand years ago.

PIKE
Ted Hughes

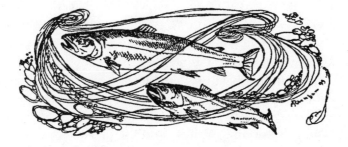

As a child Ted Hughes spent a lot of time on fishing expeditions with his brother. From this time comes his obvious sense not only of the beauty, but also the violence that lies within nature, something that is stressed in several collections of his poetry.

Having been duped by our Poet Laureate with a frozen fish as I described in the Introduction to this book, we repeated our fishing trip with better success in part thanks to Ted's skilful surgery. The entry in my diary reads:

'Dever May 24th 1988

Day began with me getting large Mayfly hook in ball of thumb, barb and all. Skilful extraction by the Laureate using the method I had read about but not believed. Hard down pressure on the eye of the hook, get loop under the bend, tremendous pull, agonised shout – A complete Success! Ted and I both had 6 fish.'

Pike, three inches long, perfect
Pike in all parts, green tigering the gold.
Killers from the egg: the malevolent aged grin.
They dance on the surface among the flies.

Or move, stunned by their own grandeur,
Over a bed of emerald, silhouette
Of submarine delicacy and horror.
A hundred feet long in their world.

In ponds, under the heat-struck lily pads –
Gloom of their stillness:
Logged on last year's black leaves, watching upwards.
Or hung in an amber cavern of weeds.

The jaws' hooked clamp and fangs
Not to be changed at this date;
A life subdued to its instrument;
The gills kneading quietly, and the pectorals.

Three we kept behind glass,
Jungled in weed: three inches, four,
And four and a half: fed fry to them –
Suddenly there were two. Finally one

With a sag belly and the grin it was born with.
And indeed they spare nobody.
Two, six pounds each, over two feet long,
High and dry and dead in the willow-herb –

One jammed past its gills down the other's gullet:
The outside eye stared: as a vice locks –
The same iron in this eye
Though its film shrank in death.

A pond I fished, fifty yards across,
Whose lilies and muscular tench
Had outlasted every visible stone
Of the monastery that planted them –

Stilled legendary depth:
It was as deep as England. It held
Pike too immense to stir, so immense and old
That past nightfall I dared not cast

But silently cast and fished
With the hair frozen on my head
For what might move, for what eye might move.
The still splashes on the dark pond,

Owls hushing the floating woods
Frail on my ear against the dream
Darkness beneath night's darkness had freed,
That rose slowly towards me, watching.

★ ★ ★

Ted Hughes wrote about the connection between poetry and
fishing in *Poetry in the Making* (1967)

NOW where did the poet learn to settle his mind like that on to one
thing? It is a valuable thing to be able to do – but something you
are never taught at school, and not many people do it naturally. I am
not very good at it, but I did acquire some skill in it. Not in school,
but while I was fishing. I fished in still water, with a float. As you
know, all a fisherman does is stare at his float for hours on end. I
have spent hundreds and hundreds of hours staring at a float – a dot
of red or yellow the size of a lentil, ten yards away. Those of you
who have never done it, might think it is a very drowsy pastime. It
is anything but that.

All the little nagging impulses, that are normally distracting your
mind, dissolve. They have to dissolve if you are to go on fishing. If
they do not, then you cannot settle down: you get bored and pack
up in a bad temper. But once they have dissolved, you enter one of
the orders of bliss.

Your whole being rests lightly on your float, but not drowsily:
very alert, so that the least twitch of the float arrives like an electric
shock. And you are not only watching the float. You are aware, in
a horizonless and slightly mesmerized way, like listening to the
double bass in orchestral music, of the fish below there in the dark.
At every moment your imagination is alarming itself with the size
of the thing slowly leaving the weeds and approaching your bait. Or
with the world of beauties down there, suspended in total ignorance

of you. And the whole purpose of this concentrated excitement, in this arena of apprehension and unforeseeable events, is to bring up some lovely solid thing like living metal from a world where nothing exists but those inevitable facts which raise life out of nothing and return it to nothing.

So you see, fishing with a float is a sort of mental exercise in concentration on a small point, while at the same time letting your imagination work freely to collect everything that might concern that still point: in this case the still point is the float and the things that concern the float are all the fish you are busy imagining.